D1590758

STUDIES IN JEWISH MUSIC:
COLLECTED WRITINGS
OF A. W. BINDER

Studies in Jewish Music: Collected Writings of A. W. Binder

Edited by
IRENE HESKES

BLOCH PUBLISHING COMPANY
New York

#3382

780
H584s

In Loving Memory of
LEAH BINDER SILVERMAN

FOREWORD

Abraham Wolf Binder (1895-1966) was a notable figure in American-Jewish cultural life. As a Jewish musician, his work was largely devoted to the traditional *nusach hatefillah*—melody of prayer—in religious services and Judaic folk song. This commemorative volume is an edited collection of his published writings on Jewish music.

As a frame of reference for the eventful period in which A. W. Binder lived and worked, two of his noted colleagues have contributed their own brief personal studies in prefatory material for this volume. Dr. Peter Gradenwitz, Israeli music critic and publisher, points up Binder's efforts to bridge Israel with American Jewry by means of Jewish music. Dr. Joseph Yasser, synagogue musician and musicologist, places into broad relief the significance of Binder's contributions in behalf of the advancement of Jewish music.

To put A. W. Binder's prodigious creativity into sharper focus in the context of his lifetime experiences, an extended biographical essay by this editor serves as an introduction. Also appended at the conclusion of the book is a bibliographical listing of Binder's musical compositions, compiled by Cantor Lewis Appleton.

In addition, it seemed a service toward greater understanding of two Jewish musicians—Ernest Bloch and A. W. Binder—to publish here for the first time one of the letters written by Bloch to Binder. It has been included in the biographical essay. For her kind assistance in this matter, this editor is indebted to the music performer and lecturer Suzanne Bloch, daughter of Ernest Bloch.

More than a volume in tribute to a distinguished American-Jewish musician, this book is intended as a source of information on various subjects within the scope of recent Jewish musical history. Among the twenty-five articles by Binder are included a wide range of important topics. From the first one published in 1927 to the last posthumous publications, there are treatments of materials which Binder gathered by study, research and professional experience during his prolific career.

Educators and school administrators, such as was Binder himself, can use this book as a textual reference for their students. Practicing musicians—ranging as did Binder in activities as composer, conductor, music director and performer—may utilize these essays as resources for their own on-going work. For lecturers and writers, Binder's own labors in those areas have left this reservoir of valuable topical literature.

Overall, Binder's articles differ as to length and style, but each one was intended as a sharing of ideas and insights. Always there are Binder's obvious efforts to induce others to become interested in particular aspects of Jewish music. The chronological placement of these materials reflects Binder's mounting zeal for his chosen work over the years of his life.

Acknowledgements

As editor, I wish to express my appreciation to the following for their kind permission to include Binder's articles which had appeared in their publications:

Lesser Zussman, Executive Director of the Jewish Publication Society of America; Chaim Pupko, Member-Executive of the Central Yiddish Culture Organization (CYCO); Helen E. Pfatteicher, Editor of the *Journal of Church Music*; Josephine Williams, Secretary of the Hymn Society of America; Rabbi Sidney L. Regner, Executive Vice President of the Central Conference of American Rabbis; Dr. Paul M. Steinberg, Dean of the School of Sacred Music and the School of Education of the Hebrew Union College— Jewish Institute of Religion; Alan Freidberg, Administrator of the America-Israel Cultural Foundation; Robert Weltsch, Director of the Leo Baeck Institute; Rabbi Ira Eisenstein, President of the Jewish Reconstructionist Foundation; Frank Cunkle, Editor of *The Diapason*; Burton L. Litwin, Director of Business Affairs for Belwin-Mills Publishing Corporation; Roy Anderson, Editor of *Choral and Organ Guide*; Cantor Arthur Wolfson, President of the Jewish Liturgical Music Society of America; Herbert Millman, Executive Vice-President of the National Jewish Welfare Board.

My special gratitude goes to A. W. Binder's daughter, Hadassah Binder Markson, and to her husband, Martin Markson, for their confidence in me and their assistance with the development of this manuscript. Unfortunately, Binder's other daughter, Leah Binder Silverman, died a short time after she enthusiastically helped to initiate this project. I am indebted also to Dr. Joseph Yasser for his supportive guidance. Finally, I take this opportunity to thank my husband for much practical aid and good patience with my editorial labors.

Abraham Wolf Binder encouraged me early in my own career in Jewish music. I feel privileged to have been associated with him in his work.

IRENE HESKES

TABLE OF CONTENTS

PART ONE

MEMOIR OF BINDER

by Peter Gradenwitz

A musicologist and active writer meets literary men, artists and musicians, fellow writers and composers, privately and professionally, on many occasions. He exchanges ideas and opinions, agrees or opposes, admires or criticizes, teaches or learns from his colleagues all over the world. Not always do these professional contacts lead to personal friendships of lasting value. When they do, the collaboration is fruitful not only for these friendly colleagues, but also for the communities in which they work, and often for an even larger circle of their fellow men. Friendships arising out of personal contacts with Abraham Wolf Binder were of that rare kind.

It was my own good fortune that A. W. Binder and I enjoyed such a fortuitous relationship. Although our actual contacts were unfortunately rare, they always led to some concrete results. We met in the Land of Israel, which Binder so much liked visiting, and we met in New York during my sporadic professional visits. We talked of Jewish music and Hebrew compositions; we discussed the new music of Israel, and the endeavors of Jewish musicians and composers in the United States of America. It was Binder's ardent desire to introduce Israeli music to American audiences and to create understanding for American Jewish music in Israel. He helped to bring Israeli musicians to America, and in turn, sent American music to Israel. He lectured in Israel and invited Israeli lecturers to New York. He advocated the creation of a living musical bridge between America, the country of his birth, and Israel, the renascence of which he greeted with love and enthusiasm.

It grieved Binder that understanding was not so quick to come as he had envisaged; there were obstacles. The Israeli musicians, naturally very much occupied with their own particular problems of style, showed too little interest in the Jewish music of American composers, who have their roots in different traditions. The Jewish composers of America, on the other hand, wondered "how Jewish" was the music of new Israel. The historian knows that developments of style and the coming-about and impact of cultural cross-influences take generations. Binder had the impatience and dynamic urgency of a true creative artist; he wished to see this musical bridge between the two great Jewish cultural societies materialize in his own lifetime.

Although musically rooted in tradition, Binder nonetheless became a pioneer in many ways. He fostered research. He advanced the cause of Hebrew singing in American schools, homes, and religious communities. As a composer, he looked to the Bible and to liturgy for inspiration. His identification with the newly-built Jewish homeland had begun long before the State of Israel became a reality; he had made visits to Palestine (*Eretz Yisrael*) years earlier. His fine choral ballet, entitled *Praise and Dance*, for voices and piano, or orchestra, is a synthesis of all he loved in Hebrew poetry and music. The texts are based on excerpts from Jewish liturgy and the Prophets; the music is in *hora* dance rhythm, and the melody has been shaped accordingly.

Binder's generosity as a critic, a fellow-composer, and a fellow-writer was proverbial. Where he disagreed, he did so vehemently but good-heartedly, and always on the solid foundation of knowledge and conviction. Where he agreed, he praised without reservation. Both his criticism and his appreciation were helpful, constructive, and thought-provoking, and that is why not only his advice, but also his criticism was widely sought and accepted.

I was proud to be called his friend and colleague, and proud also to be entrusted by Binder with the publication of some of his musical works in Israel. Sadly, his disappearance from the Jewish musical scene has lost to us an active worker who might have contributed still more to the promotion of all that is dear to American and Israeli musicians alike. He will be remembered not only by the friends and colleagues of his own generation, but also, significantly, by those younger and even very young musicians in Israel as well as America whom he helped so generously, and who benefited from his teaching and his personal interest. In the future we may all draw strength from the legacy of his efforts in behalf of Jewish music and from the inspiration of his dedication to the advancement of its cause.

A. W. BINDER IN RETROSPECT

by Joseph Yasser

Over the nearly forty years of my professional association and personal friendship with Abraham Wolf Binder, I observed his many-faceted musical activities at rather close range. This indefatigable man was not only an outstanding composer, but also a performer in both choral and orchestral conducting, as well as a lecturer, writer, educator, and a highly efficient administrator.

In 1965, on the occasion of Binder's seventieth birthday, I contributed an article to the collective manual, *A. W. Binder: His Life and Work*, published by the National Jewish Music Council of the National Jewish Welfare Board. I wrote then about his fruitful activities in behalf of the Jewish Music Forum, the founding of which he initiated in 1939, when the group known as *Mailamm*, or the American-Palestine Musical Association, was disbanded. In the formation and advancement of the Forum as a significant Jewish music organization in America, it was largely Binder who, over many years, carried almost the full brunt of the responsibilities, and gave vitality and impetus to the group. He was not above searching for the monthly meeting rooms, for free piano rentals, for speakers and performers. The printing and mailing of notices, the annual *Bulletin*, and the collection of much-needed funds occupied his seemingly tireless energies.

Especially during the first crucial years of the Jewish Music Forum, Binder handled all these functions, and more, by himself. He spurred membership, and often suggested valuable topics and music materials for the speakers, coordinating also the musical performances. Often the cause of the advancement of Jewish music has discouraged Jewish musicians, but not so Binder. When the Jewish Music Forum disbanded in 1962, he thereupon founded the Jewish Liturgical Music Society of America during the following year. Clearly, Binder was a man of action as well as of ideas, and as such, he has left his particular mark on Jewish music.

In this retrospect, I wish to evaluate Binder's status as a creative artist, and his special influence on the development of Jewish music in America over the past decades. In formulating his characteristic musical traits, the least that can be said about Binder is that he was basically one of the most *consistent*, *natural* and *practical* of Jewish composers.

By the term *consistent*, I mean that Binder never looked upon himself as a part-time Jewish composer, for whom Jewish music happened to be a mere side issue in his career as a composer. For him, Jewish music was a serious creative endeavor, the very core of his artistry. Under no circumstances did he veer away from it in the belief that he might thus win wider recognition. He firmly believed that the artist is most likely to gain universal appreciation by enhancing his own special characteristics rather than by suppressing them.

That point of view actually reinforces what the history of all music teaches us. Such composers as Moussorgsky,

Tchaikowsky, Borodin, and Rimsky-Korsakov did not acquire their world-reputations by becoming less Russian; rather, they gained much of their international stature because of their national traits. The same may be said for Chopin, Grieg, Dvorak, Albeniz, De Falla, and many others, all of whom cultivated whatever was nationally distinctive and best in their artistic natures. Even Bach, Haydn, Mozart, and Beethoven appear now to have been far more nationalistic in their musical expression than most music historians have heretofore acknowledged.

Binder became an intensely Jewish composer just because he believed music to be an international language. He was not, however, a narrow sectarian insofar as the specific choice of his Jewish musical material was concerned. He did not write characteristically Ashkenazic music because he happened to be born and brought up in an Ashkenazic *milieu.* Sephardic, Oriental, Hasidic, and Israeli musical styles were equally close to his heart, and so were the musical periods of the Biblical, Medieval, and Modern eras in Jewish creativity. He strongly believed in the melodic totality of the fundamental roots of Jewish music, and from this point of view, he may also be regarded as having been a universalist within the circumscribed Jewish field.

I consider Binder to have been a *natural* creator of Jewish music in the sense that he did not force himself to be a Jewish composer. The music of the Jews was his native predilection, the musical mother-tongue in which he was steeped most deeply. At a very early age Binder sang as a boy-soprano in a synagogue. Being the son of a *hazzan,* he had ample opportunity to learn the entire liturgical repertoire. He constantly heard Jewish music, both sacred and secular, at home and in the ghetto-like neighborhood where he spent his childhood. He picked up many Jewish melodies by ear and tried to translate them into sound on any musical instrument he could find. He was actually bound to think in terms of Jewish music as soon as he felt the urge to compose the simplest strain of music. Jewish musical expression became for Binder a spontaneous art-language, which he gradually learned to use with a singular fluency, and to which he clung faithfully throughout his entire life.

Yet, as an admirer of all musical art, and as a well-trained performer, Binder also was genuinely interested in the music of non-Jews. He was thoroughly familiar with the great classical repertoire, which he constantly performed. He benefited immensely from performances of the masters while writing his own music.

Binder was also a natural Jewish composer because his growth as a creative artist was so wisely and imperceptively gradual. Though it is quite difficult to notice stylistic changes in his chronologically close compositions, when one compares those of his works separated from each other by many years, the changes become evident. His earliest synagogue services, with their heart-felt Schubert-like simplicity, and his last services with their sporadic bits of modernistic sophistication, seem in some respects to be the work of two different composers. Yet, one finds in all of his compositions a basic quality which is uniquely Binder.

In evaluating Binder as an eminently *practical* composer, I wish to underscore the fact that he was always acutely conscious of what he was writing, and of the realistic needs of each particular composition. In his specifically chosen areas he knew well how to write for each given occasion, and how to adjust his technical means to it. This was particularly evident in his many liturgical works, which remain the most characteristic and significant of his compositions. To be sure, liturgical works for all religions are primarily creations of *Gebrauchsmusik*, or utility music, but this does not render them in any way inferior to pieces which are so-called "pure art." One might cite many well known examples to prove this point.

Binder's practical acumen expressed itself in diverse ways in his liturgical works. Apart from its dignified, spiritual quality and the ease with which it could be sung, this music was authentically wedded to the sacred texts. Significantly, Binder had a sharp sense of what could be called the "dynamic continuity of the liturgical act." He felt intuitively how long any given liturgical number should be, what proportional duration should be sustained between its instrumental and vocal episodes, how to distribute the tonal nuances throughout its entire musical texture, and how to reach its gradually approaching climax. Equally important in the liturgical field was Binder's strong leaning upon the traditional Jewish modes, of which he was doubtless one of the most reliable exponents. Within the strict melodic framework of these modes, Binder still managed to find certain ways and means for expressing his own creative individuality.

More comprehensive information pertaining to Binder's technical handling of the Jewish modes may be obtained from his invaluable little essay entitled, "My Ideas and Theories In My Synagogue Compositions," which is published for the first time in the present volume.

Binder's perpetual concern was to raise the artistic standards of Jewish music, especially of the synagogue repertoire, and even of the hazzanic performing profession. He repeatedly developed this theory in his lectures and articles. His articles on sacred Jewish music far outnumber those dealing with secular music, pointing up the areas in which his basic interests preeminently resided. Binder also paid rather close attention to the composition of a secular literature of Jewish music. He made some interesting and noteworthy contributions to that popular area, particularly with his harmonizations and elaborations in the folk music style. His true creative passion, however, was reserved for synagogue services and other religiously imbued compositions, both vocal and instrumental.

When engaged in his mission of disseminating representative Jewish music to the wider public, Binder would give equal attention to the performance (by himself and others) of *both* secular and sacred compositions. Having been, by psychological make-up and long experience, a teacher *par excellence*, Binder's invariable aim was to share with others whatever knowledge in any branch of Jewish music he himself possessed. It was also his favorite pursuit to inculcate, especially in young people, a genuine and enduring feeling for the inherent worthiness of Jewish music. A most gratifying result of Binder's efforts was that a number of professional musicians, heretofore indifferent, or at best lukewarm to this particular brand of Jewish cause, became palpably active within its bounds as composers, performers, lecturers, writers, and administrators.

These are the most vital aspects of Binder's unique contribution to the advancement of Jewish music during his lifetime. I can sum them up in the form of two concise and mutually complementary statements: First, by following his own path as a composer in a consistent, natural and practical fashion, Abraham Wolf Binder helped the total output of Jewish music to become spiritually richer and ethnically truer. Second, by serving the general public for over half a century as an energetic and trustworthy practitioner in many branches of Jewish music, A. W. Binder rendered that precious art as an impressive cultural phenomenon in our American community, and moreover, as an effective medium for lofty and far-reaching creative aspirations the world over.

BIOGRAPHICAL PORTRAIT
OF ABRAHAM WOLF BINDER

by Irene Heskes

Our early American Jewish music was established in 1654, with the arrival of the first Jews in New Amsterdam. They brought with them synagogue music of the Sephardic traditions, and Jewish folksongs in the Spanish-Portuguese style, many in the Judaeo-*Espagnol* vernacular of Ladino. A second migration of Jews from Central and Western Europe during the eighteenth and nineteenth centuries brought Ashkenazic liturgy and European-Jewish folk music. After 1870, the music of the liturgy, following upon the examples then flourishing in Middle and Eastern Europe, became a highly developed art with strong cantorial emphasis. The newer ideas of Salomon Sulzer in Vienna, Louis Lewandowski in Berlin, and Samuel Naumbourg in Paris were brought by many immigrants to these shores, where they rapidly became part of the synagogue musical literature here. Farther eastward in Europe, cantorial musical tastes were strongly influenced by such men as David

Nowakowsky of Odessa, Eliezer Gerovitch of Rostov, and Jacob Bachman of Budapest, among a legion of emerging musical talents in the field of synagogue service. As more and more of the Jewish immigrants came from these East European areas, the synagogue traditions they brought with them became increasingly influential throughout this country. Transported with the folk music of this latter era were sacred *zemirot*, holiday tunes, and secular songs, in a 700-year mixture of Hebraic, Slavonic, and Germanic elements.

These later traditions proved to be powerful catalysts which have significantly influenced general American musical ideas, as well as the music of American Jews in their secular and religious lives. Much of the musical leadership in synagogues and secular Jewish organizations in the United States has been deeply affected, and indeed vitally shaped by those cultural elements brought here during the turn-of-the-century mass-movement from Eastern Europe —specifically, the strong traditions of liturgic music evolved during centuries of ghetto life, and the ethnic vigor of Yiddish folk songs. Currently, much musical activity is still contributed by immigrants from this East European *milieu*, or by their direct musical disciples.

A distinctively American link was forged over the early years of this century between those strong immigrant-Jewish influences and the rising number of American-born Jewish musicians. This chain of cultural continuity, this human bridge between American-Jewish musicians and the older traditions of our musical heritage has strengthened immeasurably the current status of American-Jewish music. It has enabled Jewish musicians here to reach out in inspiration and renewal to what remains of viable *Diaspora* life elsewhere in the world, providing some measure of cultural consolation for the European holocaust which erased forever the once great centers of Jewish musical culture in Europe. Indeed, this newer creative musical force has also inaugurated a fruitful reciprocal relationship with the many and varied musical traditions gathered together now in the State of Israel.

In the midst of such an active Jewish music movement in America today there are two types of contributors. The overwhelmingly predominant type is the Jewish musician whose self-awareness, from an artistic point of view, has come upon him quite incidentally, and this Jewish consciousness has been met with varying degrees of response. The current American musical scene, the most prolific in general musical history, is filled with very many active musicians of Jewish parentage. Among them Jewish music, whether secular or for the synagogue, gathers its musical gleanings much as did Ruth in the fertile fields of Boaz.

Thus it is fortunate that there is the other, though much rarer type of Jewish musician. He is a Jew (or she is a Jewess!) who has taken up the cause of the advancement of Jewish music as a positive ideal, and as an individual for whom his Jewish self-expression is a totality of his creative being. With boundless enthusiasm undimmed by the passing of years, and with high Jewish musical standards, Abraham Wolf Binder in his lifetime was such a true champion of Jewish music in America. For more than half a century he actively influenced many noteworthy musical innovations. In the words of Aristotle: "Those who ever embark on new ideas and concern themselves with beginnings, deserve the chief praise."

Childhood and Formative Years

Abraham Wolf Binder was born in New York City on the lower East Side of Manhattan on January 9, 1895, into an Orthodox household. His father was a *baal tefillah* who had learned the music of the services orally from his own father, who had been a *hazzan* in Galicia. By the age of four, Binder had already begun to sing in his father's High

Holyday choir, and by the age of six he had undertaken
solos and the chanting of harmony. The music of the synagogue and its rituals fascinated the youngster, and he played
the game of *Shul*, picturing himself as *hazzan* and leading
an invisible but very grand choir of singers. He enjoyed
visits with his family to the services of the larger synagogues, which at that time were so numerous on the lower
East Side of Manhattan.

When he was seven, his father, recognizing the talents
of his young son, took him to audition for the choir of the
then newly-arrived Cantor Abraham Frachtenberg from
Galatz, Roumania. Binder sang with Frachtenberg's choir
as alto soloist until the age of fourteen. There was a wealth
of fine traditional music to be learned and performed with
that choir. In Europe, Frachtenberg had been a *meshorer*
(choir-singer) with Yeruchom Hakoton, a famous cantor
in Berditchev. Significantly, Frachtenberg was a superb
musician who trained and conducted his own choir and
composed much music for choral singing in the synagogue.
These early years were decisive for Binder in that he acquired a taste for the great traditional music of Europe, and
an appreciation of the skills of a trained and sensitive musician. His life-long concern with good choral music for the
synagogue services had commenced. Having learned some
of the musical techniques of choir training, he took on that
role when his voice changed at the age of fourteen. He then
became the choir director, with Cantor Abraham Singer of
the Kamenetzer Shul on Attorney Street in downtown
Manhattan.

Meanwhile, in 1906, Binder had become a student at the
Settlement Music School, studying piano with Elizabeth
Quaile and harmony with Angela Diller, two outstanding
music educators of that early period. Soon he also began to
study organ, and to compose some musical settings for
synagogue prayers. For his general education, he graduated
from Townsend Harris High School in Manhattan.

Commencement of Professional Life

In 1911 Binder became the organist and choir director of Temple Beth El in Greenpoint, Brooklyn. He began to teach theory and harmony, first at the Settlement Music School, and later at the Neighborhood Music School (now the Manhattan School of Music). He then assumed a musical position in 1913 with Temple Adath Israel in the Bronx, as organist and choir director with Cantor Louis Lipitz. By that time Binder had begun to realize the need for the return of authentic Jewish musical traditions to temple services. He felt that the temple services had become musically barren and imitative of the Protestant services, with the non-committal though pleasant hymns of Schlesinger and Stark. It was this strong feeling for the wealth of the *nusach ha-tefillah* (traditional synagogue musical motifs), co-mingled with an enlightened approach to modern musical techniques, which was to characterize all of Binder's professional activities in the ensuing years, and which permeated his musical ideas to the end of his lifetime.

His interests in Jewish music were not confined to the synagogue, however. In 1916, he was asked to form a choral society for the Hadassah organization, then a new institution. Binder developed a chorus—the Hadassah Choral Union—which was the first musical group to devote itself exclusively to the performance of Palestinian folk songs. During those early years he notated and harmonized many Zionist songs for the first time, and arranged them for vocal parts in concert style. He composed the pantomime *Israel* for a performance sponsored by Hadassah at the Republic Theatre in New York. It was also at that time that Binder was awarded a Mosenthal Fellowship in music composition at Columbia University, which he held from 1917 to 1920.

On June 3, 1917, one year after its formation, the Hadassah Choral Union presented a formal concert at the Wadleigh High School, part of which program was devoted to a "Palestinian Opera." This was the first of a long series of well-received public performances by Binder of his special arrangements of Zionist music. His own compositions were, over the years, to be deeply inspired by the impetus of the modern return to Palestine.

Affiliation With the 92nd Street YM-YWHA

The year 1917 was a particularly auspicious one for Binder in terms of important beginnings. Early in the month of September, Rabbi Aaron G. Robison, then executive director of the 92nd Street YM-YWHA in New York, invited Binder to organize a music department. He became the first professional musician to be a full-time staff member of a Jewish Community Center. Thereupon commenced an association which proved to be one of the most musically fruitful in Jewish Center history. When Binder formed a music department which was integrated into the framework of the "Y" itself, he began to establish various special activity groups such as a choral society, a children's chorus, an instrumental ensemble workshop, and finally an orchestral organization. All of those activities, as well as the actual school of individual musical instruction, were greatly expanded with much success over the following five decades of Binder's administration.

During those exciting years of growth and accomplishment at the "Y", Binder was to be associated with executive directors Jack Nadel and then Carl Urbont. Jack Nadel had been assistant director of the "Y" from 1917 until he became its executive director in 1922, an office he held until his own retirement in 1958. Reflecting upon those very first musical years, Nadel recalled that there had been many requests by the "Y" members for music lessons and chorus sessions for the children. Rabbi Robison decided to build up the musical services of the "Y" for all age levels as an important means of group expression. From the beginning of this association, Binder was an activist, and he proceeded to develop a program of regular musical activities. He would go to general club meetings and invite all those who had any interest or inclination toward music to attend his sessions. Working closely with Jack Nadel, the building-up over the years of the music department was for Binder a dedicated occupation. The music school became a natural part of the entire growth of that Jewish Community Center in the heart of Manhattan. Nadel recollected that with the advent of each new music project, Binder would eloquently plead the efficacy of Jewish culture, always adding, "First music, then membership!" Both music and membership flourished.

Binder's widely appreciated activities at the "Y" proved to exert a major influence upon the scope of musical activity and programming in other Jewish Community Centers throughout the country. In time, the 92nd Street YM-YWHA became a showcase music school which introduced many new concepts into music education, such as family teams for musical instruction, as well as the active study and programming of fine musical selections of particular Jewish relevance. At the time of Binder's retirement in 1966, the music school had a student enrollment of more than six hundred, and a carefully picked faculty of over fifty musicians.

In the "Y" *Bulletin* of September 1917, announcement was formally made of the engagement of the services of Abraham Wolf Binder as music director. Beside the photograph of a very young and fine looking man was the brief information that he would organize a Jewish community chorus and a "Y" symphony orchestra, and that there would be no fee for participation in these musical activities. Almost fifty years later, in the March 1965 issue of *JWB Circle*, the monthly newspaper publication of the National

Jewish Welfare Board, parent organization to Jewish Community Centers and YM-YWHA's throughout the United States and Canada, there was a feature article on Binder's Center work. The author of that piece, Bernard Postal, drew particular attention to the fact that "a significant chapter in the history of the Jewish Community Center movement has been the unique achievement of Dr. Abraham W. Binder in making a place for and integrating Jewish music into the educational programs of the Center and the YM-YWHA." The article also noted that Binder had established at the "Y" the first American conservatory of music under Jewish auspices. The "Y" music school, under Binder's leadership, became a major force for music programming that has "exercised incalculable influence on cultural programs in Jewish Community Centers around the country." Many other Centers, it was pointed out, have also been inspired to establish music departments and other music educational activities patterned after Binder's work at the 92nd Street YM-YWHA in New York City.

"Come O Sabbath Day"

In 1918 Binder supplemented his busy schedules at the "Y" with the position as music director of the then newly-formed Jewish Center Congregation, founded by Rabbi Mordecai Kaplan. Soon he also became musical director of the Temple Emanu-El religious school in New York. At that time Binder began to arrange and to compose hymns for the Reform congregational singing. One of these compositions, a song for the Friday evening services—"Come O Sabbath Day"—is now a classic sung throughout the world. Working with the music for those services was to bear fruit eventually, when Binder later assisted in the musical preparations of the third edition of the Reform *Hymnal*. Binder's first published composition, "Minuet," for violin and piano, was brought out by G. Schirmer in 1919. The following year, Binder received the degree of Bachelor of Music from the New York College of Music.

Family Life

Binder married Anna Friedman, a pianist and social worker, in 1921. They had met at the Neighborhood Music School, where she had studied piano and had been one of Binder's harmony students. Mrs. Binder taught piano, and became head of the piano faculty at the "Y" when Binder expanded the music school into a more formal organization. In 1928 they appeared together in a concert of Binder's music at the Town Hall recital hall in New York. Their older daughter Leah was born in 1922, and their younger daughter Hadassah in 1927.

It was a very musical family. Mrs. Binder taught the girls to play the piano, and Binder himself closely supervised their musical education as well as their general upbringing. He intentionally guided their musical tastes toward Jewish cultural expression. In that traditionally observant home, the religious holidays were celebrated amply with Jewish music. Both daughters became accomplished musicians. As youngsters, they gave four-hand piano concerts together, and, in their adulthood they were actively involved in musical projects with their father.

Leah Binder Silverman graduated from the Juilliard School of Music. She married a rabbi, had two daughters, and taught in the New York City public school system until her death in 1968. Hadassah Binder Markson completed studies in music at Queens College of New York, and taught piano at the "Y" school of music for many years until she became the director of that music school in 1969. She is married to an attorney and is the mother of two daughters.

Anna Friedman Binder died in 1936. Two years later, Binder married Priscilla Dreyer, the niece of Lazarus Goldschmidt, a noted Jewish scholar who translated the *Talmud* into German. Priscilla Binder helped Binder to raise his two daughters, and was also associated with him in many musical activities. She died in 1953. Binder's third marriage, to Helen F. Dayton in 1956, was terminated by divorce in 1961.

Association with Rabbi Stephen S. Wise

A chance meeting between Binder and Rabbi Stephen S. Wise led to a very productive and warm association between the two men in which were developed many lasting musical ideas for American Reform synagogues. Dr. Wise attended a performance of Binder's choral society of the "Y" and at that time met briefly with this serious young musician. That performance, presented at the Astor Hotel in Manhattan under the sponsorship of the Federation of Jewish Philanthropies, included a presentation of *A Pageant of the Strong*, with incidental music composed by A. W. Binder. Rabbi Wise noted Binder's enthusiasm and his musical qualifications. Not too long afterward, in 1921, he invited Binder to join the faculty of the newly-organized Jewish Institute of Religion in New York City, as an instructor of Jewish music. There, for the first time in America, Jewish music was made a required subject of study for Reform rabbinical students. This was one of Wise's significant innovations. He sought to make the modern rabbi better educated in the totality of Judaism.

Rabbi Wise viewed liturgical music as an important element of the Jewish religious service. In 1922 he asked Binder to become the choirmaster of the newly-formed Free Synagogue, which was then holding its services at Carnegie Hall. The Free Synagogue erected its own building in Manhattan some time later, co-adjacent to a building erected for the Jewish Institute of Religion, which subsequently merged with the Hebrew Union College. Binder continued to be the music director of the Stephen Wise Free Synagogue until the end of his life.

Because of his association with Rabbi Wise, Binder was thrust into a deeply intellectual atmosphere of Jewish scholarship, in which he was respected as an expert in his own field. Early on, Rabbi Wise established their cordial relationship and expressed confidence in Binder's capabilities. Binder, in turn, idolized Wise, and in his own subsequent dealings with younger associates in Jewish music reflected Wise's quality of extending confidence. It was not always successful, but it succeeded often enough to be justified. Joseph Yasser recalled that over the years "Binder was always ready to give someone a chance. He took a man (or woman) at his word, and gave that person an opportunity to prove himself on the job."

Binder, in time, became a scholar and researcher, both to advance himself and to project the importance of his own academic area of Jewish music at the Jewish Institute of Religion. It was part of Binder's inherent personality to grow in a particular position and to expand that position, propelling it and himself toward higher goals. Eventually his scope of Jewish musical interest became much broader, taking in the historical areas of Biblical cantillation, and the authentic liturgical chant elements of the synagogue. He studied the *piyutim*, those innovative prayers of the Middle Ages, as devotions in which Jews directed their prayers alone before God, rather than in the overt performances of rituals or sacrifices. In those prayers Jews could also create musical expressions to fit the poetic texts.

Stephen S. Wise possessed great courage and strength of conviction, particularly in regard to his vision of the future of Judaism in all its many facets. For Binder, those years of association with Wise afforded freedom to experiment in the methods of bringing greater knowledge of Jewish music (especially the traditional music of the synagogue) to the rabbinical students and to others, including his fellow members of that distinguished faculty of Jewish scholars at the Institute. One of his colleagues there, Professor Shalom Spiegel recalled, "Binder rose to the occasion and continually grew. He served, we felt, with *hidur mitzvah,* performing his work with loving dedication."

Of those earlier days Binder himself said, "I felt it was my duty to do something about letting Reform Jews hear some of the works of the masters of the nineteenth century, such as Sulzer, Lewandowski, Naumbourg and Nowakowsky. The Reform services had become saturated with music composed for them by non-Jews." In 1922, with the encouragement of Rabbi Stephen Wise, Binder re-introduced, for the first time in 100 years, the chanting of the Bible in traditional cantillation at the Saturday morning services of a Reform synagogue.

Clearly, mere musical expediency was not to be Binder's outlook, for not too long afterward he sought to inject even more of the traditional synagogue musical atmosphere into the Free Synagogue services, always with the enthusiastic approval of Rabbi Wise. Again to quote Binder, "I felt very much that in the synagogue on *Shabbes* one should feel the warmth and beauty of *Shabbes,* or indeed, the distinctive Jewish qualities of the holidays and festivals at their services, even though the prayer texts might be altered to suit the Reform or any other Jewish ritual sect." By 1928 Binder had published his first full Sabbath service.

Some years later Binder wrote, "I consider my most important contribution to synagogue music to be my association with the return to the *nusach ha-tefillah,* which is our rich musical tradition in the synagogue, and my efforts to purify it and perpetuate it. I have endeavored to use it skillfully and tastefully in all the services, not only for what it has meant to our forefathers and to the religious services of the ages past, but also significantly, for what it can do for the synagogue services of today and into the future."

Interest in Zionist Folk Song

During Binder's first visit to Palestine in 1924, he collected songs of the *halutzim* (pioneers). His first collection of arrangements of twenty-four such songs, published in New York shortly thereafter, became very popular with the pupils in religious schools. Many youngsters made their first contacts with Zionist ideas through this new Palestinian music. Binder was one of the earliest to recognize the special Jewish significance of the folk music creativity of the early Palestinian settlers. His arrangements of this music, and his public concert performances of it, helped to fire enthusiasm among Jews here for Zionist songs and dances. The quality of his early song collections also set high modern musical standards for other such publications which were intended for schools, choral groups, and Zionist organizations, not only here but also in growing Palestine. Those collections were, as were subsequent ones, the works of an experienced teacher and choirmaster with much musical skill, vocal and instrumental understanding, and a flare for quality performance. The same qualities applied in the collections and arrangements of Yiddish folk songs made by Binder over his lifetime. The extra gifts he himself bestowed upon that music were his warm enthusiasm for those Jewish musical expressions and his sensitivity to their possibilities in performance.

In 1926 the "Y" chorus participated in a New York concert at Town Hall to welcome the poet Hayim Nahman Bialik to this country. At that all-Jewish music program, Binder's arrangements of favorite Palestinian folk melodies were especially appreciated. Presented under the sponsorship of the Young Judea organization, it was a unique event. The fine reaction spurred Binder to begin to lecture on Jewish music throughout the country, carrying with him Palestinian folk music wherever he went.

Editing the Union Hymnal

In 1928 the first of Binder's Sabbath musical liturgies was published. When, in 1929, the project of a third revision of the *Union Hymnal* was undertaken by the Central Conference of American (Reform) Rabbis, Binder was asked to serve on the revision committee as music editor. To this important work he brought not only skill and wide experience with such music, but also a strong knowledge and dedication to our liturgical music heritage. Binder was determined to seek out the best qualities of our synagogue music and to infuse them into this new publication, but always in such a manner as to truly serve the ideals of the Reform movement.

The first edition of the *Union Hymnal* had been compiled in 1897 by the Conference and Society of American Cantors. It contained 129 hymns based mostly upon arrangements of known classic melodies as settings for liturgical poetry. Also included were some of the better known materials from earlier collections of hymns arranged and published during the late nineteenth century by Cantor William Sparger in New York and Cantor Alois Kaiser of Baltimore. In 1914 a second edition of the *Union Hymnal* was prepared by the Central Conference of American Rabbis, and this time the collection was expanded to 226 hymns. The additional materials of this second edition were largely derived from a hymnal published by Temple Emanu-El of New York in 1894. As early as 1924, proposals had been advanced for a completely revised third edition which would ring true to the Jewish spirit, and which would advance the idea of congregational singing, then increasingly advocated by rabbis and cantors. This new edition was also to be a guide and handbook for the children of the Reform religious schools and would contain special educational music materials.

The musical manuscript which was eventually approved by a conference of the Reform rabbis held in 1930 in Providence, Rhode Island, was the result of much dedicated effort on the part of Binder. As music editor he rearranged previous materials from the first two editions of the *Hymnal*; he contributed many new settings for the liturgical texts, and invited some outstanding Jewish musicians to make similar original contributions. Some of these new hymns were based musically upon traditional *nusach*, adapting these time-honored prayer melodies and holiday tunes to the newer Reform texts of the various services. Those new creative combinations proved spiritually appropriate and of lasting success. Added to these adaptations and new compositions were melodies from the synagogue music of Sulzer and Lewandowski. Supplementing the hymn songs of such pioneers as Kaiser, Spicker, Stark, Heller, and Schlesinger were new hymn songs by Heinrich Schalit, Jacob Weinberg, Joseph Achron, Jacob Beimel, and Gershon Ephros.

The *Hymnal* which emerged has been, with only minor emendations, the standard work for the Reform congregations since 1930, and has been distributed and actively used throughout the world. It remains also as a milestone in the history of American Jewish liturgical music. Many of these hymn tunes are now also utilized by non-Reform Jewish congregations and their religious schools. Binder's innovation in making suitable and tasteful adaptations of traditional melodies has since been taken up by other Jewish music educators and choral directors. In 1937, Binder was appointed Professor of Jewish Liturgical Music at the Jewish Institute of Religion when it combined in New York with the Hebrew Union College. He held that position until his death.

When the *Armed Forces Hymnal* was prepared for the service men during World War II, Binder served as consultant on Jewish music for the volume, which was published in 1941 and included appropriate hymns for the three faiths—Catholic, Protestant, and Jewish.

Organizing Jewish Musicians

During a second visit to Palestine in 1931, Binder conducted two concerts in Tel Aviv and in Jerusalem, presenting some of his own compositions, including the premiere of his overture *Hechalutzim*, performed by the Palestinian Symphonic Ensemble. Upon his return to this country, he published a second collection of Palestinian songs. He also appeared as guest conductor with the Manhattan Symphony Orchestra, presenting again his overture *Hechalutzim*. Later that same year Binder was one of those who formed a new Jewish music society. In association with Miriam Zunser, Solomon Rosowsky, Lazare Saminsky, Joseph Achron, and Joseph Yasser, Binder helped establish the *Mailamm* Society. That organization for the advancement of Jewish music held regular meetings, presented musical programs, and assisted Solomon Rosowsky with his research into the Biblical cantillations.

In 1939 when the *Mailamm* group disbanded, Binder initiated the formation of a new organization, the more encompassing and scholarly Jewish Music Forum. The membership was drawn not only from among Jewish composers and performers, but also from the growing ranks of musicologists and teachers. The Jewish Music Forum, through its many meetings and annual publications over the years, carried on successfully the cause of the furtherance of Jewish musical activities of the highest quality. Among those associated with the Forum, united in the cause of good Jewish music, were musicians of European birth and training as well as native-born newer generations of American-Jewish composers. That society also gradually developed interest in this country for the music of the young Palestinian (and later Israeli) musicians. When the Jewish Music Forum discontinued in 1962, Binder organized the Jewish Liturgical Music Society of America in 1963, and propounded its goals of uniting musical leaders from all branches of synagogue affiliations in the advancement of our liturgical music.

One of the more significant meetings of the Jewish Music Forum in 1940 developed into a conference on the status of synagogue music in America, held the following year. For that conference, representatives from the Central Conference of American Rabbis, the Rabbinical Assembly of America, the United Synagogue of America, the Cantors Association of America, and the Jewish Music Forum met together with noted Jewish musicians and musicologists, including Professor Curt Sachs. From these unprecedented discussions arose the idea of schools for cantorial study on a formal academic basis, similar to rabbinical academies. Delayed by the war, these plans eventually came to fruition with the formation in 1948 by the Hebrew Union College-Jewish Institute of Religion of the School of Sacred Music in New York City. As a co-founder of this school, Binder served on its faculty as Professor of Jewish Liturgical Music, teaching the *nusach ha-tefillah* to a new generation of student-cantors, who have since gone out to serve congregations throughout this country.

Because the Jewish Music Forum, through its active membership, reached out to all three branches of American Jewish affiliation, the idea of schools of cantorial study was adopted by the Conservative and Orthodox seminaries, as well as that of the Reform. In 1952 the Cantor's Institute of the Jewish Theological Seminary was formed to serve the needs of the Conservative congregations, and in 1954 the Cantorial Training Institute was established by the Yeshiva University for the Orthodox congregations.

In 1944 Binder was a co-founder of the National Jewish Music Council of the National Jewish Welfare Board. Earlier, in 1941, he had been involved in the formation of the first arts committee of the National Association of Jewish Center Workers. A prime mover in that effort had been Bernard Carp, a young social worker deeply interested in Jewish cultural activity. In 1944 Binder joined with Carp, then a field staff member of the National Jewish Welfare Board, in the establishment of the Music Council. Working with a founding board, Binder helped to delineate the practical purposes as well as the idealistic goals of that new body. The Music Council would serve to stimulate active interest in Jewish musical composition and performance throughout the United States, setting qualitative standards and providing resource information of special relevance to the programs and services provided by the many American-Jewish Community Centers.

From the very beginning the idea of an annual "Festival of Jewish Music" took form, and the first festival was celebrated for a week during the month of May 1945. In the following years the festival week was set to begin on *Shabbat Shirah* (Sabbath of Song) in the Jewish calendar. Ultimately the week was expanded to a month-long celebration, and moved on the calendar to the period from *Purim* to *Erev Pesach*.

In 1956 Binder encouraged the Music Council to make the commissioning of new Jewish musical compositions an on-going feature of Jewish music month. He was especially concerned with encouraging talented young Jewish composers to write music which would enrich Jewish cultural life, secular as well as liturgical, in this country. From 1944 to 1963 Binder served the Music Council as Vice-Chairman, and then was accorded the special designation of Honorary Chairman, in which capacity he actively served until his death. During the 1965 Jewish Music Month celebration, special national tribute was paid to Binder in recognition of his notable contributions to the advancement of Jewish music in America.

Activity During the Holocaust Era

Throughout the thirties, with the mounting crisis for Jews in Europe, Binder, like other Americans, had become increasingly concerned with efforts to assist those who had come to these shores as refugees. He helped to find work for many musicians, often drawing them for the first time into the musical orbit of the synagogue. Among a legion of Jewish musicians who fled to America at that time were cantors and choir directors, who were enabled to secure their means of spiritual and musical renewal, as well as financial aid, through the organizations which Binder activated. He aided, as well, by means of his own professional positions as head of the "Y" music school and as music director of the Stephen Wise Free Synagogue, toward which institutions he drew those valuable refugee talents.

One of those who fled the European holocaust was Heida Hermanns, the concert pianist and teacher who, with her husband Artur Holde, a music critic and musicologist, sought to rebuild a musical life here. Recalling those difficult years, Madame Hermanns wrote, "Mr. Binder was a one-man, hope-restoring institution, one place where you did not hear a 'no' before you could say why you had come for advice. He helped innumerable musicians. If later on some of them turned out to be assets for his school and for the Jewish Music Forum, it was a well-deserved result. But I am sure he helped because he *wanted* to help, with no thought of what he could gain from it. Insofar as the "Y" school was specifically concerned, the combination of Old World thoroughness with New World vitality and versatility produced happy results. During those years of the thirties and forties, the school developed from a kind of neighborhood school into a fine conservatory, offering professional training as well as general music instruction."

Over those years, Binder's concern was also extended to Palestine and to aiding those musicians who had managed to flee there before the outbreak of war. One of the combined efforts in which he was involved took shape in 1943 as the briefly constituted American Friends of the Palestinian Conservatory of Music in Jerusalem. The American Fund for Palestinian Institutions also was organized at that time. At the conclusion of the war, Binder joined in efforts to help survivors who had been musicians, and became especially concerned with the growing musical life in Palestine as the country struggled toward statehood.

It was Binder who delivered the citation tribute to Bronislaw Huberman, the famed violinist and founder of the Palestine Philharmonic Orchestra, when Huberman was awarded the Doctorate of Hebrew Letters, *honoris causa*, at the 1944 commencement exercises of the Jewish Institute of Religion in New York City.

Binder and Ernest Bloch

In 1943, Binder had been instrumental in having the Doctorate of Hebrew Letters, *honoris causa*, granted to Ernest Bloch by the Jewish Institute of Religion. The award was accepted for Bloch by a member of his family, who transmitted his feelings of pleasure at this honor, especially as a Jew. There followed some personal correspondence between Bloch, then teaching in California and residing in Oregon, and Binder in New York, concerning that award as well as other thoughts about the matter of being a Jewish composer. Binder dedicated some music he had just composed to Bloch, and planned a full concert performance by the "Y" ensembles of Bloch's Sacred Service, *Avodath Hakodesh*. After that concert, which took place in May 1944, Ernest Bloch wrote a particularly moving letter to Binder, disclosing some of his inner spiritual thoughts while creating that religious work. That letter is quoted here, with the kind permission of the Bloch family and the special interest of Suzanne Bloch, a noted musician and daughter of the composer.

Agate Beach, Oregon
May 14, 1944

My dear friend,

Both my son, who was able to stay in New York, and my daughter Suzanne, wrote to me about your performance of *Avodath Ha-kodesh* in such terms that my heart goes to you with emotion and gratitude. They'll tell me how moving it was, how deeply you had grasped the spirit of the work and been able to impart it to the interpreters, how simple and profound Rudinow had been. And I am moved also in reading the program. It shows—in the way you made it so clear, exposing the *form* (its liturgical and human bearing) and making very useful quotations from my letters—how you followed my deepest thoughts when I conceived this service. I am profoundly touched, I assure you. I had suffered so much that this "message" was offered so few opportunities to reach those for whom it was conceived, at a time when we need it so much in this age of hate and confusion! There is this absurd belief that the solution is only political or economic, when above all it is a *spiritual* drama, and only the *spirit* can heal. But men are blinded by all kinds of fetishisms; their eyes and ears are clogged.

I wonder whether I ever told you how I came about to understand the deep symbolic meaning of the *Seu Shearim*— at the time when I was studying, scrutinizing, the Hebrew text. It was not clear to me—these "doors," these "heads," that the

King of Glory may enter. I meditated and meditated. At that time (1930, August or September) I was in the high mountains, in Switzerland. I went alone each day on long trips, with my mountain stick and a knapsack—climbing and climbing, and *permeated* with the text of the service in my head and in my heart. That day, there was a deep fog everywhere—no landscape—almost darkness. Suddenly, the sun triumphed. Clouds began to rise and slowly, gradually, the mist receded; trees, rocks, mountains became clear, visible, till the sky was deep blue and darkness had disappeared! And, as if by magic, the *sense* of *Seu Shearim* was revealed to me. I was immensely moved and grateful. I had understood! Not aware at the time of the material significance of these "doors" and "heads," my ignorance had served me, helped me, to grasp a more profound symbolic meaning.

In the notes I wrote later for the New York performance, I put it: "Then the cantor intones the *Seu Shearim.* I interpret this as clouds rising—high in the sky—darkness receding out of man's heart—that the light may enter into it. Immense symbol, which poor fettered humanity, bound to its miseries, fetishisms of all kinds, is still awaiting! I wanted to express the wish that man may liberate himself from hate, prejudice, dark instincts, regression, all that lowers him and prevents him from seeing the truth, from going forward, from rising above himself."

Later, when I had gone further in my work, I consulted the eighty-four years old (and young!) Rabbi Da Fano, in Milan, of the Orthodox faith, being a little anxious at certain of my interpretations (also for my conception of the last strophe of *Adon Olam*, in which I saw the idea of death). This great and gentle scholar was very much moved and reassured me. "Your instinct has been right," he told me. "And you have miraculously guessed the underlying feelings of this text, as certain of our great scholars in the Middle Ages did."

If, by chance, you still had a few of your programs for the concert, I should be very glad to have some of them. In a short way, they say everything.

Will you please convey my message of *thanks* and deep

appreciation to all those who collaborated with you—the chorus, Cantor Rudinow, the organist—and also the organizers who helped. They and you have not only given me a joy and a consolation, but, I am sure, made a great contribution to a *cause*, which is still more important, the cause of Judaism, the cause of Humanity!

With warm regards and thanks,

Sincerely,
Ernest Bloch

Binder showed that letter to Rabbi Stephen Wise, who referred to it as a "precious treasure" and expressed his own great admiration for Bloch as a man as well as a great composer. In 1956, with the personal sponsorship of Binder, the National Jewish Music Council dedicated its annual music festival celebration to Ernest Bloch and his music.

For the January 1957 issue of the American Guild of Organists' *Quarterly*, Binder contributed an article on the Sacred Service—*Avodath Ha-kodesh*—of Ernest Bloch, in which he made the following observations: "In the synagogue music of the 19th century, its composers fell short of achieving real greatness by virtue of the fact that they harmonized this age-old synagogue musical tradition with the tonic-dominant harmonies of that day, which somehow did not reflect the true character of this music, which is basically Oriental. During the early part of the twentieth century, Jewish composers searched for a system of harmony which would reflect the true physiognomy of this music. Ernest Bloch was the first to achieve this. His music has shown the way to all Jewish composers who are engaged in this musical field of endeavor. . . . Bloch, in his quasi-recitative style in the Sacred Service, simulates the style of the cantillation of the Bible, the oldest musical type in synagogue music. . . . Yet, with all its atmosphere of antiquity and modality, there is a strong contemporary musical feeling present in this work."

Binder as a Secular Jewish Artist

Binder's *Concertante for String Orchestra* was premiered in
1943 at Carnegie Hall in New York by the National Orchestral Association, under the direction of Leon Barzin.
In 1945 the Young Artists Contest for musical performance
at the 92nd Street "Y" music school was inaugurated
by Binder. Subsequently he instituted an annual series of
concerts of Jewish chamber music at the Kaufmann concert
hall of the "Y." Throughout those busy years of service to
the Jewish musical community, Binder increasingly composed music not only for the synagogue, but also for the
concert repertoire. Many of these compositions were directly expressive of Jewish life here in America, with the
excitement of the rise of the Jewish homeland in Israel, and
with the moving responses to the desolation of world Jewry
following the holocaust in Europe.

In 1945, in Ohio, the Columbus Philharmonic Orchestra,
under the direction of Izler Solomon (one of the distinguished alumni of the "Y" music school) presented Binder's
*Lament In Memory of the Defenders of the Warsaw
Ghetto.* Also that year, Daniel Saidenberg's Little Symphony Ensemble performed Binder's *Concertino for String
Orchestra.*

The following year Binder led a series of six lectures on
the topic "Music of the Faiths" at Town Hall in New York.
The first of his choral poems *Esther, Queen of Persia* was
published and premiered at the Stephen Wise Free Synagogue. His *Six American Folk Songs*, arranged for mixed
chorus, were also published. In 1947 he recorded some
Palestinian songs under the Mercury label, and for RCA
label he did two sets of records—*Prayers and Songs for
the Sabbath* and *Jewish Holidays in Songs.*

In 1948 Binder presented the premiere of Jacob Weinberg's oratorio *Isaiah* at Carnegie Hall, with the "Y" Choral

Society. In 1949 his *Concertino for String Orchestra* was performed by the Detroit Symphony Orchestra, conducted by Karl Krueger. Other compositions premiered that year were the choral poem *Israel Reborn*, and the *Requiem-Yizkor*, composed in memory of Stephen S. Wise, which was presented at Carnegie Hall.

The non-sectarian liturgical music publication, *The Hymn*, published in 1950 an article about Binder's by-now-classic hymn *Come O Sabbath Day*. It was subsequently designated as "Hymn of the Month" by the Hymn Society of America. In 1951 the American Jewish Tercentenary Committee commissioned Binder to write the choral poem, *The Heart of America*. He also presented the radio premiere of Darius Milhaud's *Service Sacrè* (Sacred Service) over the Columbia Broadcasting System program, "Church of the Air," in celebration of Jewish Music Month. At that time Binder was honored upon the occasion of his thirtieth year of musical service to the Stephen Wise Free Synagogue.

Lecturer, Writer, and Musicologist

Throughout all those productive years, Binder was also associated with the Jewish Center Lecture Bureau of the National Jewish Welfare Board. As a lecturer he traveled extensively over this country, building interest in Jewish music among non-Jewish as well as Jewish audiences. Meanwhile he wrote extensively on various musical subjects, especially liturgical matters, for many different periodicals. Those articles constitute a body of personal opinions and experiences, as well as a vast amount of educational information. As a whole, they treat all aspects of Binder's life-long efforts in behalf of Jewish music; they, and his musical compositions, are a lasting legacy from his active and creative life.

In 1946, in association with Rabbi D. A. Jessurun Cardozo and Professor Eric Werner, Binder helped to organize the Society for the Advancement of Jewish Liturgical Music. The founding membership included such outstanding Jewish musicians and community leaders as Rabbi James Heller, Rabbi Israel Goldfarb, Isadore Freed, Cantor David Putterman, Bernard Carp, Max Helfman, and Joseph Yasser. Though this group was soon disbanded, it left its mark upon Jewish music in America through its ultimately successful efforts to set criteria for proper synagogue music, to establish the concept of formal training and curricula for the education of cantors, and to set in motion efforts toward those ends.

Two years later, a summer institute on Jewish liturgical music was sponsored by the Jewish Institute of Religion and Hebrew Union College, at which many of these important issues were presented and discussed. Binder participated by presenting papers on the history of music in hasidism, and on "Changing Aspects in Synagogue Music." In that latter lecture he stated, "There is a healthy tendency among the real composers of synagogue music of today to liberate the synagogue chant from the bar-lines behind which it has been imprisoned. This has returned to the synagogue chant some of its original physiognomy. Unfortunately, many of our contemporary composers of synagogue music have only a slight acquaintance with our musical tradition. This is to be deplored because the absence of musical tradition robs a religious service of its traditional musical color. *Nusach ha-tefillah* is the product of centuries of Jewish musical experience. We should hold it sacred and guard it zealously, for it is our musical treasure and contains the essence of our originality as a musical people."

Binder's correspondence with colleagues during that period shows his high hopes at the founding of the School of Sacred Music of the Hebrew Union College in New

York, and his personal enthusiasm at being appointed a member of its new faculty. He taught at the school until his death.

Harvest Years of Activity

In 1952, duirng his third trip to Israel, Binder lectured at Hebrew University on the developments of Jewish music in America and conducted performances of his own orchestral and chamber works at concerts of the Kol Israel Symphony Orchestra. Upon his return to America he composed his *Sabbath for Israel* for Friday evening service. In this work he endeavored to combine elements of the Israeli *melos* with the traditional synagogue chants in the belief that such a combination could be the inspirational music of our future. Retaining the traditional chants wherever ordinarily used, he added music composed in the Israeli idiom for all new texts. All of his thematic material was original, for he did not utilize specific Israeli tunes, but only their melodic mood and style. Fired with the idea of building a creative alliance with Israeli musicians, Binder helped form the Composers' Committee for American and Israeli Jewish Music. He also presented two concerts that year devoted to Israeli music at the 92nd Street YM-YWHA.

When the Doctorate of Hebrew Letters, *honoris causa*, was conferred upon Professor Binder in 1953, the Hebrew Union College citation summarized his work as, "gifted teacher, creative composer, talented conductor, pioneer in the field of Jewish folk and religious music, champion of the return of the religious music traditions to the modern synagogue, dedicated interpreter of synagogal and liturgical music to two generations of liberal rabbis, beloved teacher of cantors, builder of a bridge of music between Israel and the United States."

For an article on "Sacred Music," published in *The New York Times* that year, Binder wrote: "What should be the purpose of sacred music? It must create a religious mood and raise the worshipper to a high spiritual level by its musical substance and performance." From 1954 to 1958 he gave a course on the "Bibliography of Synagogue Music" at the Union Theological Seminary in New York. He was also elected to the executive council of the American Guild of Organists. In 1954 he conducted the choir of the School of Sacred Music of Hebrew Union College for the "Three Faiths Choir Festival" at Columbia University. He was named chairman of the department of Sacred Music of the National Federation of Music Clubs of America.

In 1954 Binder premiered his choral poem, *Hanukkah of the Maccabees*, and he prepared and presented the incidental music of the pageant *The Time Is Now* for Bonds for Israel Hanukkah Festival at Madison Square Garden in New York.

Pedagogically, Binder instituted the unique concept of family teams in music education at the "Y" music school in 1955. Subsequently he compiled a manual for parents concerning the music education of their children. He made available the materials in that manual for the later inclusion in the guidance pamphlet "It Takes Three," published in 1958 and distributed by the National Guild of Community Music Schools. Outlining significant factors as to the conditions of music practice, Binder indicated that "A child's musical education is a three-way effort in which student, teacher, and parent are involved."

At that time, in reviewing the publication *Yiddish Folk Songs With Melodies*, collected by Y. L. Cahan and edited by Max Weinreich, Binder commented "We must distinguish between 'Jewish folk songs' and 'songs which Jews sing.' What makes for a genuine Jewish folk song? I feel it must have a Jewish text derived from Jewish life and experience, and a Jewish tune which is based upon our Jewish musical tradition and is in the musical modes of the synagogue."

When Binder visited England in 1959 he met with cantors and choirmasters there and encouraged them to organize their own Jewish Music Council. That year, too, the Philosophical Library published his book *Biblical Chant*, a textual guide to the performance of the traditional East European-Ashkenazic cantillation as generally heard in the synagogues of this country. That textbook was an outgrowth of many years of instruction in the tropal chant of the Bible to rabbinical students commencing in 1937, and to the cantorial students at the School of Sacred Music since 1948. As a practical study-aid, the book has become an important educational resource also in training music teachers for the Jewish religious schools. A revised second edition was published by Sacred Music Press in 1963.

As A Mature Composer

Over the later years, Binder's larger works were composed and presented in performance. In 1956 his *Dybbuk Suite* for chamber ensemble was premiered by the Carnegie Sextet of the New York Philharmonic Orchestra, and selections from his synagogue compositions were presented at a special service in his honor at Temple-On-The-Heights in Cleveland, Ohio. In celebration of the tenth anniversary of Israel's statehood in 1958, Binder's *Sabbath for Israel* was presented by CBS Church of the Air program. His choral poem *Passover To Freedom* was premiered at the Stephen Wise Free Synagogue. Three other works were also newly performed that year. *Joy In the Land*, a cantata, was presented by the Philadelphia Philharmonic Orchestra, directed by Maurice Levine, for a *Hanukkah* Festival in that city;

Poem of Freedom for orchestra was premiered at the "Y"; and *The Israeli Suite* for orchestra was presented in Toledo, Ohio.

In 1960 Binder's one act opera, *A Goat In Chelm*, was first heard at the "Y" in a presentation under the direction of Maurice Levine. The next year, Binder was guest conductor at Temple Emanu-El of New York in a program of his own liturgical compositions. The WABC radio program, "Message of Israel," presented a special program devoted to his life and work. His piano suite *To a Lily of Sharon*, his *Three Festival Liturgy*, and the first *Bible Lesson With Music* were published.

When Binder returned for a fourth visit to Israel that year, he was tendered an honorary reception in Tel Aviv, and presented a program at the Rubin Academy of Music in Jerusalem. In 1963 his *Folk Songs in Hasidic Style*, and his oratorio, *The Legend of the Ari*, were published. The latter work was premiered the following year at the "Y." The choral-ballet, *Hora V'hodayah* was published in Israel in 1964.

During his lifetime Binder was a prodigious composer. He left a notable list of musical works which are still performed regularly in American congregations and Centers. They include four Sabbath services, a Festival service, five services for the High Holydays, many selections based on sacred texts for soloists and for mixed choirs, concert art-songs, arrangements in concert style of Yiddish and Hebrew folk songs, vocal collections and songsters, instrumental works for piano, for organ, for strings, instrumental ensemble works, larger orchestral compositions, children's choral music, and musico-dramatic works for large groups of singers and instrumentalists. Two of his cantatas, *Esther, Queen of Persia*, and *Hanukkah of the Maccabees* are annual holiday favorites throughout this country. His last works included a choral ballet, an oratorio, and a rhapsody for piano and orchestra, all of which were inspired by Biblical and Jewish themes. A second *Bible Lesson With Music* was published in 1965.

At the Biennial Convention of the National Jewish Welfare Board held in 1960, Binder received the Frank L. Weil Award for distinguished contribution to the development of American Jewish culture. The text of that citation stated, "Awarded to Dr. A. W. Binder whose work as composer, conductor and teacher has made him one of the dynamically creative forces for the advancement of Jewish music. A founder and leader of some of the earliest choral groups to perform Jewish music in this country, director of music at three major Jewish institutions, author of beloved Jewish musical compositions, and an organizer and officer of the National Jewish Music Council, he has given inspiring leadership and direction to the growth and development of Jewish music in this country and thus materially furthered the growth of American Jewish culture."

Binder at Seventy

Few American musicians have ever reached the age of seventy with as much youthful vigor in their musical creativity, and with so much unflagging enthusiasm for their life's work, as did Binder. Though he officially retired from his position as music director of the "Y" music school, he actively continued with his other music positions and responsibilities to the end of his life. In an address delivered at the Biennial Conference of the National Jewish Music Council, held in November 1964, he indicated the future direction for Jewish musical achievements: "We in America can point with pride to what our Jewish composers and performers have done here and in Israel over the recent decades. Music is a significant part of a culture of a people, for music truly is the reflection of a people's vitality, of its innate resources. Such a necessary creative art-force needs strong support. As representatives of various Jewish communities gathered here today, we must press forward in our activities on behalf of our Jewish music culture. We can do this by working, by aiding in so many ways—however nature gives us the means—toward this noble goal of developing ever wider appreciation for fine Jewish music among our people everywhere."

The National Jewish Music Council dedicated its 1965 Jewish Music Festival to the theme: "The Renaissance of Jewish Music In America—The Life And Work of A. W. Binder." In this connection, a handbook was prepared by this writer for distribution throughout the United States as a resource for the celebration of that music festival theme. As I wrote in the introductory material of that program aid manual, "This handbook, published to honor Abraham Wolf Binder as he marks his seventieth year, is more than a warm tribute to a dedicated American Jewish musician. Because Professor Binder has been a prime mover, a sustaining leader, and an invaluable source of inspiration for so many musical achievements, a publication about his life and work must inevitably present a chronicle of recent Jewish musical history. Such a survey testifies to the burgeoning renaissance of Jewish musical creativity in America. Our contemporary Jewish musicians, by enriching current Jewish life, and by preserving the heritage of our historic past, bind us in an unbroken cultural continuity with future Jewish generations."

During that festival year of 1965, many special programs and religious services presented the music of Binder in Jewish Community Centers, and especially in the numerous synagogues of all three branches throughout the country. In those liturgical service repertoires the music of Binder had increasingly become a fixed part of the American *minhag* (tradition). As a part of that year of national tribute to Binder, a gala concert of his music was presented in April at the Philharmonic Hall of Lincoln Center. Among the large roster of participating artists were the Sophie Maslow Dance Company, and a symphony orchestra conducted by Maurice Levine. The three major works performed that evening were *King David* a rhapsody for piano and orchestra, the oratorio *The Legend of the Ari*, and the choral-ballet *Hora V'hodayah (Dance and Praise)*.

Later that season, in May, the Jewish Liturgical Music Society of America held a dinner in honor of Binder at the Stephen Wise Free Synagogue. The following year Binder officially retired from his position at the "Y," continuing to act as informal advisor. However, he went forward actively with plans in his other positions at the Stephen Wise Free Synagogue and at the two schools of the Hebrew Union College in New York—the School of Sacred Music and the Jewish Institute of Religion. He also hoped to continue composing, writing articles, and guiding the activities of the various musical societies with which he was enthusiastically associated. For the National Jewish Music Council, in particular, he was engaged in preparations for the theme of a forthcoming festival which would draw attention to the contributions that Russian Jews have made to Jewish music. His interest was also drawn to encouraging the growth of the Jewish Liturgical Music Society of America, which he had founded in 1963.

Such an actively creative outlook on the part of Binder has often been manifested by other intensely dedicated individuals. The noted architect Walter Gropius wrote in a testament to be read upon his death, "Act as if you were going to live forever and cast your plan way ahead. If your contributions have been vital, there will always be somebody to pick up where you left off, and that will be your claim to immortality."

Aval Ha-manginah Nisheret—But the Melody Remains

On Friday evening, September 23, 1966, while conducting the music service for *Kol Nidre* at the Stephen Wise Free Synagogue, Binder became ill. He finished the entire *Yom Kippur* eve service, but his illness incapacitated him. Though increasingly weak and then blinded, he continued during his last days to work on his compositions, to specify the music for the rest of those holiday services, and to project future professional plans. He died on October 9, the Sunday after *Simchat Torah*.

Binder's funeral was held on October 11. Among the many eulogies offered at that service held at the Stephen Wise Free Synagogue, was that of Carl Urbont, executive director of the 92nd Street YM-YWHA. Urbont said, "It was as though Abraham Wolf Binder had responded to a secret call to put his affairs in order during the Hebrew month of *Elul*. There was surely an inner impulse for him to have requested retirement from his post as director of the music department of the 92nd Street "Y," where he served with great distinction for almost half a century. He chose the date of his retirement. It was September 1, 1966. All that swiftly followed appeared to conform to a design of unusual orderliness. He recommended and oriented his successor. He arranged every detail of our music department and of our High Holyday services at the "Y." Binder appeared outwardly to be in complete control of his physical and mental endowments, and he spoke hopefully of the future. 'I shall compose, conduct, and teach,' he said. Then, while leading his Free Synagogue chorus on *Yom Kippur*, the chorus sang a final, beautiful musical cadence to their conductor. Orderliness and design were characteristics of his personality, and these qualities formed a pattern up to his last breath. He died as he surely would have preferred it, in a blaze of creativity, with the music and poetry of our *Yom Kippur* liturgy pronouncing to him for the last time: 'Who shall live, and who shall die; who shall slumber, and who shall bestir himself.' "

As his biographer, it has seemed to me quite interesting that the first and last musical activities of Binder's life occurred during the High Holydays. He began his musical career as a four-year-old, participating in the *Rosh Hashanah* services as a member of his father's chorus; and he ended that career at the age of seventy-one, conducting a fine professional chorus in the performance of his own liturgical service for *Yom Kippur*.

In an obituary piece for the October 24, 1966 issue of *Congress Bi-Weekly*, publication of the American Jewish Congress, I wrote: "Dr. Binder served the Jewish community in a variety of capacities—composer, conductor, pianist-organist, lecturer, writer, educator, school administrator, organization founder and director—bringing to each role high musical ideals and exceptional enthusiasm and creativity. His Jewish musical interests ranged broadly, and before his death he sought to stimulate interest in the parlous state of Jewish music in the Soviet Union. Advancing age did not diminish Binder's devotion to Judaism, his zeal for Jewish music, and his enjoyment of all aspects of his varied musical career. Rather, he appeared to flourish and to bring to his labors ever greater intensity of purpose. Had he lived on, he would most certainly have guided another legion of colleagues and students. Jewish music and Jewish life have sustained a grievous loss. A. W. Binder's manifold efforts represented a significant contribution not only to Jewish music, but to Jewish culture as a whole."

A memorial-tribute concert of music by Binder was presented at the Hebrew Union College building in New York in February 1967. It was under the joint auspices of the Stephen Wise Free Synagogue, with the schools of the Hebrew Union College and other organizations. Included were liturgical selections for chorus, solo vocal works, as well as piano and violin concert music. The following year, at the April 1968 Biennial Convention of the National Jewish Welfare Board held in San Francisco, Abraham Wolf Binder was cited among those national Jewish leaders memorialized who "by example of their leadership and devotion to furthering the aims and purposes of the National Jewish Welfare Board, have bequeathed a heritage to be emulated in the years to come."

On Binder's tombstone, the words of a Hebrew folk song have been inscribed:

> *"Hayamin holfim*
> *Shana overet;*
> *Aval ha-makhelah*
> *Aval ha-manginah*
> *L'olam nisheret."*

"The days pass—a year goes by; but the chorus, but the melody remains forever."

Abraham Wolf Binder was a man of action and ideas who came upon the scene at a particularly crucial time for Jewish cultural developments in America. Binder stirred the field of Jewish music, widened its scope, and cultivated its attributes. With his own sense of direction and professional purpose, he showed the way to many others. As the protagonist, he organized and drew people together in the field. He left his mark on every aspect of Jewish musical endeavor. The sum-total of his life fully dedicated to Jewish music has earned A. W. Binder a unique place in the annals of American Jewish history.

PART TWO

1 V'SHOMRU:
A CENTURY OF
MUSICAL INTERPRETATIONS

The traditional *nusach* or musical mode of *V'shomru* which comes to us from the ages, raises the question of whether or not it conveys with it the spirit of the text as cited in the Pentateuch, Exodus XXXI: 16, 17, 18. *V'shomru* comes to us in the form of a command.

"Wherefore the children of Israel shall keep the Sabbath, to observe the Sabbath throughout their generations for a perpetual covenant. It is a sign between me and the children of Israel forever; for in six days the Lord made heaven and earth, and on the seventh day He ceased from work and rested."

Logically, therefore, *V'shomru* should be interpreted in musical terms which signify command. Such a purpose is

(This article appeared in the *Israel Abrahams Memorial Volume*, which was published in Vienna in 1927.)

usually carried out with music of a martial character—with music through which we hear trumpet sounds bearing a command, expressing the significance of a holy pact, and of a covenant never to be broken. However, our traditional mode is not at all similar to that tune, for through many generations we have heard *V'shomru* sung to the following *nusach* in this melodic version:

V'shomru
(Original Version)

arrang. by A.W. Binder.

One cannot say that the above melody is significant of a command, or even of a pact, for it unmistakably expresses a spirit of "sweet peace and rest." How impossible it would have been for our fathers to have sung *V'shomru* on the Sabbath eve in a commanding tone! Was not the synagogue on the Sabbath the only haven of refuge where the Jew could come and feel that he was among his own? That feeling of relaxation certainly could not have been attained by chanting these prayers in a stiff and commanding tone, but rather from the mode which we have just shown, a mode which gives the sacred feeling of the Sabbath day— the mode of "sweet peace and rest."

During the past century many composers of synagogue music (among whom were men of great musical ability) have interpreted the text of *V'shomru* in many ways. Significantly, however, in almost all of the many important settings to this prayer, the composer has always aimed at radiating those rays of the Sabbath "sweet peace and rest" through his composition.

Until about 125 years ago choral music in the synagogue was undeveloped and very rare. The service was carried on by the cantor with the help of the congregation. Congregational singing had always existed among our people, and it developed even more when the organ and choir were banished in the Diaspora. Some of the objections to the re-instatement of the choir into the Jewish religious services were based on the fact that the choir would do away with the traditional participation of the congregation in the musical responses of the service, to which they had become long accustomed, and which had become part of their religious experience.

One wonders how the florid recitative of the cantor's chant came about. This we may attribute to two facts: first, that the florid passages of that cantorial chant are Oriental in character, coming probably from our Oriental origin; second, that the cantor, taking advantage of the fact that he was the only one occupying the stage, made use of the situation by singing such embellishments on the traditional melodies, as we hear to the present day.

Thus we find the roots of the many musical interpretations of *V'shomru* in the early congregational participation, and in embellished chantings.

In the synagogue works of Salomon Sulzer (1804-1890) we find a strong desire to weave modern musical form through the traditional modes of the various parts of the liturgy. Sulzer was rarely free from the influences of his musical contemporaries (among them were Beethoven and Schubert), nor was he entirely free from the influence of the church music which had developed to a great extent in his day.

V'shomru

S. Sulzer.

CHOIR V'shom - ru v'ne yis - ro - el es ha - sha - bos la - a-sos es ha-sha-bos ldo-ro - som b'-ris o - - lom.

This version appears to be in the form of a stiff church chant. There might have been two reasons why Sulzer gave us such a work. In his day, the congregants were still accustomed to lending musical participation in certain prayers and responses. Consequently, he composed some of his choral works in music simple enough to be followed by the worshipers. They certainly took such advantage, and do so to the present day in his synagogue, which still stands where the old Vienna ghetto used to be. Then again, Sulzer might have had the desire to create a literal interpretation of the text according to its Biblical spirit. However, Sulzer gave us nothing but the skeleton of a form which was to be taken up and developed by his successors.

Louis Lewandowski (1821-1894), in his two volumes of synagogue music *Todah V'zimrah*, made one of the most valuable contributions to synagogue music during the nineteenth century. Not only did Lewandowski employ the traditional modes in a masterful manner, but he also laid the foundation for a most admirable form and style which was followed and developed by a great many composers of synagogue music in later years—a style which was simple, direct, sincere, and for the most part, Jewish.

Lewandowski, in his *V'shomru*, seemed to have outgrown the age when competition existed between choir and congregation. His *V'shomru* represents a compromise, for it is scored for *Chor und Gemeinde*—choir *and* congregation! The congregation and the choir begin together in a mode which interprets both the "command" and "rest and peace":

The next section is a four-measure passage for the choir voices alone, "à la Sulzer":

Passage one comes in again with the aid of the worshipers, and finally, for the last phrase, "He ceased work and rested," we have a repetition of the choral passages with a pianissimo ending. It is a rather simple and unpretentious work, but one which prophesies the day of the ideal religious service, when congregation and choir will each have their full and active share in public worship.

Samuel Naumbourg (1815-1880), deviated from the

styles of his predecessors. Having inherited a great many
Sephardic melodies, he later employed them to great advantage in his four volumes of synagogue music. In his
V'shomru, in F minor, he has given us a most refined
recitative for the cantor, in the "rest and peace" mode,
which at once ushers in a lovely Sabbath spirit:

This solo is followed by a chorus for male voices based
on one of the tunes of the *Kaddish*, which is known today
throughout the modern synagogue world:

Naumbourg's *V'shomru* ends in the quiet and dignified
manner (suggesting in many ways the Sephardic chant)
that we find over and over again in his works. This interpretation of *V'shomru* is typical of the *V'shomru* of the
Diaspora, for in it we get to feel the sacred joy with which

the Jew welcomed the Sabbath. It was to hear these beautiful tunes that he hoped and looked forward during the preceding six days of labor. Naumbourg's *V'shomru* is not elaborate, but it is very beautiful, almost cameo-like.

Samuel Alman of London (b. 1877) has given us in his volume of synagogue music an interpretation of *V'shomru* which is quite different from those of his predecessors, but which at the same time adheres to the traditional modes in the most Orthodox manner:

In his opening phrase, which takes the form of a bass solo, we hear, although in the minor mode, martial strains. Alman has taken the skip of the fifth, which we find in the first and original version of *V'shomru*, and has constructed it in such a way as to give the effect of a command, or even a warning. This figure of the monotonous triplet and the jump of the fifth is later beautifully developed through the choir.

What seems to be most significant in Alman's *V'shomru* is the fact that through his genuine musicianly qualities he has introduced the coloratura style of the cantor into the beginning of this work, and then has developed it with much ingenuity through the choir. This passage certainly deserves citation, for it is one of exalted beauty:

The major mode which we find in the original version receives due attention from Alman. In a passage of trumpet-like sounds running through the inner voices of the choir, we hear *"Ki Sheshes Yomim,"* bringing before our imaginations the forming of an eternal pact never to be broken:

When Alman returns to his original key, it is a "blessed" return. His ending, *"Shovas Vayinofash,"* is really restful and refreshing. This musical setting of *V'shomru* is musically notable, as well as characteristically Jewish.

In the *V'shomru* in C minor, by David Nowakowsky (1848-1921), famous choir master to Cantor Minkowsky of Odessa, we find a work of supreme beauty attained by superb musicianship and majestic Jewish feeling. Nowakowsky adhered strictly to the traditional mode and coupled that with the fine sense of musicianship and musical knowledge so prevalent among the serious Russian composers who were his contemporaries.

Here we have something utterly new. The male chorus sings a chorale, while above it the high voices chant in unison in almost recitative style, in the true traditional mode:

The theme of his fugue on *"Ki Sheshes Yomim"* is based on the actual *nusach*, embodying the middle section of the original version which changes to major:

The tenor's answer in the fifth seems to be the most natural thing that could be expected, and helps in a large measure to establish the traditional Sabbath eve atmosphere. There are four announcements of the above theme, and some slight development, all wrought in a manner worthy of a master, giving proof of the extraordinary contrapuntal ability of Nowakowsky, which runs through all of his works. The close of this beautiful composition ends in the usual quiet manner which has become characteristic of the modern interpretation of *V'shomru*. However, it is different from the others inasmuch as it is polyphonic in style. Its mode is similar to that of the rest of the work.

In an effort to acquaint the musical world with some of the beauties of synagogue music—its beautiful modes, its subtle harmonies and exotic expressions—I set out in on of my own five *V'shomru* compositions to create one in th

form of an art-song. This work was conceived in the traditional mode, and opens with a quiet melodic line:

he melody continues according to the meaning of the
down to *Os Hi L'olom*—I return to *Beni Uven Bene*
el, and interpret that in a melody of the recitative
e, very fervent, reaching an exalted climax:

This passage represents solemnity—the solemnity which one feels throughout this beautiful text. After the climax, we hear part of the original motif again, and finally there is a closing passage representing the "rest and peace" mode.

Seeing all these works which have been analyzed here from a bird's-eye view, we find that Sulzer and Lewandowski fall into a form entirely their own. We must give both these masters of synagogue music credit for the great work which they accomplished in founding the classical school of composition for the synagogue. They were able to weave the traditional motifs through the recitatives for the cantor, which we find in their volumes. In very few and brief instances, however, do their choral works indicate that these composers were capable of that abandon, that complete embodiment of the Jewish spirit where we find the Jewish soul expressed. Their choral music was kept in forms with a watchful eye on their musical neighbor—the German church-chorale.

It was not so with Naumbourg, nor with Alman and Nowakowsky. The Jewish spirit speaks in their works, without restriction or imitation, without the fear of Wagnerian criticism, such as was aimed at Meyerbeer and Mendelssohn. Everything, everything is felt in Nowakowsky, both in solo passages and in his choral treatments. His harmonies are genuinely semitic, containing that wonderful subtlety, coupled with simplicity. In Alman, as well, we feel the Jewish soul; we hear the Talmudic student at study, and all such other beautiful touches that Jewish life reveals.

We are happy to find that synagogue music is on the march forward. We are happy to feel that we have had our Sulzer and Lewandowski, who were builders of firm foundations. We are happy that after them came such creative spirits as Naumbourg, Weintraub, Alman, Gerovitch, Loewenstamm, Dunajewski, Schorr, Nowakowsky. They were the builders of a structure which is still being built, and which hopefully will in the future tower to exalted musical heights.

II HANUKKAH *IN MUSIC*

In ancient days, as in our own, victory over the enemy was always the signal for an outburst of poetry and song. The musical instrument and the battle-song always played an important part in the conduct of warfare. Even during the Maccabean period, war trumpets were placed on coins as symbols of victory.[1] When Israel crossed the Red Sea after throwing off the yoke of Egyptian bondage, Moses and the Children of Israel burst into the immortal "Song of the Sea."[2] It is said that the prayer *Alenu*, recited at the end of every service, was composed by Joshua after the victory of Jericho,[3] while the Song of Deborah bears witness to Israel's victory over the Canaanites.[4] David's dance before the Ark of the Covenant, after he recaptured it from the Philistines, was another act of thanksgiving.[5]

(This article originally appeared in the book *Hanukkah—the Feast of Lights*, by Emily Elvira Solis-Cohen Jr. and was published by the Jewish Publication Society of America in 1937.)

When Judas Maccabeus entered Jerusalem with his followers and recaptured the Temple, it was indeed the signal for festivity and song. This celebration was both vocal and instrumental.[6] The singing consisted of the *Hallel* (Psalms 113-118), for it was a belated observance of *Sukkot*, a festival always celebrated with the singing of *Hallel*.[7] Psalm 30, the Psalm of Dedication, which was most likely sung at the rededication of the Temple by the Maccabeans, thereafter was assigned especially for *Hanukkah*.[8] "The circumstances which had preceded the Maccabean achievements and the solemnity of *Hanukkah* sufficiently explain the selection of this Davidic Psalm with its tune of thankful but self-abasing joy."[9]

If there were some surmise that the name Maccabee was derived from *Mi Chamocha Ba-elim Adonay* (Who is like Thee among the mighty, O Lord?), and that this might have been the rallying cry of Judah and his followers, it could also be assumed that "Who is like Thee among the mighty, O Lord?" was a battle song as well as a song of victory.[10]

With the appearance of the legend about the cruse of oil, and the consequent injunction to kindle lights during *Hanukkah* week, the three benedictions were adopted for the beginning of the *Hanukkah* service. These benedictions, as well as *Ha-nerot Ha-lalu* and *Al Ha-nissim*, were known as early as the days of the *Amoraim*. *Ha-nerot Ha-lalu* was originally recited after the first benediction.[11]

How these benedictions were chanted originally is unknown. The tune generally used today by Ashkenazic Jews in Western countries is followed by the chanting of *Ha-nerot Ha-lalu*. In accordance with the Hebraic custom of including laws and philosophies with prayer, this contains injunctions to govern one's conduct during the hours the lights are burning.[12]

The service then continues with the hymn of thanksgiving *Ma'oz Tsur*, "Rock of My Salvation," as a late addition to the service of the Kindling of the Lights.[13] It was composed in the Middle Ages by one Mordecai, whose name as author appears in an acrostic. It was first sung in the home, and later was introduced into the synagogue. *Ma'oz Tsur* is known to have had in 1450 a tune other than the one now popular. The present tune, obviously of German origin, may be traced to two German folk tunes of the sixteenth century.[14] As very often happens, two strands of these tunes were joined, and the last four bars attached, making the tune which we know now. Besides the *Hallel*, which is recited at the morning service on all eight days of *Hanukkah*, *Al Ha-nissim*, the only special addition made to the regular liturgy, is added to the *Amidah*. In this prayer thanks is given to God for the miracle of deliverance through the sons of Mattathias, and the important points of the *Hanukkah* story are beautifully set forth, stressing the fact that idealism and heroism are not always to be found in the multitude.[15]

This being the only special prayer in the *Hanukkah* liturgy, it was naturally dwelt upon and elaborately sung. It was also added three times daily during the week of *Hanukkah* to the grace recited after all meals. I have included an arrangement of a popular Eastern European version in my *Hanukkah Songster*, a collection of choral music for children.

The Jew was never content just to sing the hymns and prayers which the liturgy prescribed for each holiday. He also invented songs and poetry about each of his holiday celebrations to supplement his liturgy. The earliest published collection of poems with music, specifically designated as folk songs, was Elchanan Kirchan's *Simhat Hanefesh*, published in Fuerth in 1727.[16] This book consisted of songs and melodies (notated) for all holidays and such special occasions as weddings and circumcisions.

These poems were set to popular melodies of the day,[17] as for example, the special song to be sung during the eight days of *Hanukkah*. The song develops thus: the time when

Hanukkah should be celebrated; the way it should be celebrated; rules about kindling of the lights; ritual; women's
duties on *Hanukkah*; the story of the Syrian invasion; the
miracle of the cruse of oil; the story of Judah; Antiochus'
edicts; moralizations on ablutions for women; Hannah and
her seven sons; alms for the poor; conditions of the day.
The last stanza gives us a clue to the conditions existing in
the community where Kirchan lived: "We are hated in the
exile. Dear Lord, turn it away. Day and night we are in
turmoil. Send *Mashiah* in our day."

The other songs in this book, which in their day were
very popular and also highly considered, are in the same
style, containing laws and customs for each holiday, and
always some moralization. During the evenings of *Hanukkah* week, songs such as these were heard around the tables,
as well as puzzle-songs.[18] Games and riddles also provided
amusement. Special foods, such as latkes, cheeses, and
roast duck, varying with the locale, were prepared during
this week. Yiddish folksongs of the nineteenth century tell
of these household customs.

The Jewish community looked forward eagerly to the
celebration of *Hanukkah*, for it was the first relief from
the bleakness of the late fall and early winter. The preparations for it were elaborate, and the expectations were high.
The children looked forward to a full or half vacation during this festival week. If they did go to *heder*, most of the
time was spent in playing *Hanukkah* games.[19] Then there
was the *Hanukkah gelt*, which the children received from
parents and relatives.

The lighting of the *Hanukkah* candles was, and is still,
chiefly a home ceremony. Every morning and evening,
however, the *Shamash*, or beadle, without much ceremony,
also kindled lights in the synagogue. This synagogue ceremony was performed once during *Hanukkah* week with
pomp and musical ornamentation, if the city fortunately
possessed a cantor and choir.

Between the sixteenth and the eighteenth centuries it was the custom in certain European congregations to chant the service of welcome to the Sabbath (*Kabbalat Shabbat*) with orchestral accompaniment.[20] The orchestra consisted of a fiddle, contrabass, clarinet, drum, and perhaps a trumpet. Most likely what later in the nineteenth and twentieth centuries became known in Europe and America as "the *Hanukkah* concert" had its origin with these customs.

The *Hanukkah* concert usually began with Psalm 30, the Psalm of Dedication. This was generally followed by the elaborate chanting of the benedictions for the kindling of the lights by cantor, choir, and orchestra, and then by the singing of *Ha-nerot Ha-lalu*. Very often the evening's program was rounded out with the chanting of one of the Psalms of the *Hallel*, particularly the last section of Psalm 118, followed by *Al Ha-nissim*. This was also the occasion upon which congregations had the opportunity of giving *Hanukkah gelt* to the cantor and choir. These customs still persisted into the twentieth century in many European countries.

In America, however, a new *Hanukkah* musical literature has gradually been evolved to keep the light of *Hanukkah* alive. Emma Lazarus, in her *Kindle the Taper*, was one of the first in the New World to give a poetic rendering to the *Hanukkah* story. This poem was set to music by Dr. Jacob Singer. There have been later poets to use the theme in English verse, notably Solomon Solis-Cohen, Philip M. Raskin, and Emma Ehrlich Levinger. They have been of untold help in interpreting the spirit of Jewish life to our younger generation.

The story of the Maccabean victory was the subject of one of the greatest oratorios, *Judas Maccabeus*,[21] the work of George Frederick Handel (1685-1759). It was composed in thirty-two days, between July 9 and August 11, 1746, in honor of the Duke of Cumberland upon his return from Scotland after the victory of Culloden. The libretto,

written by the Reverend Thomas Morell, is based on the
Maccabean narrative as given in the first book of Maccabees
and the twelfth book of *Antiquities of the Jews*, by Jo-
sephus. After its first performance at Covent Garden on
April 1, 1747, it was repeated six times during that year.
Handel conducted it thirty-eight times over the following
years, and its success was greatly due to the support of the
Anglo-Jewish community.[22] Despite the fact that it is almost two hundred years old, many of the solos and choruses
in this oratorio are sung frequently throughout the musical world, as for example, Judas' call, "Sound an Alarm";
the triumphal chorus "See, the Conquering Hero"; the
duet, "O Lovely Peace"; and the bass solo, "Rejoice O
Judah", followed by a final chorus, "Hallelujah."

Anton Rubinstein also utilized the Maccabean story for
his opera *The Maccabees*.[23] The same text as that used by
Handel, but somewhat abridged and rearranged, was used
as an oratorio for children in 1917 by the author of this
article; it was first performed at the New York YMHA
in that year, under the direction of the composer.[24]

The *Hanukkah* melody of *Ma'oz Tsur* was sufficiently
interesting for Max Bruch (1838-1916) to have incorporated it into his *Three Hebrew Melodies* for chorus and
orchestra.[25]

In Palestine, *Hanukkah* is one of the important and colorful holidays of the year. The spirit throughout the land
during *Hanukkah* week is festive. Carnivals, concerts, and
gala performances are the order of the day. For the modern Palestinian rebuilding the ancient homeland, the Maccabean spirit is a daily inspiration. It is the heroism of the
Maccabeans, rather than the miracle of the oil, that pervades
the songs and touches the spirit of present-day celebrations. Not alone during the festival of *Hanukkah*, but every
day, is the example of the Maccabees brought to the boy
and girl in Palestine. So it has come about that a boy
scout organization in Palestine is known as "Maccabee."

During its frequent parades through the city of Tel Aviv, the members of this scout organization sing *Kadimah Maccabee*. Some other new Palestinian folk songs contain references to the spirit and days of the Maccabees.

Through the ages, music has voiced Israel's gratitude to the Lord for the heroic spirit of the Maccabees, and for God's deliverance from a blow which, if successful, would have meant annihilation. By means of music, Jews were able to forget (if but briefly) the torment of the exile during the eight days of *Hanukkah*. Today, also through song, our people endeavor to keep alive the spirit of the Hasmoneans.

FOOTNOTES

1. Sachs, *Musik des Altertums*, Breslau, page 90. During the summer of 1931 when I visited the excavations of Beth Tsur, which was at one time a Maccabean encampment, Dr. Sellers showed me some coins of this type ascribed to the Maccabean period.
2. Exodus 15.1; 17.10.
3. *Sefer Kol Bo*, 16.
4. Judges 5.
5. II Samuel 6.14.
6. I Maccabees 4.54.
7. II Maccabees 10.6; cf. above pages 40-41.
8. *Soferim* 18.2.
9. Jennings and Lowe, *The Psalms*, Book I, pages 117-118.
10. Shoiss, *Das Yontef Buch*, New York, page 259, note 1.
11. *Soferim* 20.6.
12. Singer, *Daily Prayer Book*, London, page 274.
13. *Ibid.*, pages 274-275.
14. Idelsohn, *Jewish Music*, page 205.
15. Singer, *op. cit.*, London, pages 51-52.
16. Republished in 1926, New York, edited by Dr. J. Shatzky.
17. *Ibid.*, pages 44 and 47.
18. *The Jewish Encyclopedia*, volume VI, s. v. *Hanukkah*.
19. *Ibid.*
20. Levy, *Travels in Israel*.
21. Upton, *Standard Oratorios*, Judas Maccabeus.
22. *Ibid.*
23. Two excerpts from this opera may be found in the *Lieder-Sammelbuch*, Yuval, Tel Aviv.
24. Binder, A. W., *Judas Maccabeus*, Oratorio for Children, New York, Bloch Publishing Co.
25. Bruch, Max, *Hebraeische Gesaenge*, Breitkopf and Haertel, Leipzig.

III SOME JEWISH CONTRIBUTIONS
TO THE ART OF MUSIC

The question of Jewish contributions to the development of the art of music has been largely ignored by musical historians. Perhaps that is partially due to the fact that intensive research into ancient Jewish music was only begun in our own time. Little is still known by the outside world of the great musical structure of cantillation modes, prayer modes, traditional tunes, folk songs, and art music built up by the Jew during his sojourn in the Holyland and during the Diaspora.

Many of the early Christians were formerly Jews, and when they separated from the household of Israel they brought with them into their new houses of worship modes and melodies which they had known as Jews in the

(This article was published in the *Bulletin of the Jewish Academy of Arts and Sciences*, number three, in 1937. As a paper, it was read before that Academy on May 24, 1936, upon the occasion of the induction of Leopold Godowsky as a Fellow of the Academy.)

synagogue. The debt of the liturgy of the church to the liturgy of the synagogue is an established fact. It has from time to time been acknowledged by Christian music scholars that with the text of the Psalms the ancient church adopted the corresponding chants and manner of antiphonal singing.

Recent research into ancient cantillation[1] and comparison studies made with Gregorian chants,[2] have proven conclusively the debt which early church music owes to ancient Jewish music. To acknowledge this fact is to throw new light upon the entire history and development of the art of music.

Biblical texts served as inspiration to the early Italian composers, who utilized these texts for their musical compositions. The Bible served, too, as the basis for the texts of most of the great oratorios, such as Handel's many great choral works, as well as for Haydn's *The Creation*, and *Elijah*, by Mendelssohn.

Some of the great composers of the nineteenth century acknowledged in several of their works the influence of Jewish song. There is a definite suggestion of *Kol Nidre* in one movement of Beethoven's C# minor quartet, opus 131. Max Bruch's *Kol Nidre*, originally composed for cello and orchestra, is a familiar masterpiece. He also composed *Three Hebrew Melodies* for chorus and string orchestra. Modeste Moussorgsky, a great Russian composer, utilized a Yiddish folk song[3] in his cantata *Joshua*, for chorus and orchestra. Strange as it may seem, the theme of this cantata is engraved upon his tombstone. Rimsky-Korsakov composed a song entitled *Chanson Hebraique* and Balakirev also had a "Hebrew Song" among his compositions. There are many examples of such Jewish influence among other composers as well.

Active Jewish participation in general development of art music does not begin to appear until the early part of the nineteenth century. This was due to the fact that

all singing and instrumental playing was banned from
every-day Jewish life after the Jew was exiled from his
land and driven to the four corners of the earth. Singing
was permitted, however, at religious services and on special
occasions. But instrumental music playing was forbidden
in the religious Jewish home. There were, of course, the
town *klezmer* (musicians), who played at various festive
occasions, but they belonged to the lower stratum of Jewish life, simply because they did something which was
forbidden.

And so we find that Jewish musical talent, wherever it
was manifested, spent itself entirely upon the music of the
synagogue. If one did show musical ability coupled with a
good singing voice, he became first a choir singer and then
a cantor. Jewish musical history tells us that there were
at all times cantors with unusual voices who were greatly
admired not only by Jews, but also by the non-Jewish
world. Israel Lovy (1773-1832), cantor of the great synagogue in Paris, was invited by the Duke of Bavaria, Maxi-
millian Joseph, to sing the tenor part at a performance of
Haydn's oratorio, *The Creation*. Salomon Sulzer[4] (1804-
1890), cantor of the Vienna *Kultes-Gemeinde*, was the
first recognized interpreter of the songs of Franz Schubert,
whose contemporary and friend he was. It was Sulzer who
persuaded Shubert to set the 92nd Psalm, *Tov L'hodot*
to music in the original Hebrew. This setting may be found
in the first of Sulzer's two volumes of synagogue music,
entitled *Shir Zion*.[5] Franz Liszt was greatly moved by
Sulzer's singing when he heard him on Friday evening
in the synagogue on the Judenstrasse of Vienna; and he
wrote at length about this experience.

Jewish participation in the musical life of Europe began,
however, with the period of Jewish emancipation and the
period of Reform and enlightenment. Two composers who
contributed much toward the development of the opera in
Europe during the nineteenth century were products of the

early Reform movement of Judaism in Germany. One was Giacomo Meyerbeer, son of Herz Beer of Berlin who in 1815 opened a synagogue in his own home with Zunz and Kley as the preachers. Herz Beer had his son write special music for these services. Meyerbeer, at that time a young man, believed that the instrumental music of the synagogue should be limited to the types of instruments which were used at the Temple in Jerusalem, namely: trumpets, horns, and harps. This theory made very little impression at that time, for the organ, the musical instrument of the church, was soon made the accompanying instrument in the Reform temples of Germany.

The second significant composer of that era was Jacques Offenbach, the son of Isaac Offenbach,[6] cantor and rabbi of Cologne during the first half of the nineteenth century. Jacques Offenbach, too, received his early musical inspiration from the synagogue, and benefited from the possibilities for musical development which the new theories of Jewish life at that time afforded. Karl Goldmark, son of a cantor in Vienna, and Jacques Fromenthal Halevy in Paris, contributed two successful operas during the nineteenth century which are still retained in the operatic repertoires of the great opera houses of today— Goldmark for his *Queen of Sheba* and Halevy for *La Juive*. Halevy also wrote a number of works for the synagogue, which may be found in Samuel Naumbourg's synagogue collections.[7] Felix Mendelssohn, grandson of Moses Mendelssohn, might also be permitted to join this circle.

Now that musical instruments were brought back into Jewish religious worship, instrumental playing became part of Jewish home life. This was especially true among Jews who joined the Reform movement, or were carried along with the period of enlightenment, which had begun to shine through the walls of the ghettos of Europe.

At that time, Jews began to excel as interpreters of the great masters of the musical art. In the foreground among the pianists were Ignatz Moscheles, (who was the pupil and friend of Beethoven), as well as such pianists as Carl Tausig, Emil Sauer, Anton Rubinstein, and scores of lesser lights. Among the great violinists of that period may be mentioned Heinrich Wilhelm Ernst, Joseph Joachim (who was the great friend of Brahms), Henri Wieniawski, and Leopold Auer; among the cellists were David Popper and Carl Davidoff.

In America, Jews have contributed considerably toward the fostering of an appreciation for good music. Leopold Damrosch, who arrived in this country in 1871, was the founder of the New York Symphony Orchestra, and later also of the New York Oratorio Society. He did much toward raising the standards of musical organizations and performances, and was responsible, as was later in our own time his son Walter Damrosch, for the introduction in this country of great musical masterpieces and performers.

Among other first performances in this country, Leopold Damrosch gave the first presentation of Berlioz's oratorio *The Damnation of Faust.* His son, Walter, presented the first performance in this country of Wagner's *Parsifal,* Saint-Saëns' *Samson and Delilah,* the symphonies of Brahms and Elgar, and Tchaikowsky's sixth symphony, *The Pathetique.* In 1891 Walter Damrosch helped to dedicate Carnegie Hall with the New York Symphony Orchestra, and was responsible for bringing Tchaikowsky to this country to conduct some of his own works during the ceremonies of that dedication.

Jews have done much in this country to advance the operatic art. Oscar Hammerstein, opera impressario in the early days of this century, was responsible for the introduction of many modern operatic masterpieces. He presented for the first time in this country Debussy's *Pelléas et Mélisande,* Strauss's *Elektra* and *Salome.* He also gave America the opportunity of hearing such great voices as the tenor Bonci, and the soprano Tetrazzini. As general director of the Metropolitan Opera House in those days, Heinrich Conried did much toward advancing the status of that organization, and helped to stimulate popular interest in opera, which was then limited to the privileged few.

Jews have contributed much to the personnel of the symphony orchestras of this country.[8] In the ten major symphony orchestras of this land, we find that 34 percent of the string players are Jews, in the woodwind sections 9.6 percent, in the brass 9.4 percent, in the percussion 25.7 percent; among the trumpet players of these orchestras we find that 16.7 percent are Jews. It is interesting to note that the largest percentages of Jews are to be found in the string, percussion, and trumpet sections of these orchestras; perhaps, this proves that Jews have a preference for the instruments which were played during the Temple of pre-Diaspora times.

Among the conductors of these orchestras, 45.9 percent are Jews. There are such leaders as Bodansky, Damrosch, Dobrowen, Golschmann, Hertz, Klemperer, Koussevitzky, Kolar, Monteux, Smallens, and Walter. Among the violin soloists may be found many Jewish names, such as: Flesch, Kreisler, Menuhin, Heifetz, Elman, Huberman. Among the pianists we have Bauer, Busoni, Godowsky, Horowitz, Hess, Samuel, Levitzki, Landowska. In the field of the operatic art we may also find some Jews—Braslau, Gluck, Jadlowker, Kipnis, Schorr, List, and Raisa.[9]

Jews have made their influence felt in American musical composition, too. Outstanding contributions to American music are Bloch's symphonic poem *America*, Gruenberg's opera *Emperor Jones*, Gershwin's Opera *Porgy and Bess*, and the jazz elements in Copland's works. Is there need to point out that the American jazz idiom, which is the most interesting musical phenomenon of these decades, has been greatly developed by George Gershwin and Irving Berlin, who stand at the head of a long list of Jews who constantly give to America its popular songs?

In the field of musical education, two Jews have contributed conspicuously in recent years. The late Rubin Goldmark, who was a Fellow of the Jewish Academy of Arts and Sciences, was the teacher of many young American composers who are now helping to shape the American music idiom. Outstanding among these are Copland, Gershwin, Berezowsky, and Jacobi. Ernest Bloch has also been active as a teacher during his residence in America. In the field of violin teaching, Kneisel, Persinger, and Auer have helped develop almost all of the significant violin talent which America has produced in the last decade.

Lastly, in the field of piano pedagogy, Jews have also excelled. Of them, the name of Leopold Godowsky will certainly be remembered in the history of the art of piano playing in this country.

FOOTNOTES

1. "Music of the Pentateuch," Solomon Rosowsky; Proceedings of the Musical Association of London—Session LX, January 18, 1934.
2. "Manual of Musical Illustrations," A. Z. Idelsohn; Hebrew Union College, Cincinnati.
3. *Vus Bistu Azoi Broigez?* (Why Are You So Angry?) is the name of the song so used.
4. "History of the Jews in Vienna," Grunwald; Jewish Publication Society, Philadelphia.
5. *Shir Zion*, Salomon Sulzer; Volume one. Published in Vienna.
6. "Isaac Offenbach," A. W. Binder; *The Jewish Tribune*—1930, New York City.
7. *Zemiroth Yisrael*," three volumes, Samuel Naumbourg; published by S. W. Kaufman, in Leipzig.
8. "Jewish Musicality in America," Keith Sward; *Journal of Applied Psychology*, Volume XVII, pages 672-675, December 1933.
9. *Famous Musicians of a Wandering Race*, Saleski; Bloch Publishing Company, New York City.

IV CHANGING VALUES
IN SYNAGOGUE MUSIC

Religious groups and peoples very frequently lose sight of the aesthetic changes which take place around them. They zealously adhere to forms and traditions without taking cognizance of the changes and evolution which take place day by day. The result is that such groups begin to wither, until a revival is initiated by someone who realizes the danger of gradual extinction.

We are here concerned with keeping the music of the synagogue alive and in tune with the development of the musical art. We realize and appreciate the beauty and originality of the cantillation modes of the *Torah* on the Sabbath. We do not advocate any change in that direction whatsoever, outside of the fact that this very important

(This article was published in the December 1941 issue of the *Bulletin of the Jewish Music Forum,* and was based upon a lecture paper and discussion presented to a meeting of that society during the season 1940-1941, which had been devoted to a "Conference on the Status of Synagogue Music In America.")

function ought to be performed by one who knows the tropes and can sing them with a beautiful voice. Nor do we wish to interefere with the pure and almost naive beauty of the *nusach ha-tefillah* as we hear it chanted by the ordinary congregant who is by instinct musically endowed. Our quarrel is with most of the vocal and instrumental music which we hear in many synagogues throughout the country—Orthodox, Conservative, and Reform.

Most of the choral music which is heard in our synagogues today is not at all Jewish in idiom or style. Even the music of the great classicists and pioneers of synagogue choral music—Sulzer, Lewandowski, and Naumbourg—is not thoroughly Jewish in the light in which we understand it today. They created their works during an assimilationist period, and obviously kept off the tracks of synagogal musical tradition to suit the theories of the then-active reformed rabbis and laymen. Their congregants were taught not to want to hear those "Oriental modes and melodies," but rather tunes in the style of the purely European chorales and folk songs. A large literature of this synagogue music exists.

It was only toward the latter part of their lives that Sulzer and Lewandowski, after they came in contact with East European *hazzanim* and *hazzanut*, began to realize the beauties of the Jewish musical tradition which they had forsaken. In their later works, when they did employ the old modes and melodies, they disguised them behind the European harmonic system, which snuffed out their very life and destroyed their Jewish character.

True, their influence penetrated into Eastern Europe, and for a while everything there too, was *à la* Sulzer-Lewandowski. But the East Europeans, too, recognized that the Jewish soul was lacking in this new music. Soon such personalities as Gerovitch, Rosowsky, and Nowakowsky appeared in the large Jewish communities of Eastern Europe. They not only had musical erudition, but also endeavored to keep the Jewish soul in their synagogal works. This they achieved in part through their fidelity to Jewish melody when they noted it down, as well as in their choral adaptations in which one senses a deep Jewish spirit. This was also achieved when some of these composers deserted the harmonic paths of their immediate predecessors. They, too, created a tremendous literature which in our own day, however, is sadly neglected.

In our own country, the composers of synagogue music who immigrated here toward the last quarter of the nineteenth century were of rather meager musical stature. Men like Welsh, Kaiser, and Sparger did their best, indeed, but the best they achieved resulted only in a mediocre imitation of Sulzer and Lewandowski. We cannot call men like Kitziger and Schlesinger composers of synagogue music, for they were merely artisan-organists called in to play and direct. With a new liturgy, and no music to suit it, they were forced into an unfortunate situation. In this emergency they had to compose, and nobody attempted to guide them.

The Reform synagogues, and to some extent Conservative synagogues in America, have been brought up on the Kitziger and Schlesinger type of synagogue music. That music is not liturgical and is even anti-liturgical. At its best, it is quasi-operatic, saccharine and sentimental. Many of the tunes in these works were actually lifted from various Italian operas.

With regard to music borrowed from foreign sources, let me say that every type of music creates its own specific mood. When we hear Moussorgsky or Rimsky-Korsakov we are immediately transplanted to a Russian atmosphere even if by chance a Hebrew text were set to this music. The same is true of an air or chorus from a French or Italian opera when treated, or rather mistreated, in this manner. Why should such incongruities be permitted when our own musical heritage is so rich.

When planning the music for the synagogue, we must take the following facts into consideration. In former days our people, and other people as well, heard very little music. Perhaps, the only music which the Jews of former days did hear was the music of the *hazzan* and his choir when they came to the synagogue. That is why they demanded on Sabbath, Festivals, and the Holy Days, elaborate chanting by the cantor and his choir, something which is almost extinct in our own day, even in many of the Orthodox synagogues where this had been customary. Everything was acceptable in those days too—a cantor with a throaty voice who sang out of tune most of the time; shrill boy sopranos; hooting falsetto singers; and raucous basses. Anything in music was accepted too, so long as it was tuneful, and the more familiar the better.

Conditions have changed today. Our people do not depend on the synagogue for their musical fare. They go to concerts and opera, and through the means of radio everyone can hear the best singers, instrumentalists, choruses, and orchestras, as well as the loftiest in music. And so, musical taste and musical listening habits have greatly changed.

Youth has been particularly subjected to these changes. Our young people represent the Jewish congregations of the future and the future leaders in synagogues and community life. We must do our utmost not to frighten them away by music which is outmoded, but rather to attract them to the synagogue with a lofty religious atmosphere which can largely be created by good music. If our New York Philharmonic Society were to present the same type of inferior music which we hear in many of our synagogues in this country, their subscription list would hardly pay for the rental of one row of seats in the concert hall.

Our synagogues must take these changes into consideration if they want our people to maintain their respect for the synagogue as the most important institution in Jewish life. We should not engage bad singers as cantors or as choir singers, for they simply become an annoyance at the service. People with fine musical taste might actually refrain from attending the synagogue in order not to hear that "terrible tenor," or that "hooting soprano."

The music, too, should be chosen with great care. Musical laymen, rabbis, and cantors should take full advantage of the synagogue music literature which has recently been composed by our contemporary generation of Jewish composers. This is modern synagogue music, composed by talented and dedicated Jewish composers whose ideals have been, without exception, to elevate and to dignify the music of our houses of worship. They aim to bring into their music that Jewish spirit which is found in the ancient modes and melodies. Moreover, Jewish musical scholars are gradually unearthing our musical treasures of the past and propounding guiding theoretical principles for the future.

The Central Conference of American Rabbis has recognized that by altering the prayer book in the cause of making it "palatable" for their congregants, they deprived it of many of its original liturgical treasures. The new edition, therefore, restores much of the traditional Sabbath and Holyday liturgy. Our attitude toward music is the same. We do not wish to rob our people of their traditional melodic treasures by substituting music which is merely "palatable."

As to cantillation, it presupposes, naturally, an adequate performance for its proper appreciation. Beethoven's symphonies, great as they are, would not stand up under faulty performance. Our recognized Jewish composers, in harmony with the trend toward tradition among our liberal rabbis, are gradually veering away from the pseudo-melody, so characteristic of the American synagogue of the last half century. They are now utilizing, in their new works, the unjustly abandoned traditional musical sources.

This music opens new vistas and enriches the religious

experiences of the worshipers. It is not always cloyingly sweet, nor does the Bible exude that type of sweetness. This music frequently comforts, but it also cries, cajoles, chastises, and shouts aloud like the voices of the great prophets of old.

Wherever possible, full services of our new synagogue music should be presented, but it is advisable to proceed step by step. At first, the responses from these new services such as *Barchu* and *Shema* should be introduced. Then we should proceed to the larger items in these works. These excerpts should be repeated and repeated often. Rabbis should explain the elevating values of this music, the necessity of having this music sung until it is understood, appreciated, and it becomes a natural part of the service. These works represent truly contemporary thought in Jewish music.

The synagogue must recapture its place as the fountainhead of Jewish inspiration. We should go to the concert hall for good concert music, to the opera for operatic music, and for real synagogue music to the synagogue. The important bodies in this country should devise ways and means to encourage our talented Jewish composers to write new works for the synagogues. This could be done by means of specific commissions, or by contests.

The fact remains that our synagogue music must not be allowed to stagnate or to deteriorate, but must be constantly raised to higher levels of pure religious art. In our modern synagogue, we should look back to the glories of the past, and onward to new glories for the future.

V HOW CONGREGATIONS CAN
BE MADE TO SING

Since time immemorial man has given vent to musical expression in all moods and circumstances. The innumerable songs of the nations bear witness to this fact. Still, the majority of men and women of today will deny their ability to utter a musical sound, and even less to sing a tune. While most people will not sing by themselves, however, many will join when caught up in a singing crowd, sometimes unconscious of the fact that they are doing so. From this premise we shall see how people can be made to sing.

A congregation can be taught to sing in three ways:

(1) By preparing itself as a whole at special rehearsals. These may be combined with Bible classes,

(Published in the December 1943 issue of the annual *Bulletin*, publication of the Society for the Advancement of Jewish Musical Culture, also known as the Jewish Music Forum. The text is based upon a lecture presented to the Society earlier that past year, in connection with a conference held on the "Status of Congregational Singing.")

lectures, and meetings which are held during the week. The rehearsals may also take place after the late Friday evening service when new congregational music (chants, songs, hymns) can be introduced, or at *Oneg Shabbat* get-togethers on Saturday afternoons.

(2) By following a specially-trained choral group. The latter learns the music for congregational singing, and then serves as a collective leader or instigator of song at the service. This method works very successfully when the members of the special choral group do not sit together as a separate body at the services, but distribute themselves throughout the congregation, serving as regional leaders.

(3) By following the cantor right at the services. This can be done either by following the cantor in unison-singing or in the form of alternate (antiphonal) singing, repeating each musical phrase introduced by the cantor. This third method is the slowest and, unless preceded each time by a sufficient number of repetitions, has not much possibility of success.

Congregational singing can never be substituted for choral singing, inasmuch as congregations are incapable of singing the great choral works of the nineteenth and twentieth centuries which should adorn our services. Nor can congregational singing, or a choir, be a substitute for a cantor. The cantor is the mainstay musically of our synagogue service. He should be the musical specialist in the synagogue.

The person who is chosen to teach and lead the congregational singing is very important. Upon him will depend the success of this venture. Aside from having a pleasing voice, he must be a real musician with adequate knowledge of the techniques of teaching and conducting, and with a good deal of patience. Above all, he must be able to elicit the necessary enthusiasm for the musical works.

Children should also be organized into special groups for the purpose of learning congregational singing, for they represent our congregations of the future. The training of the children in this field should be for their own junior services, as well as for the purpose of joining in the congregational singing at the regular services with their elders.

By teaching our congregations the right kind of synagogue music, and by having it sung properly, we may look forward to more interest in the service on the part of the adults, more enjoyment of it by our children, and generally a greater spirit of devotion in our synagogues.

VI THE NEGLECT AND NEED OF JEWISH MUSIC

Music has always played an important part in the life of the Jewish people. During Biblical days there were songs and instrumental playing in religious as well as in secular life. In Diaspora exile, as time went on, much more was developed and added to this already established musical life in all spheres of Jewish existence. As a matter of fact, music accompanied the Jew in every move of his daily routine. He sang when he prayed and when he hoped for the return to his native land. He hummed when he thought. The smallest religious act was accompanied by a prayer which was either sung or chanted.

It is to this penchant, which actually accompanied him

(This article appeared in the September 1944 issue of *The Jewish Center*, published by the National Jewish Welfare Board. It expresses the author's ideas which he expounded at that time in helping to form the National Jewish Music Council.)

throughout his life, that the inherent musicality of the Jew may be attributed.

When the period of enlightenment broke upon the ghettos of Europe at the beginning of the nineteenth century, our people were thrown into direct contact with European culture in all its phases. Their contact with nineteenth century music made a terrific impression upon them. There were immediate repercussions of this in the music of the synagogue. It was early in that century when Salomon Sulzer of Vienna made his appearance upon the scene, bringing his musical reforms into the music of the synagogue. He was soon followed by many other innovators, who from that time into the present era have added a great amount of musical literature to the synagogue liturgy.

The Jew had been singing a folk song, too. Very few had bothered to gather and write it down until the spirit of nationalism in music became prevalent toward the end of the nineteenth century, primarily among the smaller nations of Europe. Folk song collecting began to take place among the Jews, too. This culminated in the establishment of the Jewish Folk Music Society of St. Petersburg, Russia, in 1908.

Those pioneers, notably Joel Engel, began to collect all types of Jewish folk songs sung particularly by Jews in Eastern Europe. Having among them many Jewish musicians with great creative talents, they set about to create a Jewish national musical art. They utilized, in compositions of various kinds, much of the material which had been gathered. Piano pieces, violin and cello selections, songs, trios, quartets, and orchestral works were composed. Much of this music was published, and is available to us today.

The Jewish Folk Music Society of St. Petersburg exerted a strong influence upon Jewish composers all over the world, both in its own time and in the years which followed. Those composers sowed the seed; and from that time to our own day, a fine literature of Jewish art music has come into being, encompassing music of every description and dimension. The "labeled" Jewish composer was now upon the scene. While some of this music is published, the greater part of it lies on the studio shelves of the composers, unpublished and unheard.

Who is to blame for the neglect of this part of our cultural life? Is it the composer, or the Jewish people for whom this music was written primarily? Of course, the composer may be blamed to some extent for not bringing his music to the attention of our people; but those who have tried will tell you that their pleas for a hearing have fallen upon deaf ears. The majority of our people are not interested in Jewish music! Even when special concerts of Jewish music are arranged, our people do not patronize them. When publishers finally undertake to publish Jewish music, Jews do not buy it. The result is that the publishers desist from publishing Jewish music because of lack of support from the public.

We speak of the nationhood of the Jewish people, of Palestine as the center of Jewish culture, and of Judaism as a civilization. All of these theories presuppose a folk music and a musical art. Without a distinctive Jewish art we are not a nation; we cannot speak of a complete culture, nor can we call ourselves a civilization.

Why do Jews sidetrack and disregard their own music? Why do they take so little cognizance of their artists, be they painters, sculptors, or musicians? Why, for instance, is a Jewish composer of the stature of Ernest Bloch given no recognition by his own people, save for an honorary degree which was awarded him in 1943 by the Jewish Institute of Religion?

It is no wonder that talented Jewish composers who have wanted to devote their abilities to Jewish music are alienated and driven from the Jewish fold by lack of support and recognition on the part of their own people. A Jewish composer cannot hope for much encouragement from the non-Jewish world.

What is the remedy? Jews must become aware of the fact that music is an important element in their secular as well as their religious life. Jewish Community Centers should set aside funds for activities which would specialize in Jewish music. Adequate budgets should be set aside in synagogues for capable singers to present the genuine music of the synagogue. Jewish music should be performed at all Jewish functions, wherever Jews gather and where there is a musical program. Jewish music should be demanded from the performers. Choruses in Community Centers should perform Jewish choral music (which is readily available in printed form), purchasing copies for each member and avoiding the mimeographing of parts. Jewish communities throughout the country should organize concerts of Jewish music at which the larger Jewish chamber and orchestral works may be heard. Prizes should be established for Jewish musical works, and new compositions should be commissioned from Jewish composers.

The recent experimental "Jewish Music Week" programs instituted by the Arts Committee of the National Association of Jewish Center Workers, in collaboration with the National Jewish Welfare Board, under the direction of Dr. Bernard Carp, is a long step in the right direction. Why cannot Centers subscribe to a fund in return for which they would receive several issues of new Jewish music in various forms? I have in mind particularly Jewish chamber music, orchestral music, and other forms suitable for the groups found in Jewish Centers, for whom Jewish music is sorely needed.

In this way will we create the demand which will in turn create the supply, for a composer can develop only when his works are heard. When our people will begin buying

Jewish music, the publishers will begin publishing it. Only by becoming conscious of our Jewish composers and their music may we hope to develop this important part of cultural expression among our people.

VII THE MUSIC OF
THE SYNAGOGUE:
AN HISTORICAL SURVEY

The Bible and the Talmud are replete with references to singing and to instrumental playing. This points to the important part that music played in the daily life of ancient Israel. That music consisted chiefly of modes upon which were based certain melodic figures, in some cases (according to headings of the Psalms) specific melodies.

Certain portions of the Bible were read in public in a chant-like manner which we call *cantillation*. It was considered a desecration to read Biblical text without a chant. This cantillation was finally written down with the text in the ancient *neume* system, during the ninth century of the Common Era by Aaron Ben Asher of Tiberias in Palestine. According to some of the early church fathers,

(This article appeared in the Fall 1945 issue of *Diapason*, published by the American Guild of Organists. It is based upon a lecture delivered by the author on May 1965 at Guild Hall of St. Thomas Church in New York City.)

and acknowledged in their studies by musical historians of the nineteenth and particularly the twentieth century, these cantillation modes of the Bible are the basis of the Gregorian Chant which we know today. Historically, the early Christians were considered only another sect in the total household of Israel. When they organized their own places of worship they brought with them the songs and chants which they had sung in the Temple and in the early synagogues in Palestine.

Among the Jews, these ancient cantillation modes and synagogue melodies have best been preserved in the Jewish communities of the Near and Middle East, which is their original climate. As soon as those melodies and modes began to roll toward the West, they gathered up western influences. Today, the cantillation modes of the Jews of Persia may on the surface sound radically different from those cantillation modes which we may still hear in the Orthodox and Conservative synagogues in our own country. Yet, upon comparison, their similarities and common origin can readily be recognized.

The synagogue, in turn, has benefited from the development of the music of the church. Until the beginning of the nineteenth century, synagogue music was largely improvisational. A traditional mode was prescribed for a certain prayer or service, and the cantor improvised accordingly in that mode. There were also melodies invented in these modes which have become part of tradition. The accompanying singers to the cantor also improvised their harmonies.

With the impact of the classical period of the eighteenth century and the development of the cantata, mass, and oratorio, the synagogue, too, began to face the need of organizing its music according to the musical standards of the day. Salomon Sulzer of nineteenth century Vienna is considered to be the father of classical synagogue music, although the way was prepared for him by a number of predecessors. Sulzer was the first to take the ancient modes and melodies and to shape them into well-formed choral works. He even inspired Franz Schubert to compose a choral setting to the original Hebrew text of Psalm 92. Sulzer was followed later by Lewandowski in Berlin, Naumbourg in Paris, Nowakowski in Russia, and scores of others, who during the nineteenth century built a tremendous literature of excellent choral music for the synagogue service.

Toward the end of the nineteenth century, serious synagogue musicians began to feel the incongruity between the Oriental *melos* of their musical tradition and the German harmonic system which was being employed as harmonic background. The same thing happened in Russia, where the German harmonic system also did not suit the Russian type of melody. Incidentally, it was Moussorgsky who found a solution to that problem, making his music more Russian than the works of his contemporary Russian composers.

It was that special harmonic problem which agitated and occupied the minds of Jewish composers at the close of the nineteenth and the beginning of the twentieth century. Experiments in this direction were made by many musicians in both religious and secular Jewish music. The one to solve the problem best was Ernest Bloch, in such works as his cello rhapsody *Shelomo*, the symphony *Israel*, the *Three Psalms* for voice and orchestra, and, above all, his *Sacred Service*, which was written for the Sabbath morning service according to the *Hebrew Union Prayer Book*. In this great oratorio, which is indeed one of the greatest choral works written in our time, Bloch expresses the Jewish *melos* with a harmonic background which reflects its true spirit.

Over the past decade the synagogue has attracted many musicians of excellent talent and training. They have contributed to synagogue music literature many services of

importance from the musical as well as the traditional point
of view. Music which by no means can be considered as
genuine synagogue music has been displaced. The new
third edition of the *Union Hymnal* has also aimed to create
the Jewish hymn to be sung to an English text. In it we
have many wonderful Hebrew poems translated into English and set to the appropriate traditional mode or melody
shaped into a hymn-tune.

Both church and synagogue are aiming to raise the level
of their music by attracting to their service highly-trained
musicians. And both church and synagogue must come to
realize that, with all the good music which people hear
today over the radio and in the concert halls, they can fulfill a specific human need by giving worshipers sacred music
of a very high level, finely performed.

VIII   THE SABBATH IN MUSIC

"I will sing, O Sabbath, songs of love unto thee,
For it is fitting, O day that art precious to me."

(Jehudah Halevi)

Early in the history of the Jewish people the Sabbath was called a delight and a day of good cheer. It was never a day of mortification or sadness, as among the Babylonians of ancient days. In the Temple at Jerusalem special sacrifices were offered, excerpts from the Bible were read, and a special "Psalm for the Sabbath Day" was sung by the Levites. This was Psalm 92, still recited as the Psalm of the Sabbath. Significantly, Psalm 92 is one of the ten Psalms which begin with the words *Mizmor Shir*, both words meaning "song." This was interpreted to mean that the Sabbath was to abound in song and praise, and so to be a delight. It was also considered significant that this Psalm contains much musical terminology. In it are found such words as: *Asor*, meaning ten-stringed instrument;[1] *Nevel*, large harp;

(This article originally appeared in the book *Sabbath: the Day of Delight*, by Abraham E. Millgram, published in 1944 by the Jewish Publication Society of America.)

Higgayon, meditative music; *Kinnor*, small harp; *Aranen*, "I shall sing," or "I shall be joyful."

Many other reasons for music on the Sabbath were offered at a later time. A few typical ones are worth quoting. "There are," it was said, "seven gates in the head of a human being: two ears, two nostrils, two eyes, and a mouth. The last is the seventh, with which it is incumbent for the Jew to bless the seventh day."[2] Then there is a passage in the Song of Songs—"I am dark but comely"—which the *Midrash* interprets, "Dark am I during the six days of the week, but beautiful am I on the Sabbath with my songs and prayers." Thus music became an integral part of the celebration and of the very spirit of the Sabbath day.

It seems highly probable that more than the usual amount of singing characterized the Sabbath service in the synagogues as well as the Temple of Palestine. The prescribed portion of the Law had to be read "with a sweet tune,"[3] and this reading played an important part in the service. There was gaiety, singing and dancing on the Sabbath day in the public squares, too. Finally, Levites were permitted to play their instruments on the Sabbath, and even to mend a broken string of an instrument.[4] While the three trumpet blasts which were sounded at intervals on a Friday afternoon were a warning to cease work in preparation for the Sabbath, such prohibitions did not apply to the Temple.

After the destruction of the Temple, the Jews went into mourning. Singing and instrumental music, which were a sign of joy, were prohibited. On the Sabbath, however, which was a day of rest and which was called "a delight," Israel was permitted to cast off its mourning and welcome the day in holiness and joy. *Ein Avalot B'shabbat*, "Mourning on the Sabbath is prohibited!"

Music became the great aid to this principle of temporary surcease from sorrow. In the synagogue the Pentateuch and the Prophets continued to be read with a sweet tune, as commanded. We still hear these modes in our synagogues;

they are known as "cantillation modes."[5] The ever-growing liturgy, which replaced the sacrifices, was sung and chanted. We today have but faint traces of this music, because musical notations did not come into existence until the eighth century, Common Era. The *Kiddush* over wine, in the synagogue as in the home, must always have been chanted in rather elaborate and festive style.

In the home the Sabbath meal, too, was made to contribute to the delight of the day. *Zemirot*, or table songs, had begun to develop as far back as the days of the Second Temple.[6] Thus it is believed that *Tsur Mi-shelo*, one of the group of *zemirot* for the Sabbath eve whose author is unknown, belongs to the early Tannaitic period, perhaps even before Yabneh. The poem is based on three benedictions of the grace: *Ha-zan*, *Al Ha-aretz*, and *Boneh*. There is no reference at all to the Sabbath in this poem. Most of the *zemirot*, however, are products of a much later day.

The idea of making the Sabbath a day of delight and joy through music gained momentum as time went on. As mounting persecution made the burden of the Jew increasingly heavy, it became necessary to emphasize those elements in the Sabbath which could give him some respite from his troubled existence, some way of restoring his self-respect. The Sabbath was to bring sweet peace and rest and remind him that he was a prince of God. It is therefore significant that the gayest *zemirot* were written during the gloomiest times.[7]

The eleventh century witnessed the beginning of the great period in the history of Hebrew poetry, both sacred and secular. The vogue in those days was to compose religious poetry to the rhythm and melody of popular secular songs and to imitate their phonetic sound in Hebrew.[8] At first the rabbis censured such practices, but the poets won. One rabbi, after having been persuaded of the worthiness of the practice, said that he saw "no reason why the devil should have all the beautiful tunes." Many of these sacred poems became popular; some found their way into the liturgy, and a number became *zemirot* for the Sabbath.

Another factor in the development of *zemirot* was the growth of the *Kabbala*, whose mystic ideas became popularly associated with the Sabbath. One kabbalistic belief was that a *Neshamah Yeterah*, an additional soul, or a Sabbath soul, descended upon the one who observed the Sabbath day according to law. Many kabbalists believed that such a soul could be attained only through song on the Sabbath. The Lurian kabbalists of the sixteenth century laid particular stress upon the power of music. Isaac Luria himself encouraged his disciple Shelomo Alkabetz (c. 1503-1580) to compose the famous poem, *L'cha Dodi*. This poem, along with the Song of Songs, *Azamer Bi-shevahin*, and *An'im Zemirot* constitute the center of a group of love songs by which the Jew expressed his love for God and the Sabbath. *L'cha Dodi* spread rapidly to all Jewish communities and, in later centuries, became a favorite text for composers of synagogue music. Isaac Luria also composed *zemirot* for each of the three Sabbath meals: *Azamer Bi-shevahin, Asader Li-se'udata,* and *Bene Hechala.*

Not only the poetry but also the tunes of certain *zemirot* have been attributed to Isaac Luria and his kabbalist followers, including Israel Najara, the composer of *Yah Ribbon Olam*. While this may be doubted, it is clear that the *hasidim,* the spiritual descendants of the Lurian kabbalists, contributed much to the music for the *zemirot.* Hasidic tunes for *zemirot* are almost always joyous and rhythmic. Characteristic of the method of singing them is the frequent interpolation of stretches of wordless song where there is melody to spare between the phrases or verses of a poem. The *hasidim* were careless in choosing their melodies. They adapted to their needs military marches, waltzes and other popular tunes of the day and land in which they lived; consequently the rhythm of the

song or the length of the melody did not always fit. Yet to
the *hasidim* this did not seem to matter.

Among the *HaBaD hasidim*, however, one does find melodies with mystic elements of the kind which colored their
beliefs. The most mystic tunes were reserved for the
Aramaic poems in the *zemirot*, such as *Azamer Bi-
shevahin*, and *Yah Ribbon*. This may have been due to the
Lurianic origin of these poems.

Whether among *hasidim* or *mitnagdim*, *zemirot* served
as the bridge between table talk and religious discourses,
between the human and the divine, between the jocular
and the serious. It has been pointed out frequently that a
Jew must honor God with the beauty of his soul and the
beauty of his throat:[9] "While Israel feasts, he always sings
songs of praise to God."[10] The chief singers at the table
were the father and the sons. Mother and daughters might
join in the refrains or sing their own *zemirot*.[11] Such were
the customs as the singing of *zemirot* gained ground during the Middle Ages, particularly in Germany and Italy.[12]
The Ashkenazim sang *zemirot* all year round, while the
Sephardim sang them only in winter and summer.

There are *zemirot* for all three meals of the Sabbath.
However, the most important and colorful group, from the
poetic and musical points of view, are those associated with
the Friday evening and Saturday midday meals. At the
Sabbath eve meal, the master of the home welcomes the
Sabbath with the chanting of a group of prayers beginning
with *Shalom Aleichem*. The *Kiddush* follows. The actual
zemirot are introduced with a meditative poem—*Kol
Mekadesh* for Friday evening, and *Baruch Adonay Yom
Yom* for Sabbath afternoon. The tune of each of these is
reminiscent of a liturgical mode. *Kol Mekadesh* is sung
in the *Magen Avot* mode on the Friday evening service,
suggesting the "sweet peace and rest" attitude of the Sabbath; *Baruch Adonay* is likewise associated with a Friday

evening synagogue mode, that af *Adonay Malach*, suggesting Israel as the "Prince of God."

Generally, the *zemirot* melodies which follow the introductory ones are lively, and bear the unquestionable
stamp of the country or locality whence they stem. The
Sabbath guest used to be asked to sing the *zemirot* with
the melodies customarily used in his native town. If the
Sabbath guest was a good singer, his hosts and their neighbors would gather to learn his songs. This is how melodies
frequently spread through Jewish communities.

It is not within the province of this discussion to specu-
late on the origins or authors of the poetry of the *zemirot*,
but a few remarks on this aspect of Jewish music may be
in place.

Israel Najara (1555-1628), the author of the very beautiful and popular poem, *Yah Ribbon*, holds a unique place
among the authors of poetry in the *zemirot* period. He
composed not only poetry but also melodies. He followed
the favorite custom of his period in composing poems to
existing rhythms and melodies of popular songs. In 1587, in
Safed, he published the first edition of his *Diwan: Zemirot
Israel*, which became very popular in Oriental Jewish
communities. It was the first Jewish song book to be published in the East.

One poem in the Sabbath *zemirot* which deserves special mention is *Mah Yafit*, which is the work of Mordecai
ben Isaac, whose name is found therein in an acrostic. One
melody for this poem was of Polish origin and gained no-
toriety among the wealthy Polish *pans* in the seventeenth,
eighteenth, and nineteenth centuries. At their wild orgies
these *pans*, who were the Jews' landlords, frequently would
compel a Jew to sing and dance to the *Mah Yafit* melody.
Almost every Pole knew that a Jew could sing *Mah Yafit*.
Even Chopin was led to remark: "Poor Polish airs, you do
not in the least suspect how you will be interlarded with
Mah Yafit."

Zemirot were sung not only at the Sabbath midday meal, but also at the *Shalosh Se'udot*, the third meal of the Sabbath. This meal usually took place after the Sabbath afternoon service, and almost always in the synagogue. The singing of *zemirot* was kept up until sundown, and thus the *zemirot* always had the character of a prelude to the outgoing of the Sabbath. The evening service usually followed and after the *Havdalah*, which ushered in the secular days of the week, *zemirot* again were sung. Later in the evening, at the *Melaveh Malkah*, still more were sung to indicate the accompanying of "the Bride" back to her abode where she would remain until her return on the following Sabbath. As a matter of fact, there was always a great deal of singing at the outgoing of the Sabbath, for it was considered appropriate to chant hymns and thus fittingly to accompany the Sabbath "Bride" upon her departure.

The music for the various occasions had distinct character and atmosphere. For the greeting of the Sabbath and for the Sabbath day itself, joyous melodies were generally employed, but for the outgoing of the Sabbath, mystic and nostalgic tunes were sung. The post-*Havdalah* group of *zemirot* dealt with the coming of Elijah the Prophet to deliver Israel from exile. Elijah songs are the most ancient of these *zemirot*, since the Jew hoped and sang of his return to his Homeland from the very moment of exile. Of this group of songs, *Eliyahu Ha-navi* is the most ancient.

The table-songs of the Sabbath comprised the Jewish song book. The Jew sang them through joy and tears. These poems and songs are the mirror of the soul-life of "Universal Israel," for through them the Jew attained the *Neshamah Yeterah*—Sabbath Over-Soul—which descended upon him on the Sabbath day.

There are very few parallels to the Jewish *zemirot* among other nations. Many nations have their drinking songs, but we have our *zemirot*. In these we find the genial piety combined with the good cheer and thankfulness, which were usually separated in the table-songs that existed among the other nations. They combine tragedy and joy, the material and the spiritual, changes of taste and progress of thought. All these elements are mirrored in the songs, and through it all the general theme is "The Sabbath."

Turning to Sabbath music in the synagogue, we find that the precentor or cantor always occupied an important position in Jewish religious worship. He led the people in prayer and read portions of the Law to the congregation "with a sweet voice." His importance increased during the early centuries of the exile, when the liturgy replaced the sacrifices. This liturgy had to be chanted. Precentors were also required to know the prayers by heart, and later on to improvise or compose prayers for special occasions. Under these circumstances, scholarly qualifications were paramount in precentors. Frequently the offices of rabbi and precentor were combined in one man. As time went on, however, two conditions in the Jewish community led to the rise of the cantor, who specialized only in chanting the prayers on Sabbaths and holidays. The first condition was the general development of the art of music in Western Europe, which made its influence felt upon the Jewish communities who sojourned in various parts of the continent. Secondly, as part of his *Oneg Shabbat*, the Jew wanted the cantor to entertain him on the Sabbath. The better the cantor's voice and the more elaborately the prayers were chanted, the better the Jew like it.[13]

Gradually, toward the end of the seventeenth century, the offices of rabbi and cantor were separated from each other, and gifted cantors and choirs began to bring joy and comfort to their communities in the synagogues on the Sabbath. Cantor, choir and musicians, in certain communities during the eighteenth century, would lead the congregation in the *Kabbalat Shabbat* (welcoming of the

Sabbath).[14] The most elaborately sung part in this section of the service was the *L'cha Dodi*. Congregations in Eastern Europe witnessed the development of the choir and the specialized cantor toward the end of the eighteenth and the beginning of the nineteenth century.

Salomon Sulzer (1804-1890), in Vienna, was one of the first to bring technical order into synagogue music. His rendition of the service on the Sabbath was a delight to those who came to hear him.[15] His influence penetrated into all the progressive communities in Europe. Soon Sabbath eve and Sabbath morning were anticipated with special eagerness and interest in the synagogue. Cantor and choir satisfied the great love for music which the Jews had since the days when they lived in Palestine as a nation among nations. A Jew was not permitted or wanted in the opera houses or concert halls, nor would the pious Jew have taken advantage of such a privilege even if it had been granted.

The special music on particular Sabbaths of the Jewish calendar year was musically colored by the resourceful cantor and his choir with special modes and melodies. On *Shabbat Shirah* when the "Song of the Red Sea" was read in the weekly portion of the *Torah*, it was chanted by the reader elaborately, with a special tune. On *Shabbat Hagadol*, the Sabbath before Passover, the cantor would give the congregation a foretaste of some of the *Seder* melodies when he reached *Hasal, Va-amartem Zevah Pesach*. On *Shabbat Hazan*, the Sabbath preceding *Tisha B'av*, he would chant the *L'cha Dodi* at the welcoming of the Sabbath with the tune of *Eli Zion* of the *Kinnot*; and on the Sabbath day, the focal point of the synagogue service was the reading of the *Maftir, Hazan Yesha'yahu* to the cantillation mode of the Book of Lamentations, which is chanted on *Tisha B'av* eve. This set the scene for *Tisha B'av*.

On the next Sabbath, *Shabbat Nahamu*, "the Sabbath of Comfort," the heavy veil of mourning was lifted. All was cheerful and hopeful. The major mode returned to *L'cha Dodi* on the Sabbath eve, and gone was the lament from the *Haftarah* on the Sabbath day. In the East European town, immediately after *Tisha B'av*, joyous strains could be heard from the rehearsal room of the cantor and choir, who would be preparing some special joyous composition to be sung on *Shabbat Nahamu.* The town musicians, too, would be tuning up for many weddings which would take place on the Friday afternoon of *Shabbat Nahamu* and on Saturday evening.[16]

Shabbat Mebarechim, the Sabbath on which the new moon was announced, which naturally came once a month, also had its special importance and significance musically. The cantor considered it the most important Sabbath of the month, and on it special musical works were sung. The focal point of the service was, of course, the section which dealt with the benedictions for the new month. These were sung as follows: *Yehi Ratzon* (May It Be Thy Will) in the *Ahavah Rabbah* and *Selichah* modes; *Mi She'asah* (He Who Wrought Miracles), the announcement of the New Moon, and *Yehadshehu* (May He Renew) all in the *Adonay Malach* mode.

When the new moon or *Rosh Hodesh* occurred on the Sabbath, the day was called *Shabbat Rosh Hodesh*. On it, the *Hallel* (Psalms 113-118) was chanted and special changes were made in the *Musaf* prayers to conform with the character of the day. The general atmosphere in the synagogue on that Sabbath, as soon as the *Hallel* Psalms arrived, was like that of the Three Festivals: *Pesach*, *Shavuot* and *Sukkot*. This spirit was created by the cantor who ushered in the *Hallel* Psalms with the Three Festival cadence. From then on, all was festive.

Of the enormous amount of liturgical synagogue music which was created during the nineteenth century, we find about 80 percent set to the Sabbath liturgy. The reason for this abundance is the fact that cantors did not see any necessity for varying the music of the festivals and holidays, which came but once a year, but did find it necessary, for the sake of variety and interest on Sabbath after Sabbath, to have various versions of certain parts of the liturgy in their repertoire.

When the Reform movement began to flourish in Germany, it aimed to obliterate as much of the Oriental color in synagogue music as possible. As a step in this direction, the cantillation modes of the *Torah* and the *Ahavah Rabbah* mode in the liturgy were eliminated. Salomon Sulzer in Vienna and Louis Lewandowski in Berlin were the composers who accommodated themselves to these theories and reforms and became instruments for them. In their synagogue works one finds very little trace of the traditional Sabbath modes. Consequently, their music cannot be considered typical of the synagogue. While larger communities in Eastern Europe liked the musical order which Sulzer and Lewandowski brought into the synagogue, they could not accept the music itself, which lacked the synagogal Sabbath spirit. We find in the works of Samuel Naumbourg (1815-1880) in Paris, a desire to utilize the Sulzer and Lewandowski method, but only by applying it to the ancient Sabbath prayer modes. It was left to men like Weintraub in Koenigsberg, however, and later to cantor-composers of Eastern Europe to start applying modern methods of musical composition to the ancient Jewish modes and melodies. Among these musicians were Schorr, Nowakowsky, Dunajewsky, Gerovitch, Belzer, and scores of lesser known cantors.

Although even these men were under the influence of European form and harmony, still we find in their works a constant striving to adhere to tradition. The literature which these cantors and choir directors created forms part of the tremendous structure of Jewish music.

Surveying the American scene, if it were possible to observe the Sabbath according to tradition, we would find our Sabbath music far richer than it seems, but because the Sabbath is inadequately observed in our day, we find an attitude of satisfaction in a musical *status quo*.

In Orthodox synagogues the music of the nineteenth century prevails. What is laudable in the Orthodox synagogue is the fact that the cantillation modes and prayer modes are rather strictly adhered to. In the Conservative synagogue, where a mixed choir and organ are employed, the Orthodox musical method is peppered with some Episcopal hymns and Unitarian anthems. The music of the Reform synagogue moved away from tradition almost entirely until about a decade ago.

The Reform synagogues, however, have had the greatest facilities for the presentation of good music. Some Jewish musicians, sensing these possibilities, have tried there, since the early part of this century, to create and to present music which is truly representative of the synagogue. This work began with the efforts of Edward Stark (1863-1918), cantor of Temple Emanuel in San Francisco, California. In our own day, there have been men such as Ernest Bloch, Jacob Weinberg, Isadore Freed, and the writer. The Reform movement has begun, though slowly, to realize its musical shortcomings. In an effort to provide a remedy, its leaders have revised the *Union Hymnal* twice in almost half a century. The present edition contains a special Sabbath section of hymns based on the traditional Sabbath modes and liturgy, appropriate for synagogue and home.

In the American Jewish home, music has receded into the background on the Sabbath. One may still hear *Shalom Aleichem* and the *Kiddush* chanted on the Sabbath eve, but the *zemirot* have vanished almost entirely. In some Jewish homes the custom of chanting the grace after meals still prevails; but on the whole, Jewish music flourishes mostly in the synagogue, where significant contributions are now being made to Sabbath music by a small group of Jewish composers.

Curiously enough, we find very little folk music dealing with the Sabbath in Hebrew or Yiddish. The reason for this is that folk songs came under the classification of *Shire Hol*, "everyday songs," while on the Sabbath only *Shire Kodesh*, "sacred songs," were sung, and only in Hebrew. Whatever folklore did spring forth out of the Sabbath was sung either before the Sabbath eve or after *Havdalah*, when the Sabbath was actually over. The only exception in using the Yiddish song on the Sabbath is found in the chant *Got Fun Avrohom*, "God of Abraham," which the women recite or chant just before the *Havdalah*. The song *Shreitzhe Yidn Shabbes*, "Cry Out Sabbath," is a marvelous assertion of the faith of the Jew in the Sabbath. The *Melaveh Malkah*, "Seeing Off The Queen," a song attributed to the hasidic Rabbi Levi Yitzchok of Berditchev, is a picture of the Jew as he returns to his regular weekday routine. *A Chazendl Oif Shabbes*, "A Cantor For the Sabbath," is a satire on Jews who ran from one synagogue to another on the Sabbath in order to hear various cantors, and on those Jews who were the followers of certain cantors.

In the Hebrew language we find very few modern poems dealing with the Sabbath which have been set to music. Most magnificent are the two poems by Bialik: *Shabbat Ha-malkah*, "The Sabbath Queen," and *Yesh Li Gan*, "I Have A Garden," which have become popular folk songs. *Shabbat Ha-malkah* has even taken its place in certain Jewish communities at the late Friday evening services, or at *Oneg Shabbat* gatherings. It is also now, deservedly, among the regular *zemirot* in homes where they are still sung. This poem is really a paraphrase of *Shalom Aleichem*. *Yesh Li Gan* is an idyllic love song, which undoubtedly has no place on the Sabbath but is widely sung.

It has also become the custom in this country to sing

appropriate new Palestinian Hebrew folk songs at Sabbath gatherings. The great poet Bialik, remembering the
sacred impressions which the Sabbath had made upon him
in his early youth, felt a void in the Sabbath as it developed in Palestine, and particularly in the city where he
lived, Tel Aviv. He missed the gatherings of great multi-
tudes of Jews on the Sabbath day in the *Bet Ha-midrash*
to listen to the Holy Word and to sing together the Sabbath *zemirot*. The *Oneg Shabbat* which he initiated in
1929 was an institution to supply this need.[17]

About fifteen hundred to two thousand Jews would
gather in the *Ohel Shem* auditorium at about five in the
afternoon. They then began with the singing, led by a
group of men and boys banded together for the purpose of
leading the gathering in Sabbath *zemirot*. They always
included the prayer *Attah Echad*, "Thou Art One," an
excerpt from the Sabbath afternoon liturgy, sung to a
melody in East European style. That tune represented the
sanctity of the Sabbath and the longing which the Jew
always had for the spiritual rewards of the day. This excerpt from the afternoon service was in lieu of the afternoon service proper. The tune was at first sung by a few,
then was gradually caught up by more and more, until the
tremendous voice of an entire people was carried away on
the wings of song to upper levels, where "dwells the Sabbath soul of the Jew."

Then a discourse would take place. When that was over,
there would be more singing. By this time, twilight had
descended on the Holy Land, and the "Holy Spirit" rested
on this multitude as it accompanied the Sabbath upon its
departure. When the first three stars became visible, the
flicker of the *Havdalah* candle appeared suddenly, and a
golden voice was lifted in the opening phrases of the
Havdalah: *Hine El Yeshu'ati*, "Behold The God Of My
Salvation." The entire congregation was now standing.
When the words *La-yehudim Hayetah Orah*, "To The

Jews There Was Light," were chanted, a blaze of light suddenly illuminated the gathering; all the lights in the auditorium had been lit. When the *Havdalah* was over, there would be singing of *zemirot* in which the entire multitude participated, and that was followed by instrumental music—for the Sabbath was over.

The great Bialik realized the power of song and made it an integral part of this celebration of the Sabbath.

In the Diaspora this idea caught hold, and has since been instituted in many Jewish communities throughout the world. It has helped to bring the song back into the Sabbath. We are beginning to witness the realization of: *Ki Mi-tsion Tetse Torah, U'dvar Adonay Mi-yerushalayim.* "For out of Zion shall go forth *Torah*, and the word of God out of Jerusalem."

FOOTNOTES

1. Curt Sachs, *The History of Musical Instruments*, New York, 1940.
2. Moses Azulai, *Lehem Min Ha-shamayim; cf. Sefer Ha-shabbat*, Tel Aviv, 1936.
3. *Megillah* 32a.
4. *Mishna Erubin* 10.13.
5. Solomon Rosowsky, *The Music of the Pentateuch*, London, 1934.
6. Abraham Zevi Idelsohn, *The Ceremonies in Judaism*, Cincinnati, 1929.
7. Herbert Loewe, *Mediaeval Jewish Minstrelsy*, London, 1926.
8. Aguilar-De Sola, *The Ancient Melodies of the Liturgy of the Spanish and Portugese Jews*, London, 1857.
9. *Zohar*, II, p. 93a.
10. *Cant. Rab.* 8.15.
11. Israel Abrahams, *Jewish Life in the Middle Ages*, New York, 1917; London, 1932.
12. *Ibid.*
13. The kabbalistic cantor and rabbi of Frankfurt-Am-Main of the sixteenth century, Rabbi Herz Treves, bitterly complained against the new movement and the strange view which the *hazzanim* took of their holy functions. "They have ceased to be writers of *Torah*, *Tefillin* and *Mezuzah*, nor do they care for the correct grammatical reading, nor for the reading of the prayers, only for their songs, without regard for the real sense of the words. They neglect the traditional tunes of their ancestors." Idelsohn, A. Z., "Songs and Singers in the 18th Century," in *Hebrew Union College Jubilee Volume*, Cincinnati, 1925.

14. In the library of the Jewish Institute of Religion, New York City, may be found the manuscripts of Isaac Offenbach, cantor at Cologne during the early part of the nineteenth century. He was the father of Jacques Offenbach, famous composer. Among these manuscripts are found violin parts to the *Kabbalat Shabbat* which Isaac Offenbach played as a young man, most likely in his home town, which was Offenbach, Germany.

15. "In Vienna we knew the famous tenor, Sulzer, who served in the capacity of precentor in the synagogue, and whose reputation is so outstanding. For moments we could enter into his real soul, and recognize the secret doctrines of the fathers. . . . We went to his synagogue in order to hear him. Seldom were we so deeply stirred by emotion as on that evening, so shaken, that our soul was entirely given to meditation and to participation in the service." Liszt, Franz, *Die Zigeuner Und Ihre Muzik in Ungarn*, Leipzig, 1883, translated by L. Raman.

16. A. S. Sachs, *Worlds That Passed*, Philadelphia, 1928.

17. Ernest Simon, *Der Entfuehrung Des Oneg Shabbat in Tel Aviv*, in *Juedisches Fest Buch*, Berlin, 1936.

IX   THE SPIRIT OF THE
SABBATH EVE SERVICE

The reason for the observance of the Sabbath is closely linked with creation, for in Exodus 31:16, 17 we find, "The children of Israel shall observe the Sabbath. . . . For in six days the Lord created heaven and earth, and on the seventh day He rested and was refreshed." It is interesting to note that in our own day Igor Stravinsky, in his musical credo, links music with creation: "For my part, music is a force which gives reason to things, a force which creates organization, which attunes things. Music probably attended the creation of the universe."

Here we find the Sabbath linked with creation, and creation linked with music. The link between the Sabbath

(Published in January 1951, as part of the *Summary of Proceedings* for the Second Annual Institute on Jewish Liturgical Music held June 12-14, 1949 in New York City, by the Society for the Advancement of Jewish Liturgical Music, in cooperation with the Hebrew Union College—Jewish Institute of Religion.)

and music is a very old one, dating back to Biblical days when the Psalm 92, which is full of musical references, was chosen as the Psalm for the Sabbath. Throughout the ages, music was the chief aid toward the realization of Isaiah's injunction, "And ye shall call the Sabbath a delight."

We Ashkenazic Jews have, according to our musical tradition, two modes associated with our Friday evening liturgy. They are the *Adonay Malach* mode, based on the mixolydian mode, and the *Magen Avot* mode, based on the aeolian minor mode. Here we have the logic and the creative order of which Stravinsky speaks in his musical credo. The origin of these two Jewish modes goes back to our ancient musical source, namely: cantillation. The *Adonay Malach* mode derives from Pentateuchal cantillation, and the *Magen Avot* mode from the cantillation of the Prophets, or *Haftarah.*

Each of the two modes have their specific purposes. The *Adonay Malach*, which according to our present musical patterns is a major mode, is a majestic mode. It signifies Israel as the "Prince of God." It is applied to the first part of the liturgy which is called, "Welcoming of the Sabbath," and it helped the Jew to extricate himself from the mire of ghetto life and to don his Sabbath attire. It helped prepare him to receive his special Sabbath soul. The *Magen Avot* mode, which is specifically applied to the second part of the Sabbath liturgy, that is the evening service, is in the aeolian minor scale; but it is far from having as its purpose sadness, which is commonly attributed to minor. The origin of this mode is very old, and according to A. Z. Idelsohn, "is the deepest expression of the Jewish soul, and will live as long as the Jewish people lives." Its purpose is to create for the Jew the spirit of Sabbath rest and peace.

There are today those who advocate the disregard of our musical tradition. They counsel Jewish composers "to do whatever they want" when writing for the synagogue. There were also those in the days of Theodor Herzl who advocated that a Jewish State be established any place where land could be gotten. Yet the deeply-rooted Jews wanted only Palestine (*Eretz Yisrael*), for there was the land which contained our roots and our spirit. It was that land which our ancestors trod, and which was tied up with our history.

I say that our musical tradition is our musical homeland. If we are to build a synagogue musical liturgy, it must be built upon our ancient musical roots, which have been nurtured and developed by our ancestors through many centuries, and which exude the Jewish spirit as does no other musical medium. I do not say that we are to sing or perform our musical traditions exactly as they were sung or performed centuries ago. I rather advocate that we build upon our musical traditions in our present day, developing this synagogue music according to those traditions, but in the best musical standards of our own day.

What should be the purpose of the music on the Sabbath eve? It should relax the mind, create a religious mood of peace and rest, raise the worshiper by its musical substance and performance to high spiritual levels, and above all, it should serve as an aid toward a deeper concentration in devotion. If all those concerned in making a Friday evening service do not have these goals, then the entire purpose of the service is defeated. Rabbi, cantor, and choir must be united in those purposes.

Being a synagogue musician is, in a sense, a full-time profession. One cannot step into the role at 7:00 PM on Friday evening and wash it off on Saturday at noon. If you do not feel the spirit of the Sabbath, you cannot transmit it to a congregation through your music. You must believe in it in order to be believed. Only by our becoming conscious of the real role of Sabbath music can we expect our congregations to begin to realize its importance. When they begin to realize its importance, they will want only the kind of synagogue musical personnel who are capable of giving to each service its genuine spirit. When that happens, we shall not be discussing "raising the level of synagogue music," but rather "rising *to* the high levels of synagogue music."

X PURIM *IN MUSIC*

Despite the fact that instrumental playing, singing and joy-making were forbidden to the Jew after the destruction of the Second Temple in Jerusalem, these restrictions were lifted from almost the very beginning of the exile, on at least two occasions in the Jewish calendar year: on *Simchat Torah* and *Purim*. Joy became unlimited and uninhibited on these two holidays, the latter gradually approaching, often with official sanction, close to hilarity. The joyous spirit of *Purim* began with the reading of the *Megillah* (Book of Esther) in the synagogue, and gradually reached into the home. As time went on, it extended into the *purimspiel* and into the various parodies and songs which form an important part of the music that grew out of the celebration of this festival.

(This article appeared in *The Purim Anthology*, by Philip Goodman, published in 1949 by the Jewish Publication Society of America.)

The reading of the *Megillah* is preceded by three bene-dictions, in a major mode in which one immediately feels the joyous and carefree atmosphere of *Purim*. The traditional manner of reading the *Megillah* is, like that of a letter or document, animated and hasty.[1] In Oriental communities it is read in almost *parlando* style, with melodic variations at half and full stops.[2] The dorian and phrygian modes are used by some Orientals, while the Ashkenazic Jews use the system of cantillation based on the dorian mode. This mode is, however, embellished by borrowing from the cantillation of the Book of Lamentations and from certain liturgical motives. These borrowings are primarily used to give expression to certain key phrases and sentences of the *Megillah* to make them accord with the talmudic and midrashic interpretations of the text.[3] *Midrash Esther* 2.11, for example, tells us that the vessels used at Ahasuerus's feast were those taken from the Holy Temple when Jerusalem was captured by Nebuchadnezzar in 586 B.C.E., which accounts for the melodic change from the joyous *Megillah* mode to the sad mode of Lamentations. According to tradition, those additional phrases which depict the gloom and despair of the Jews are also to be chanted with motives from the cantillation mode of Lamentations.

At the beginning of Chapter 6.1, we are told of the sleeplessness which King Ahasuerus suffered on a certain night. According to *Midrash Esther* 10.1, God, the King of kings, also suffered sleeplessness on account of the terrible plight of His people in Persia. Therefore, the Ashkenazim chant this sentence with the elaborate melody used for *Ha-melech* (The King) at the opening of the second section of the morning service on *Rosh Hashanah* and *Yom Kippur*. According to the musical tradition in some communities, *V'yitlu Et Haman* (Chapter 7. 10) is chanted in a joyous and exalted style.

These are some of the special musical detours made by

the reader while reading the *Megillah*. The congregation
which listens to the reading also has its say at these points,
and recites these verses aloud before the reader. These
phrases were also either read by the congregation or sung to
snatches of popular songs of the day.[4] Such congregational
interruptions gave the Jews opportunities to express their
distaste for the many "Hamans" of their own day. The
phrases were often sung to simple tunes for the purpose
of amusing the children.[5] Everything was done during the
reading of the *Megillah* to make it happy and expressive
of Israel's gratitude for past and future deliverances.

After the reading of the *Megillah* a special hymn,
Shoshanat Yaakov, is sung to a joyous and sometimes even
hilarious melody.

Noisemaking at the mention of the name of Haman
dates back to the earliest days since the *Megillah* reading
became customary. In Deuteronomy 25.19, we are com-
mended "to erase" the name of Amalek, who was the first
enemy of the Jews after they left Egypt. Thus we find that
some Oriental Jews write the name of Haman (who was
supposed to be a descendant of Amalek) on a slip of paper
and erase it at the mention of Haman's name, or they write
it on the soles of their shoes and rub and stamp on it. The
practice of using the *grogger* at the mention of Haman's
name, as we know that custom today, however, goes back
to the thirteenth century in France and Germany.[6] In view
of the fact that the *grogger* is now classified among musical
instruments as a percussion instrument, it should be interesting to trace its origin here.

The *grogger* is a combination of two primitive instruments: the bull-roarer and the scraper.[7] The bull-roarer
consisted of a long stick at the top of which was attached
a string and at the end of the string a thin board. When this
was twirled, it made a weird noise. The faster it was
twirled, the higher was the pitch of noise. The scraper
consisted of a notched shell, bone, or gourd, which was

scraped with a rigid object. The *grogger* combines both of these rattles.

Noisemaking of this kind was an old custom among primitive people at the outgoing and incoming of new seasons, in order to scare away the evil spirits. *Purim*, which comes at the beginning of springtime, most likely adopted the *grogger* from primitive practices at this period of the year.[8] Many such primitive instruments have turned up among children's toys.

It took the Oriental Jews a long time to change their practice of knocking two stones together and stamping their feet at the mention of Haman's name. Today in Palestine, they have turned to the *grogger* which they buy from the Ashkenazic Jews. In Persia, Jews still do not use the *grogger*. Children wearing masks go from house to house beating drums.[9] In Italy, when Jews on *Purim* circle round an effigy of Haman, trumpets are blown.

Included in the joy-making on *Purim* were parodies which go back to the fourteenth century. These were usually composed according to patterns taken from the synagogue liturgy or from the popular songs of the day. These parodies were usually put to the melodies of the original songs or prayers. A parody on the *Hanukkah* hymn entitled *"Ma'oz Tsur For Purim,"* by Gabriel Pollack,[10] to be sung at the table, is an interesting example. These parodies were full of the good humor of the festival, caricatures of the wicked characters in the *Megillah*, and the idealization of its heroes. Many of these parodies were in the form of wine songs.

The *Purim Rab*, who was a take-off of the local rabbi, was an important character in *Purim* parody. He would deliver a humorous sermon in the style of the local rabbi, and sing the *Purim Kiddush*, which was a potpourri of several versions of the *Kiddush* for the holy days and the Sabbath.

The birth of opera in the sixteenth century immediately

began to exert an influence on Jewish music in and out of the synagogue. We hear of cantors at this time indulging in excessive vocal pyrotechnics in operatic style during the chanting of the service, to the delight of the congregation and the chagrin of the rabbis. It was also at this time that the office of cantor and rabbi were divorced from each other in many of the large communities in Europe. Often communities wanted the cantor to possess a beautiful voice and to be able to sing some of the prayers with melodies taken from the popular songs of the day, no matter whether they were secular or sacred.[11] When *Purim* came, therefore, and joy and hilarity reigned, outside musical influences made themselves strongly felt, especially in the *purimspiel*.

The influence of opera may be detected when we discover choral numbers used as *entr'actes* as well as epilogues in *Dos Purim Lied Fun Yosef ben Binyomin*, found in Eisik Walich's collection.[12] *Der Ashmedai Spiel* had two such interludes which were sung by the chorus. *Shoshanat Yaakov*, the *Purim* liturgical hymn, usually ended all *Purim* plays, and during the seventeenth and eighteenth centuries, it was frequently arranged and sung for solo and chorus, in the operatic style of the period.

Acta Esther (Prague, 1720)[13] which, we are told, was known by the famous Rabbi David Oppenheim of that period and performed by his students, contains two songs in aria form;[14] it calls for the accompaniment of *Kol Mine K'le Zemer V'hatsotsrot* (trumpets and all types of musical instruments). In *Hokmat Shlomo*[15] we find a death march for David, and trumpets for the crowning of Solomon. Jacob Dessauer in Amsterdam, in the eighteenth century, calls for music by various composers in his *purimspiel*, "Mordecai and Esther, the Greatest of Jews."[16] Many popular melodies of the day must surely have been included.

Who were the participants in the *purimspiel*? The musical accompaniment was played by the *klezmer* (musicians of the town),[17] although in some cases, as in Bukowina, the *purimspiel* was accompanied by gentile musicians.[18] The acting was done by the *letzim* (jesters)[19] and *badchonim* (folk minstrels) in the town, and much of the singing was also done by these, as well as by the *meshorerim* (choir singers).

Details of musical customs in the celebration of *Purim* vary not only from country to country, but from city to city, and even from community to community.

Singing was the main means of individual and collective expression, and was an aid to creating the joyous *Purim* spirit. The main singing was done during and after the *Purim* feast, which took place a little before sundown on the day of *Purim*. Songs in the vernacular were permitted on this festival, and in various parts of Europe and the Orient songs in Judeo-Italian, Judeo-Spanish, and Judeo-German were sung.[20] In Persia, *Purim* songs could be heard in the streets of the Jewish quarter weeks before *Purim*.[21] In Amsterdam, in 1804, humorous songs were circulated in the community before *Purim* in a *Purim* almanac. Solomon Doklar became famous for his "purimiads" which were to be "read, sung, and retold."[22]

The hasidic sect, which was founded in the eighteenth century, developed its own manner and customs in the celebration of *Purim*. *Hasidim* found spiritual qualities in the hilarities of a *Purim* celebration. They, for example, believed that all of the prayers and requests of the *rebbe* were granted to him in heaven at the conclusion of his *Purim* dance. They also believed that the Divine Presence rested on a joyous and happy face, and they took special advantage of this interpretation on the festival when joy was unlimited. They began in the synagogue by singing passages such as *V'yitlu Et Haman, V'ha-ir Shushan, La-y'hudim, Ba-laila Ha-hu* (Esther 7.10; 8.15; 8.16; 6.1) very elaborately and with a good deal of noise and enthusiasm.

Rabbi Levi Yitzhok of Berditchev, in the early part of the nineteenth century, danced while he chanted *Al Mikra Megillah*, the first of the three benedictions preceding the reading of the *Megillah*.

Rabbi Abbush Meir of Sanz, who was extremely musical, composed a new melody for *Shoshanat Yaakov* every year. His *hasidim* would gather at the *Shalosh Seudot* (third meal) on the Sabbath preceding *Purim*, and at that time he would teach them the new tune. This would, of course, be sung *ad infinitum* during the *Purim* celebration. The tune would again show up at the following Sabbath eve service in *L'cha Dodi*.

On the night of *Purim* a flood of songs was released. At that time the *Shoshanat Yaakov* held the center of attraction. Later, they sang Psalms—7, 33, 121, and 124, among others. There would also be songs, hasidic and others, in the vernacular. *Hasidim* would frequently entertain the *rebbe* and the other *hasidim* with a *purimspiel*, which was often accompanied by singing and even instrumental playing.

On the following day, *Shushan Purim*, joy and hilarity were still unabated. A climax was reached at the *Mincha* (afternoon service), when one of the *hasidim* would act as cantor. He would first of all dress in a *kittel* (white shroud used on the High Holy Days) and chant the prayers with the serious High Holy Day melodies in burlesque style. These were some of the ways in which the *hasidim*, whose credo it was to "serve God in joy," made joy unbounded on this day, the most joyous of holidays.[23]

In Israel *Purim* is celebrated in carnival style, particularly in Tel Aviv. On *Purim* eve one hears the *Megillah* read over loudspeakers throughout the streets surrounding the Great Synagogue for the benefit of those who cannot be

accommodated in the synagogue proper. In the evening
the whole city is a blaze of light in accordance with the
verse in the *Megillah*, "And unto the Jews there was light
and joy." Mass singing envelopes the city. Choruses from
roof-tops join those in the streets. Here and there, groups
of young people may be seen whirling about to the tune
of a *hora*, which the band coming down the street is playing. On a platform erected in one of the main streets the
characters of the *Megillah* sing and dance and entertain the
crowds till the wee hours of the morning.

It is hard to visualize any *Purim*, no matter how far
back, without the singing of folk songs by the people. Unfortunately, our sources for *Purim* parodies,[24] which were
indeed the first songs sung on *Purim* in both synagogue
and home, do not give us the melodies. The *Purim* folk
song, as we know it, dates back to the sixteenth and seventeenth centuries; examples may be found in Eisik Walich's
collection[25] and in Elchanan Kirchan's *Simchat Ha-nefesh*
(Joy of the Spirit).[26]

Fundamental in Yiddish songs of *Purim* is the folk song
based on the greeting "*Gut Purim*," with which Jews have
greeted each other on *Purim*, and which the *purimspieler*
sang when they entered a home where they were to perform. The folk songs then proceed to tell of the joy of the
day, the revenge on Haman and his wife Zeresh (purported
to be a shrew), King Ahasuerus the drunkard, and the
hero and heroine of the story, Esther the Queen and Mordecai the Prince. The songs also tell how the tables were
turned on Haman, who plotted to destroy the Jews, but
who himself met with destruction. The latter subject has
been especially popular in folksongs, in view of the fact
that Hamans have never been lacking in Jewish life in any
generation. In one song we are actually asked why we
cannot have *Purim* every day, in view of the ever-present
Haman! Many songs tell also of the custom of sending

gifts on *Purim*, and of the special *Purim* delicacy, the *hamantash*.

Many of the Yiddish folksongs were the creation of the *purimspieler*. Early Yiddish playwrights made use of the *Purim* theme. In Yiddish plays such as *Ahasuerus*, by Abraham Goldfaden, we find the popular folksong, *Heint Iz Purim*. In Hurewitch's very popular play, *Ben Hador*, a stanza in the famous song, *Min Hametzar* is devoted to the subject of Haman.

Over generations, little children, masked, went from house to house, rapped at the door and sang: "Today is *Purim*; tomorrow is none. Give me a penny, and I'll be gone." Variations came where children at different times and places substituted for the word "penny," the words *kopek, groshen, krepel, hamantash*, etc.

The melodies of the Yiddish *Purim* songs lost their ghetto pathos on *Purim*. Since there were few joyous tunes in the Jewish folk song repertoire, such melodies had often to be borrowed from foreign sources for these joyous texts.

Hebrew folk songs for *Purim*, as we have pointed out, began with the Hebrew parodies of the Middle Ages. *Purim* songs in Hebrew began to be composed also at the time when the first *Purim* was celebrated by the early Palestinian pioneers of 1881. Since then, many songs have been composed for this important and happy Palestinian festival. These songs fall into three groups—original poems with original melodies; poems translated from Yiddish to the accompanying melody; and parodies on Yiddish folk songs sung to the accompanying melody.

While the Hebrew *Purim* songs deal with all themes enumerated in the Yiddish folk songs, there are a few additional ones to be found, as for example: the general "tipsy" feeling of carnival times, the description of the *adloyada* in Tel Aviv, the colorful costumes, and the moods and pictures which the *Megillah* characters portray.

In the many children's songs which are sung in Israel weeks before *Purim*, we find the idea of personalizing the *grogger*, the *hamantash*, and the *shalah manot*. *Purim* is also idealized in a song as *Pur Pur Purim*, in which birds and fishes, too, are pictured as celebrating the festival. One cannot say that Palestinian melodies, extremely rhythmical and vibrant as they are, are not a new element in Jewish folk song as compared to those folk songs of the ghetto.

Too much originality has not been displayed in America, where a musical literature for *Purim* has been growing steadily. While many of the *Purim* lyrics by Samuel S. Grossman are good, and admirably catch the spirit of *Purim*, the melodies for the most part are banal and undistinguished in character. The texts of our American *Purim* songs deal for the most part with the same subjects as those which we found in the Yiddish folk songs. A number of attempts have been made to translate some of the Yiddish and Hebrew songs into English[27] in order to enable our children to catch some of the true *Purim* spirit. An effort has also been made to utilize the cantillation mode of the Book of Esther in one English song,[28] so as to accustom the ears of the younger generation to a branch of Jewish song unfamiliar to them. In American Jewish Sunday schools, hymns of faith and deliverance are also sung on *Purim*.[29] A favorite musical custom on *Purim* in Sunday schools, clubs, Hebrew schools, and other gatherings, is to sing *Purim* parodies to popular American folk songs, nursery rhymes, and songs of the day. We find *Purim* parodies set to such songs as "The Man on the Flying Trapeze," "Tit-Willow," "It Ain't Gonna Rain No More," "Polly Wolly Doodle," "Farmer in the Dell," "A Bicycle Built For Two," "London Bridge is Falling Down," "Here We Go Round the Mulberry Bush," and "Ten Little Indians."

An attempt has even been made to make a *Purim* parody out of the popular comic operetta *The Mikado*, by Gilbert and Sullivan. This was done by Mabel H. Meyer and has been re-named *Ha-Ha Hadassah*.[30]

Serious musicians have not neglected the subject of *Purim*. At the head of the list of art creations inspired by the story of *Purim* is George Frederick Handel's early oratorio, *Esther*, composed in 1720. Two cantatas by Bradbury and Stoughton were composed in our country during the last century, and more recently, two operas were composed by the German Jewish composers Jacob Knoller and Frederick Bloch. Operettas by various composers have also been written, and an overture entitled *Esther*, to Grillparzer's *Esther*, by Eugene D'Albert is to be found. The author of this article has just completed a dramatic narrative with music, entitled *Esther, Queen of Persia*.

All in all, Purim has made its contribution to Jewish music by the very joyousness of its nature, which, better than anything else, is expressed in the cantillation mode itself for the Book of Esther.

FOOTNOTES

1. *The Jewish Encyclopedia*, Funk and Wagnalls Company, New York, 1905, Volume X, page 276.
2. Idelsohn, Abraham Zevi, *Jewish Music*, Henry Holt and Company, New York, 1929, page 65.
3. Beimel, Jacob, "*Mesorot Zimratiyot Bi kri'at Ha-megillah*," *Hadoar*, New York, March 3, 1929.
4. Idelsohn, A. Z.—see footnote number 2.
5. Abrahams, Israel, *Jewish Life In the Middle Ages*, Goldston, London, 1896, page 47.
6. Roth, Cecil, "Down With Haman," in *American Hebrew*, February 19, 1937.
7. Sachs, Curt, *History of Musical Instruments*, W. W. Norton, New York, 1940, page 41.
8. We still make noise on New Year's Eve, at the outgoing and incoming of the year. The *grogger* is one of the principal noisemaking instruments used at such festivities.
9. Schauss, Hayyim, *Dos Yom Tob Buch*, New York, 1933, page 212.
10. This ms. was to be found in the Municipal Library of Frankfort-

Am-Main before World War II. Included in his *Torah Or*, Amsterdam, 1857.

11. Low, Leopold, *Die Lebensalter In Der Juedischen Literatur*, Szegedin, 1865, page 313. Rabbi Judah Starkes (1640) justified the use of a Polish melody in the synagogue. On setting new Hebrew poetry to popular songs of the day, see the preface to *The Ancient Melodies of the Spanish and Portugese Jews*, by David de Sola, London, 1857.

12. This collection is in mss. in the Bodleiana, Oxford. See Neubauer *Catalogue of Hebrew Manuscripts*, number 2420. See also Shipper, Isaac, *Geshikhte Fun Yidisher Teater-Kunst*, Kultur-Liga, Warsaw, 1927, page 53.

13. Shatzky, Jacob, *"Di Ershte Geshikhte Fun Yidishen Teater,"* in *Philologishe Shriften*, YIVO, Wilna, 1928, Volume II, page 239.

14. Cf. Shipper, page 250. Cf. Shatzky for disagreement with Shipper as to whether *Acta Esther* was to be considered an opera.

15. Cf. Shatzky, page 255.

16. Shatzky, Jacob, *"Purim Spieler un Letzim in der Amsterdamer Getto"* in *YIVO Bletter*, volume 19, number 2 (1942), pages 212-220.

17. For an interesting discussion on *Klezmer*, their music, organization, etc., see M. Beregowski, *Yiddishe Instrumentale Folks Musik*, Verlag fun Wissenshaft Academie, Kiev, USSR, 1937.

18. Kamal, R. F., *Die Yuden in der Bukowina*, Globus, 1905, page 158.

19. See *"An Ahashverosh Spiel in Prag Mit 100 Yohr Zurik,"* by Jacob Shatzky in *Arkhiv far der Geshikhte fun Yiddishen Teater un Drame*, YIVO, Wilna, 1930, Volume I, page 162.

20. For Judeo-German songs see Elchanan Kirchan, *Simchat Ha-nefesh*, Fuerth, 1727. Newly edited by Jacob Shatzky, Maisel, New York, 1926.

21. Cf. Schauss, page 212.

22. Shatzky, Jacob, *Purim Spieler un Letzim in der Amsterdamer Getto* in *YIVO Bletter*, volume 19, number 2 (1942), pages 212-220.

23. Geshuri, M., *Zemirot Purim Ezel Ha-hasidim*, Haaretz, Tel Aviv.

24. Davidson, Israel, *Parody in Jewish Literature*, Columbia University Press, New York, 1907.

25. Cf. footnote number 12.

26. Cf. footnote number 20.

27. *Heint Iz Purim* has been translated into English by A. M. Dushkin, and *Pur Pur Purim* by Mabel H. Meyer.

28. Binder, A. W., *The Jewish Year In Song*, G. Schirmer, New York, 1928, "I Love the Day of Purim," page 16.

29. *Union Hymnal*, Central Conference of American Rabbis, Cincinnati, Third Edition, 1940, Hymns 95, 123.

30. Bloch Publishing Company, New York, 1937.

XI JEWISH MUSIC:
AN ENCYCLOPEDIC SURVEY

I. Music in The Bible

During the past century and a half, Jewish musicians have played an important part in the musical life of the world. In all European countries, as well as in the Americas, Jews have contributed significantly to the development of musical art. Jewish names first appeared prominently among performers and conductors, and later among the leading composers of every country. The emergence of the Jews on the world musical scene has not been accidental; music has held a vital place in Jewish life from the

(This article originally appeared in the publication, *The Jewish People: Past and Present*, volume III. It was published in 1952 by Jewish Encyclopedic Handbooks—Central Yiddish Culture Organization (CYCO), in New York.)

earliest periods of history, from the days when the Jews wandered in the wilderness to the present.

When Moses led the children of Israel from Egyptian bondage, the Bible tells us, "Then sang Moses and the children of Israel this song unto the Lord, and spoke, saying, I will sing unto the Lord, for He is highly exalted; the horse and his rider hath He thrown into the sea" (Ex. xv, 1). This was the first great song of freedom in the history of civilization. To celebrate Barak's great victory over the Canaanites, Deborah sang a song of praise to God, "Hear, O ye kings; give ear, O ye princes; I, unto the Lord will I sing; I will sing praise to the Lord, the God of Israel" (Judges v, 3).

King David, too, the "sweet singer in Israel," excelled from his earliest youth in the playing of the *kinnor* (a small harp). It is David to whom the Book of Psalms is attributed. In it we find songs of prayer and praise that have soothed the hearts of men for many centuries. Singing and instrumental music were also used to inspire prophecy. "But now bring me a minstrel," said the prophet Elisha, "and it came to pass, when the minstrel played, that the hand of the Lord came upon him" (II Kings III, 15).

In the *Mishnah* we find the following description of a musical performance during the service in the Temple, in the last century B.C.E. After the priests recited a benediction, the Ten Commandments, the *Shema* (Deut. vi, 4-9), the priestly benediction (Num. vi, 22-26), and three other benedictions, they began the acts of the offerings. When the sacrifices were over, the *magrepha* (a kind of pipe organ) was sounded. This was the signal for the priests to enter the Temple and prostrate themselves. Now the Levites began their part in the service. Two priests took their places at the altar and blew the trumpets *tekiah-teruah-tekiah*. After this, they approached Ben Azra, the cymbal player, and stood on the right and left side of him.

At a signal with a flag by the superintendent, Ben Azra who was a Levite, sounded his cymbal and all the Levites began to sing the Psalm of the day. When they finished a part of the Psalm, the priests blew the trumpets, and the people bowed and worshipped.

Not only the Psalms were sung by the Levites, but also portions of the Pentateuch. The *Mishnah* describes the composition of the orchestra in the Second Temple as follows: *nevel*: minimum two, maximum six; *kinnor*: minimum nine, maximum limitless; *cymbal*: one; *halil*: minimum two, maximum twelve.

This indicates twelve instruments as the required minimum, with the *halilim* added on twelve festal days. It is clear that Israel did not stress loud orchestral instruments during the service, as did her idolatrous neighbors. Just as sacrifice was secondary to prayer, so was instrumental music secondary to song.

The following antiphonal forms were used in public singing during the services:

A. The leader intoned half a verse, and the congregation repeated it. He continued with half lines, and the congregation repeated the first half verse as a refrain.

B. The leader sang half a line at a time, and the congregation repeated it. This, according to Rabbi Eleazer, son of Joseph ha-Galili, was the manner in which children were instructed.

C. The leader read the first line, and the congregation responded with the second, and so on. According to Rabbi Nehemiah, this form was used in reciting the *Shema*. It is still employed by the Babylonian Jews for chanting the *Hallel* on Passover.

At public services, such refrains as *Amen, Halleluyah, Hoshiah Na* (O, help!), and *Anenu* (answer us) were chanted by the people. In later times, we find *Ki Le-olam Hasdo* (for his mercy endureth forever) used as a refrain (Psalm cxviii, 1-4). The responses, *Amen, Halleluyah*, and

Hoshiah Na (Hosanna) have become significant elements of Christian liturgy.

II. Biblical Cantillation

It was customary in the ancient days to study prayers, poetry, and laws with the aid of song. Through association with the melody, the words were more easily remembered and the meaning more clearly understood. "Now therefore write ye this song for you, and teach thou it the children of Israel," Moses admonishes the children of Israel (Deut. xxxi, 19). The people studied and read the *Torah* in a kind of unrhythmic melody known as cantillation.

Portions of the Bible were read in this musical fashion during public services early in the history of Israel. We know, for instance, that the Song of the Sea, the Ten Commandments, and certain Psalms were sung at the daily service in the Temple in Jerusalem.

According to the *Talmud*, "The Bible should be read in public and made understood to the hearers in musical and sweet tones. . . . He who reads the *Torah* without tune shows disregard for it and its vital values." Moreover, "Whosoever intones the Holy Scriptures in the manner of secular song offends the *Torah*."

"The accentuation of the *Torah* is as sacred as its text," it is further stated in the *Talmud*. A discussion follows as to whether a man may receive payment for teaching the meaning of the *Torah* accents, which leads us to believe that there were special teachers who taught the meaning of Biblical accentuation.

The system of Biblical cantillation as we know it today evolved slowly. At first only three signs were known: *pesik*, which indicated a short stop; *etnahta*, a half-stop;

and *sof pasuk*, a full stop. Cantillation signs or tropes are known in Hebrew as *taame ha-neginot, taamim,* and *neginot.*

The *neginot* or *taamim* served to mark all the nuances in the interpretation of the meaning of a phrase. When these signs were introduced into the text, they also indicated a sort of punctuation. Later, in the eleventh century, ibn Ezra said: "All interpretations which are not in accord with the cantillation signs are not valid and should be disregarded."

The *taamim* were preserved traditionally by memory, and were taught by special teachers of accentuation. Over a period of time, however, a system of chironomy was developed and used at public readings. One or two *tomechim* (helpers) stood beside the reader and indicated the direction of the trope for each work by the rise and fall of a finger, or a twist of the palm of the hand. In *Berakot* 62a, we are told, "He indicates with the right the *Torah* tunes." This system of chironomy was carried into the Middle Ages. It was practiced in Baghdad in the twelfth century, and is still used today in Yemen. Rashi tells us that those who came from Palestine used this method in his day.

The only books of the Bible that have come down to us with traditional cantillation are those that were read in public services. The modes, or the musical interpretation of the tropes, differ. Special cantillation modes are provided for the Pentateuch, Prophets, Esther, Lamentations, Ruth, Ecclesiastes, Song of Songs, Psalms, and, in some Oriental communities, for Job, Proverbs, Ezra, and Nehemiah. Chronicles have no cantillation modes since they are never read at public services.

Unlike our modern musical notation, where each sign represents only one note, the Biblical *neginot* represent groups of notes, the minimum being two (as in *pashta*), and the maximum, eighteen (as in *shalshelet*).

Two systems of accents are employed in the Bible, one for the twenty-one books and another for Job, Proverbs, and Psalms.

III. Biblical Cantillation and Early Christian Music

The questions of the relationship between Biblical cantillation and the Byzantine and Gregorian chants have occupied the attention of musicologists and theologians throughout the ages. The Christian theologians were the first to accept the theory that the music of their churches had originally been brought from the synagogue by the early Christians.

It has been shown by A. Z. Idelsohn (*Jewish Music*, New York, 1929) that the Yemenite and other Near Eastern Jewish communities have preserved hundreds of melodies that are identical with the Byzantine and Gregorian chants. The fact that these Jewish communities were never influenced by either of these two churches, together with other evidence cited below, could be regarded as proof that the synagogue chant was the parent of both the Byzantine and the Gregorian chant.

When the early Christians separated into their own synagogues with their special form of Judaism, they took with them not only the Jewish liturgy, which was the only liturgy they knew, and in which the Book of Psalms was a principal element, but also the melodies with which it was sung and chanted. The early Christians in Jerusalem continued to attend Temple worship until at least 60 C.E.

In the preface to his book *Byzantine Music and Hymnography*, Egon Wellesz writes, "The most important decision was to deal with the origin of Christian music in a separate work, which was to show that both Byzantine and Western chants ultimately derived from a common source, the music of the synagogue."

The church also inherited the melismatic type of singing that is particularly characteristic of the *Halleluyah*. In his exposition of Psalm 99, Augustine describes the character of the songs of exultation: "He who jubilates, speaks no word; it is a song of joy without words." The spiritual songs to which he refers were obviously the melismatic melodies of the *Halleluyah* and other exultant songs of praise which had been brought by the Jewish Christians from the Temple and the synagogue into the church (cf. Wellesz). Like *Amen, Cherubim, Seraphim*, and *Hosanna*, the Hebrew word *Halleluyah* has been left untranslated by the Greek and Roman churches, and it has always been assumed that the chants for *Halleluyah* were derived from the Jewish liturgy. Bishop Isidore of Seville said, as early as 636 C.E., "The melodies of the laudations, that is, the chants for the *Halleluyah*, are Hebrew canticles." This view is supported by the musical structure of the *Halleluyah* of the Ambrosian rite, the oldest examples of this type surviving in manuscripts.

The famous poet, Immanuel of Rome (c. 1260-c. 1328), says of the relations of church music to the synagogue chant, "What says the art of music to the gentiles? 'I have been stolen from the land of the Hebrews.'"

The derivation of Christian music from Jewish liturgy has also been accepted by modern writers on the subject. In his *Music in the Middle Ages* (New York 1941, p. 114), Gustave Reese writes, "The influence of Hebrew music has been acknowledged by the most modern writers, among them Wagner, Gastoue, Ursprung. . . . Circumstantial evidence of a connection is afforded by the derivation of the post of . . . cantor . . . from the analogous position in the synagogue, and by the admission into the liturgy of portions of the synagogue service, such as the '*Alleluia*' and the 'Holy, Holy, Holy,' the latter having been adopted, as indicated, by a letter from Clement I, about the end of the first century."

Another noted musicologist says, "We must not forget
. . . that the origin and heritage of Christianity is an Oriental one, or, more precisely, Hebrew; consequently, the
first Christian hymns and songs were taken from the Jewish liturgy or were direct imitations of it." (Paul Henry
Lang, *Music in Western Civilization*, New York, 1941,
p. 23)

It thus becomes clear that the ancient synagogue chant
provided the foundation for the music of the church,
which in turn formed the basis for the development of the
art of music as we know it today.

IV. The Musical Tradition of the Synagogue-Nusach Ha-
tefillah

The great musical structure which the synagogue has developed around its liturgy throughout the ages is a precious heritage, enshrining Jewish hopes and aspirations
and, above all, the Jewish song.

This musical tradition comprises three main elements:
it rests on the Biblical cantillation modes; from these came
the *nusach ha-tefillah*, or the prayer modes; and the two
combined gave rise to the authentic synagogue melodies
we know today.

Different cantillation modes are used in chanting the
various sections of the Bible.

We find the Pentateuch cantillated in one way in
Yemen, another in Spain, and still another in America.
Again, among Ashkenazic Jews, the system of its cantillation on High Holy Days is entirely different from that
followed at ordinary Sabbath services. And yet, despite
the variations due to custom, occasion and geography,
the cantillation modes are closely related, however great
the distances that separate the people who use them. On
comparison, we find common musical figures and intervals
that are characteristic of the systems.

In the course of time the synagogue ritual was gradually developed and enriched. By the seventh century it comprised these elements: *Tefillah* (prayer); *Hallel* (laudation); *Tehinah* or *Tachanun* (petition); *Selichah* (prayer for forgiveness); *Viddui* (confession); *Kinah* (lamentation); and *Zemirot* (hymns).

Because the synagogue liturgy stems from the Bible, it is quite possible that the *nusach ha-tefillah* (traditional prayer modes) evolved from the Biblical cantillation modes. We constantly hear cantillation modes and figures in all the authentic prayer modes.

In the Ashkenazic tradition there are five fundamental liturgical modes: 1) the *Adonay Malach* mode; 2) the *Magen Avot* mode; 3) the *Selichah* mode; 4) the *Ahavah Rabbah* mode; and 5) the *Viddui* mode. These modes, which are sung differently in the Sephardic tradition, also vary according to occasion and, to some extent, according to geographic location.

These are the oldest elements in the Jewish musical tradition as developed and preserved through generations. The *Adonay Malach* is derived from the Pentateuch mode; the *Magen Avot* mode, from Prophets, Lamentations, and Psalms; and the *Viddui* mode, from the Oriental mode of Job.

The *Ahavah Rabbah* mode, which contains the augmented second interval that has become so characteristic of Jewish music, is the most recent of the modes, for it does not occur among the Biblical modes. It came from southwestern Europe. When Jews from Western Europe moved eastward toward Russia and the Ukraine, they encountered families of Jews who were of Tartar, Persian, and Byzantine origin. In the music of these peoples one finds church and folk melodies in a mode similar to our *Ahavah Rabbah* mode.

When the *Magen Avot* mode, or Prophetic mode, was used by cantors in these Eastern areas, they frequently changed to the *Ahavah Rabbah* mode by raising the third on the way up and lowering the second when going down.

Our synagogue melodies have been called *Mi-sinai* tunes, on the basis of the tradition that at Mount Sinai Moses spoke and God answered him in a voice in which Moses heard our entire musical tradition. These melodies are also termed *scarbove*, from a corrupted version of the word *sacre*, meaning "holy."

In this group of *Mi-sinai* or *scarbove* melodies we find special tunes for various holidays and occasions, setting the specific atmosphere of the day.

Sometimes these tunes were originally borrowed from the songs of the countries through which exile had carried our people. Before they were incorporated into the liturgy they went through a process of integration into Jewish style and spirit.

The birthplace of numerous *Mi-sinai* melodies was southwestern Germany—the old communities of Worms, Mainz, Speyer, and the Rhineland, where Jews had lived for several centuries and had developed centers of Jewish scholarship. Many of the *Mi-sinai* tunes for the High Holidays, such as *Ha-melech*, *Musaf Kaddish*, and *Avot*, are attributed to Rabbi Meir of Rothenburg (ca. 1220-1293), who lived in Worms. He was one of the leading *sheliche tsibbur* of his day, and helped to order the synagogue musical tradition.

V. The Development of Cantorial Art Up to the Nineteenth Century

A. The Precentor

In the Temple in Jerusalem the liturgy was intoned by the priests and Levites, but in the local synagogues in Palestine a learned and prominent man of the community was usually selected to lead the prayers. He was called the *sheliach tsibbur*, messenger of the people, or precentor. The prayer modes, which were in the musical style of those days, were uniform and known to all.

It was a very high honor to be called upon to lead in prayer, and the man thus chosen had to be well versed in the prayers and their meanings. After reciting the first benedictions, the precentor had to improvise prayers according to the need of the hour, and then he closed with the final benedictions, to which the community listened silently, with occasional short responses.

Many learned and respected men served as precentors during the Talmudic period, among them Honi ha-Meaggel, Rabbi Hiya, and Rabbi Akiba. At the end of the first century C.E., Rabbi Zenon was an important precentor in the court of Rabban Gamaliel in Yamnia. These great personalities improvised remarkable prayers, many of which have come down to us by tradition.

In the second century, Rabbi Judah ben Ilai, in Palestine, enunciated the qualifications of the *sheliach tsibbur* (precentor). He had to struggle for existence and be of fine character, humble, well bred, and kind. He had to be learned and know the prayers by heart, as well as to have a sweet voice, clear articulation, and clean garments. Blindness or deformities were no reason for disqualification.

When the sacrificial ritual was discontinued after the destruction of the Second Temple, all instrumental music was forbidden. The precentors now took the place of the priests and Levites.

When the prayers were finally formulated and written down at the beginning of the Middle Ages, the problem of who was to conduct the services was simplified. More of the common folk could now serve as precentors.

Beginning with the ninth century, we find Hebrew poets imitating Arabic poetic rhythms in their liturgical poetry. This influence was a strong and decisive one, for it not

only changed the prayer forms employed in the Hebrew
liturgy, but also introduced a more regular rhythm into
the synagogue song. Up to that time the unrhythmical
chant predominated in Jewish song. During the twelfth
and thirteenth centuries it was fashionable among Hebrew
poets to begin their poems with Hebrew words that were
similar in sound to the words of the Spanish song, the
melody of which was to accompany the poem. At first this
practice was strongly condemned by the rabbis, but the
secular melodies finally gained acceptance. As one rabbi
put it, "Why should Satan have all the beautiful tunes?"

B. The Earliest Professional *Hazzanim*

The great rabbis who had served as precentors up to
this time considered it below their dignity to use popular
or alien types of song, but the new poetry was beautiful,
and they wished to include it in the service. In many cases,
therefore, the poets themselves became *hazzanim*, feeling
that they were best qualified to interpret their own songs.

Here we have the beginnings of the office of the professional *hazzan* as we know it today. While many congregations engaged professional *hazzanim*, the practice of select-
ing an honorary precentor from among the synagogue
laity never disappeared. Another factor that led to the appearance of the *hazzan* in the pulpit of the synagogue in
the Middle Ages was the widespread ignorance which
resulted from the persecutions and made necessary the
presence of a professional leader in the religious service.

Rab Yehudai Gaon, head of the Academy of Sura (760-
764 C.E.) was one of the leading precentors of his time,
and is credited with codifying and ordering the musical
tradition. He favored the new practice of professional
hazzanut and supported it with his authority.

The reading of the prayers and the reading of the Pentateuch in the synagogue were now separated. The *hazzan*

chanted the prayers from a lower level, and the *Torah* was read and the sermon preached from an elevated platform called *Almemor* or *Bimah*.

The influence of Italy's musical development at the end of the Middle Ages was making itself felt throughout Europe, and it reached the synagogue as well. More and more cantors brought into the service secular melodies and the style that was heard from traveling Italian singers and troubadors. In fact, at this period, in the fourteenth and fifteenth centuries, we also find traveling *hazzanim*. These itinerant cantors carried melodies and customs from one community to another, and thus contributed to the stabilization and unification of the musical tradition of the synagogue.

Many rabbis looked with disfavor upon the practice of singing secular melodies in the synagogue and the new style of cantorial singing, which the congregations seemed to approve. They censured the *hazzanim* for introducing these innovations. The kabbalistic rabbi and cantor Herz Treves of Frankfort on the Main (1470-1550) complains bitterly about the new movement and the strange attitude of the *hazzanim* toward their holy functions. "They have ceased to be writers of *Torah*, *Tefillin*, and *Megillot*, nor do they care for the correct grammatical reading of the prayers. All they are concerned with is their songs, without regard for the true meaning of the words. They neglect the traditional melodies of their ancestors."

The protests of the rabbis proved unavailing. The Jews began to grow accustomed to going to the synagogue on the Sabbath for prayer and for musical enjoyment. Their innate love of music, dating back to Biblical days, found satisfaction on the Sabbath, for they heard no other music save that of the itinerant bands of street singers. Their chief source of music, therefore, was the synagogue, and when they came there on the Sabbath, they expected the cantor to entertain them. The office of cantor rose in importance among the people, and he became a valued member of the community. In many cases he was preferred to the rabbi.

Jacob ha-Levi Molin (ca. 1356-1427), also known as the *Maharil*, who was rabbi and precentor in Mainz and Worms, was a great adherent of the *nusach ha-tefillah*, the musical tradition of the synagogue. It was said of his renditions of the prayers that they elevated the spirits of the hearers and moved the worshipers to devotion.

The *hazzanim* were not paid on a regular basis out of the synagogue budget. Instead, their earnings were pieced together in various ways that often belittled the dignity of their service. The sources of their income included weddings and circumcisions. At a certain time during the feast, the cantor sang a blessing for each of the guests gathered around the table, after which a plate was passed, and the guests contributed as they saw fit.

In some communities the cantor received a percentage of the dowries. He also received gifts from the local householders on *Hanukkah* and *Purim*. On the latter holiday he went from house to house with the members of his choir to entertain the important members of the congregation, who gave him a gift of money. In certain communities he received a percentage of the money that was paid for slaughtering (*shechitah gelt*), and part of the money collected in the charity boxes in the synagogue. During the month of *Elul*, the month before the High Holidays, he went to the cemetery to chant prayers for the dead, for which he received payment. On *Yom Kippur* eve a plate was placed for him among the other charity plates on a table at the door of the synagogue.

This manner of earning a livelihood corrupted many *hazzanim*. In the seventeenth century Rabbi Ephraim Lentshitz, the author of *Olelot Ephraim*, remarked that "The *hazzanim* care not for their prayers, but only for their songs, so that they may get greater praise and gifts."

On the other hand, in Amsterdam, in 1783, Hazzan Solomon Friede was installed in his office with great pomp and ceremony, attesting to the high regard in which the cantor was held in that community.

VI. *Cantorial Art in the Eighteenth and Nineteenth Centuries*

The impact of the musical progress of the eighteenth century, led by such great musical personalities as Bach and Handel, made itself felt among the *hazzanim* as well. Many of them began to study music and instrumental playing. Influenced by the musical style of the period, they began to bring into the synagogue the popular melodies of the day. It was not unusual at the time to hear a prayer sung in minuet or gavotte rhythm. Ahron Beer (1738-1821), who became a cantor in Berlin in 1765, was one of the first cantors with a technical musical training. In his collection of prayers he had many tunes for each Sabbath. He explained that he did this intentionally, to prevent the congregation from learning the melodies and singing along with him at the service. Most of the cantors of this period were musically unschooled, though they were endowed with native musical talent, often remarkable voices, and were usually learned and extremely pious men.

Hazzanim who combined outstanding musical gifts, learning, and piety became great celebrities. Such a man was Hazzan Salomon Kashtan (1781-1829), cantor in the town of Dubno, Russia, who traveled extensively throughout Lithuania, Poland, Austria, and Hungary. He possessed a remarkable tenor voice with which he was able to perform the most incredible coloratura passages. His compositions were highly original, yet steeped in musical tradition and dignity, and moved the listeners to deep devotion. Fortunately, many of his works were preserved by his son, Hirsch Weintraub.

Another great cantorial light of that time was Bezalel Schulsinger (ca. 1791-1860), otherwise known as Bezalel Odesser. He was born in Galicia. While he had no formal musical training, he possessed great native talent, and is remembered as one of the greatest *hazzanim* of the period. His style was graceful, full of emotion, and of great vocal warmth. He composed extensively, but unfortunately none of his music was published. Some of it is preserved in manuscript. Almost all of the prominent Eastern European *hazzanim* of his time were his disciples.

A special form of improvisation was practiced by Boruch Karliner (died in 1879), who served as cantor in Karlin and Pinsk, in Russia. He would signal to one of the better singers in his choir to improvise a *shtel* as an introduction to an improvisation that he himself was about to begin. Frequently, during the service, Boruch would give his choir a new tune, and the singers would proceed to develop it.

Another great nineteenth century cantor was Yeruchom Blindman, or Yeruchom Ha-koton. He was very short in stature, and when he stood on the pulpit, he always used some elevation. While he, too, had almost no musical education, he composed many synagogue works that were steeped in the synagogue musical tradition. He conducted his own choir without the aid of a choir director. Thanks to his remarkable voice, Jewish learning and innate musicality, he became one of the leading exponents of the cantorial art.

Yeruchom's contemporary, Nison Spivak, also known as Nisi Belzer, possessed some of the same qualities, but his voice was small and was said to have been very raucous. He won widespread fame nevertheless, and has gone down in cantorial history as one of the greatest *hazzanim* of his time. He compensated for his lack of voice with extremely elaborate compositions, a finely trained choir, and wonderful improvisations which were tremendously moving despite his vocal deficiencies.

Yeruchom and Nisi were competitors as well as contemporaries. Their stylistic influence on cantorial art was tremendous and lives on in the hearts and voices of many cantors even to this day.

At this period, in the middle of the nineteenth century, cantors not only with good but also with poor voices held the attention of their congregations in Eastern Europe. They were also composers and sang their own works at the services. Their individual compositions were rather long, sometimes taking from fifteen minutes to a half hour.

These cantors, on the whole, had very little musical education, yet they even managed to write contrapuntal passages, primitive as these sometimes were, and also succeeded in developing some harmonic choral effects. What they lacked most, however, was musical form. Their compositions went from melody to melody without relationship, development, or integration. This is why their works, while valuable historically, are of little practical use to us today. After the first few minutes they lose coherence, and the listener's attention begins to wander.

We have seen that improvisation was an important element in Jewish prayer from the earliest days of the synagogue. A precentor had to be able to improvise a prayer to answer the needs of the moment; later, he was expected to give it either a tune or a chant in a special mode.

Improvisation, both in religious and in secular music, originated and developed principally because at first melodies were played and sung from memory. Even when religious melodies were reconstructed from *neumes*, the fact that each sign represented a group of notes rather than a single note made it necessary for the performer to depend to a large extent on his imagination and invention.

Musical improvisation was continued in later centuries,

and has survived to our day. In the seventeenth and eighteenth centuries singers and solo players were permitted to improvise special passages in a musical composition, while the others waited silently. Improvisations on well-known melodies were demanded at concerts of instrumentalists like Beethoven, Liszt, and their contemporaries. In our own day, in our country, the jam-session in jazz bands is also improvisation.

In the synagogue, the professional *hazzan* developed a special type of musical improvisational style. It is what we call *hazzanut*, or the real art of the cantor. First of all, it is the linking of the tone to the meaning of the word. It is highly florid, coloratura in style, with unique curves and figures, modulatory, intricate, brilliant in execution, and very moving. The coloratura style derives from two sources —our Oriental origin, and the influence of the opera and oratorio to which our people responded strongly in European countries at the close of the eighteenth century.

VII. The Rise and Development of the Synagogue Choir Up to the Nineteenth Century

Mass participation in prayer and public celebrations is frequently mentioned in Biblical literature. After the destruction of the Temple, music was prohibited: "The ear that listens to music shall be deaf," says the *Talmud*. It was for this reason that all choral, and especially instrumental music was discontinued. On Sabbaths, holidays, and at wedding celebrations, however, musical performances were allowed. "There should be no mourning on the Sabbath." It was therefore primarily in the synagogue that Jewish music was able to develop.

While no choral singing was formally permitted, we find that as early as the third century the precentor was assisted by two helpers, called *tomechim* or *mesayim*, who aided him whenever necessary in remembering the prayers. The *tomechim* probably often joined in singing the prayers and thus became the foundation for the synagogue choir that was to develop in later centuries.

The earliest mention of a professional choir is found in Babylonia in the ninth century. In *Sefer Yuhasin* a detailed description is given of the installation of the *Exilarch*, which includes what seems to be the first account of choral participation in Jewish religious service.

The introduction of choir singers in the synagogue musical service always provoked violent controversy. Even in Italy, where more and more Jews began to participate in the country's musical life, departures from the accepted order of synagogue service met with considerable resistance, but nevertheless, influenced by the Renaissance, the synagogues in Venice, Mantua, Ferrara, Padua, and Casale Monferrato tried to introduce choral singing in their services. With the encouragement of Rabbi Leon of Modena (1571-1648), the celebrated musician Salomone Rossi organized a choir for which he set various Psalms to music in arrangements for choirs of three to eight voices. It must be said, however, that these compositions contain no Jewish characteristics, but are decidedly in the style of the art music of the period.

This innovation in the service of the synagogue met with a great deal of criticism from both rabbis and communities, though Rabbi Leon of Modena defended it tirelessly. The dispute was finally brought to the rabbis in Venice, who decided in favor of the innovation. The synagogue as a whole, however, was not yet ready for the choir. Another 200 years had to pass before it was generally accepted.

Rossi's Psalms were published in Venice in October, 1622, under the title, *Shir Ha-shirim Asher Li-shelomoh*. The volume was dedicated to Mose Sullam, and the introduction was written by Leon of Modena, who also did the proofreading.

The synagogue choir at that time usually consisted of a singer (a boy's voice), a bass, and the *hazzan*. The opposition of the rabbis took many forms. In 1602 Rabbi Ephraim Lentshitz of Lublin spoke of the choir derisively as "the three who yell while no one answers."

In the meantime, through the combined influence of traveling singers, the developing church music, and the *ars nova* that was then sweeping Europe, this type of choral body began to find favor in many Jewish communities in Western Europe.

In Amsterdam the try-outs of singers before they were engaged drew tremendous audiences. On October 20, 1790, a rabbinical decree abolished the use of choristers in the synagogue, but the interdiction did not long remain in force.

The *hazzan* and his two choristers frequently had to travel from place to place, since no one community could support them. Even when they were engaged solely for the service of one community they received no fixed salaries, but as we have said above, had to depend on contributions from various sources.

The musical style of the synagogue choir at this time was mainly improvisatory. Most of the singing was done in unison; when harmonies were used, they were either in thirds or in sixths, with an occasional chord. There were rehearsals, but it was never certain that the performances achieved at the rehearsals would be reproduced at the service, for the music was not written down because very few of the *hazzanim* or singers were able to read music. The singers were also used for humming a root tune at certain points while the *hazzan* sang an emotional passage, and for the repetition of key words at significant places in the prayer, or at a cadence. Good singers were often permitted to improvise an introduction to an improvisation by the cantor.

Singers with good voices were lured away from cantor to cantor. When they changed posts, they brought popular compositions and melodies from the previous *hazzan* to the new one.

The usual synagogue combination of three or more choristers seldom presented what could be considered an artistic performance; even their best was far below the quality of the choral singing that was already heard in many non-Jewish places of worship in Europe. It was against this musical chaos and inadequacy that Israel Lovy and Salomon Sulzer revolted some years later.

VIII. Synagogue Music in Europe in Modern Times

A. The Reform Movement in Western Europe

With the emancipation of the Jews in Central Europe came experiments in reforming the synagogue service. The first experiment took place in Westphalia, in Western Germany, on the initiative of Israel Jacobson (1768-1828), a wealthy merchant.

At first these reforms consisted mainly of the introduction of a sermon in German, German hymns, and a mixed choir with organ accompaniment. The choirs which had hitherto been limited to two voices—a boy's and a basso's—supporting the cantor who improvised harmonizations as they sang, was now replaced by a four-part choir which read music, rehearsed the repertoire, and strove to present an artistic performance at the synagogue service. This four-part choir consisted of either boys' and men's voices or, as in Westphalia, of male and female voices.

Much of the early influence in this direction came from

the Protestant church, the choral music of which had attained a high artistic level in the works of Bach, Handel, Mozart, and Haydn—the musical luminaries of the period.

The reformers sought to raise the musical standards of the synagogue. They also strove to eliminate all Oriental features from the synagogue song, including the cantillation modes in the reading of the *Torah*. These, however, were the very foundations of the kind of music that this new reform movement was trying to bring into the synagogue. They succeeded in their efforts, but partly to the detriment of synagogue music in their century.

The first real effort to institute a four-part choir was made by Cantor Israel Lovy (1773-1832), who was also known as Israel Glogow, or Reb Yisroel Fuerth, or Israel Strassburg (according to the cities where he had served as cantor). He possessed a beautiful tenor voice as well as fine musical education, played several instruments, spoke many languages, and had received an excellent Jewish education. His was the spirit of a reformer; in addition to the ordered four-part choir, he also attempted to introduce into the service the style of the classicists of his day. He attained a certain measure of success, although the actual accomplishment of sweeping musical changes in the synagogue service must be attributed not to him, but to Salomon Sulzer.

Jacobson's experiment in Westphalia took root, but an attempt to open a Reform synagogue in Berlin in 1815 was frustrated by the government. Later, this idea was taken up by Jacob Herz Beer, again in Berlin. He organized a Reform service at his home, with music by his son Giacomo, who later became famous as the great opera composer, Meyerbeer. (He had added his rich uncle's name, "Meyer" to his own last name, "Beer.")

The Reform ideas spread throughout Germany, and were

everywhere met by strenuous opposition on the part of Orthodox communities.

B. Salomon Sulzer and Louis Lewandowski

At the beginning of the nineteenth century the community in Vienna decided to institute a Reform service, following the pattern of the temple in Hamburg, which had become a model for the Reform synagogues of Europe. In 1826 the Viennese community dedicated a new temple and resolved to engage a *hazzan* who would be capable of bringing about the desired reforms. Salomon Sulzer (1804-1890) was brought to Vienna for this task. He was a pupil of Salomon Eichberg who, in turn, was a pupil of Israel Lovy.

The Vienna synagogue did not eliminate the cantorial chant or the cantillation of the *Torah*, but it introduced a four-part choir of boys and men, the German sermon, and an orderly procedure in the service.

Sulzer contributed much toward creating the pattern of the Vienna service. Thanks to his rich and beautiful light baritone voice, his understanding of the cantorial chant, his love of beauty and dignity in the service, and his artistic nature and good taste, his service became the envy of all communities, east and west.

Instead of *hazzan*, Sulzer called himself "cantor," a designation used by Johann Sebastian Bach for himself. A synagogue which employed a four-part rehearsed choir became known as a *chor-shul*.

Sulzer gave dignity to his post and demanded respect for it. The community gladly gave him the respect his post deserved. As a matter of fact, he was not permitted to sing or speak outside of the synagogue. Sulzer, who was also a distinguished *Lieder* singer, had to decline, therefore, an invitation to sing at the royal court.

As a friend of Franz Schubert, Sulzer was one of the first to interpret his songs. In the course of their friendship, Schubert composed for Sulzer a choral musical setting of *Tov L'hodot* (Psalm 92), using the original Hebrew text.

Many noted musicians came to the synagogue to hear Sulzer, including Franz Liszt, who said of the experience, "Only once were we given the opportunity to see what true Judaic art could be. We have seldom been moved as deeply as we were that evening; so stirred that our soul was entirely immersed in meditation and participation in the service."

Salomon Sulzer is generally known as the father of modern *hazzanut* and synagogue music. His chief contribution to the cantorial chant and to synagogue music was form— a thing that was lacking up to that time. Yet the process of modernization also brought the infusion of a German style, foreign to synagogue music, and eliminated certain characteristics of the synagogue chant, such as the *melisma* and traditional modulations. In his choral music Sulzer set the *nusach*, when he employed it, behind bar lines. To the traditional Jew his music sounded un-Jewish. Many of Sulzer's works are in ¾ time, which give further evidence of the tremendous influence exerted by Johann Strauss and the Vienna waltzes upon him and his followers. Later in life, when he had closer contact with East European *hazzanim* who came to study with him, he learned to value traditional *hazzanut* and incorporated it in his work, adapting it to his own style.

Sulzer was venerated by the entire Jewish world. His opinion on musical matters was sought by all, and very many in the cantorial profession came to study with him. It was his lifelong aim to raise *hazzanut* to a high level of dignity and art.

Louis Lewandowski (1821-1894), another musical reformer, was born in Wreschen, in Posen, and lived and worked in Berlin. He did for the German synagogue what

Sulzer did for the Austrian. While he possessed great talent and a personality of his own, his work was strongly influenced by Sulzer. He was principally a choir director, but he also officiated as assistant cantor. The post of choir director was not yet definitely established at that time as a separate office.

In 1864 he was invited to become choir director of the New Synagogue in Berlin. He was given an organ to accompany his choir, and it was here that he came into his full powers. It was here, too, that he composed and published his two volumes of synagogue music, *Kol Rinnah* (Sabbath services) and *Todah V'zimrah* (holiday services).

Two men influenced Lewandowski's music—Sulzer and Mendelssohn, both of them his contemporaries. While he followed Sulzer's patterns and principles, he further developed the musical forms evolved by Sulzer, and infused them with deeper expressiveness in interpreting the texts. In Lewandowski's work, also, there are many German substitutes for the musical tradition of the synagogue, and too many bar lines where the cantorial recitative should be free.

One of the chief defects in Lewandowski, as in Sulzer, was the application of a Western harmonic system to the musical tradition, which disguised the true spirit of the synagogue chant and melody. In a German tune such as *Seu Shearim* (*Todah V'zimrah*, p. 214), this system is very appropriate, and even emphasizes the German derivation of the tune; but where he employs traditional modes or melodies, as in the *Three Festivals Maariv* recitative (*Todah V'zimrah*, p. 8), or the *Tal Kaddish*, his use of the Western system of harmonization distorts the character of the music. Despite these flaws, melodies by Sulzer and Lewandowski are extremely popular and are sung regularly in synagogues throughout the Western world. Lewandowski was also influenced by Strauss' ¾ rhythm.

C. Samuel Naumbourg and Hirsch Weintraub

In Paris at this time Samuel Naumbourg (1815-1880) was accomplishing reforms similar to those of Sulzer and Lewandowski in Vienna and Berlin. Paris was considered the musical capital of the world, and was most active in the field of opera. Those operatic influences are strongly and frequently evident in Naumbourg's work. His compositions, collected in four volumes entitled *Zemirot Yisrael* (1847), follow to a great extent the forms of Sulzer and Lewandowski, but he had a greater sense of that Jewishness which was lacking in the works of his contemporaries. He made frequent use of traditional melodies, or *mélodies anciennes*, as he called them, and his harmonic settings do not disguise their origin. Especially Jewish in its harmonic atmosphere is his famous *Ana Tova* (*Zemirot Yisrael*, Vol. II, p. 323), which surpasses any synagogue composition written up to that time from the point of view of Jewish style and form.

Naumbourg was one of the first composers to study Jewish musicology, publishing in Paris, in 1874, his *Précédeés D'une Étude Historique sur la Musique des Hebreux.* In 1877, in collaboration with Vincent D'Indy, he edited and published Salomone Rossi's *Shir Ha-shirim Asher Lishelomoh*, originally published in Venice in 1622, thus making available to the musical world the oldest published choral music of the synagogue.

On the recommendation of Jacques Fromental Halévy, the French-Jewish composer of the opera *La Juive*, he was appointed cantor of the synagogue on Rue de Temple, in Paris, in 1845. Halévy's famous operatic setting of *Min Ha-metzar* (Psalm 118) is included in Naumbourg's *Zemirot Yisrael* (Vol. I, p. 74), as are some compositions by one of his predecessors, Israel Lovy.

Samuel Naumbourg was the first of the nineteenth century composers in Western Europe to show the way toward preserving the musical tradition of the synagogue within the framework of contemporary musical development.

The musical reforms introduced by Sulzer, Lewandowski, and Naumbourg exerted a deep influence in all synagogues which employed a choir and cantor at the Sabbath services. Their effect was felt even in Eastern Europe—in Russia, Poland, Hungary, and Rumania—where Orthodox Judaism was firmly entrenched. The new music was accepted only in part in these countries, however, for it lacked the essential element of the synagogue spirit, its *nusach ha-tefillah* (musical tradition), without which this spirit cannot survive.

Those who felt this deficiency took the first steps to remedy it. They strove to preserve the synagogue musical tradition where it was still retained and to bring about a return to it where it had been abandoned. The former path was followed by Hirsch Weintraub (1811-1882), a cultivated musician with a beautiful voice and great interpretive talents.

Two factors combined to produce the Jewish style of many of Weintraub's works. He was the son of Salomon Kashtan, one of the greatest cantors of the time, and was therefore profoundly steeped in the musical tradition of the synagogue. From earliest childhood he had heard his father sing, and the impression remained with him throughout his life. Furthermore, he served as cantor in Konigsberg, Germany, a city in close proximity to the highly traditional centers of Eastern Europe.

Weintraub was not entirely free of the Sulzer-Lewandowski influence, and many of his compositions were in poor taste. In his arrangements of his father's works, however, or in his own work in a Jewish vein, he began to evolve a Jewish melodic line and specifically Jewish harmonies. His *Barchu* for the Sabbath morning, or his *Ve-*

nislach, for *Yom Kippur* eve, found in his three volumes
entitled *Shire Bet Adonay,* illustrate these aspects of his
work.

D. The Way Back to the *Nusach Ha-tefillah*

The way back to the musical tradition of the synagogue
within the framework of existing musical conceptions of
form and interpretation was found by the cantors and
choirmasters of Eastern Europe. Among the first of these
was the cantor Eliezer Gerovitch (1844-1913), who lived
and worked in Rostov-on-Don. Most of his works adhere
to tradition, with simple but suitable harmonic background.

Meanwhile, the art of *hazzanut* was making progress in
Eastern Europe, which produced at that period a large num-
ber of distinguished *hazzanim.* These included Yeruchom
Blindman, called Yeruchom Ha-koton (1798-1891), Nison
Spivak, called Nisi Belzer (1824-1906), Nison Blumenthal
of Odessa (1805-1902), Boruch Schorr (1923-1904),
Pinchos Minkowsky (1859-1924), and Jacob Bachman
(1846-1905).

It was David Nowakowsky (1848-1921) who integrated
all the previous efforts to further the progress of synagogue
music. Nowakowsky was born in Malin, in the province
of Kiev, Russia. He received his early musical training as
a choir-boy in Berditchev, but acquired most of his musical
knowledge through his own efforts. In his twenty-first year
he became choir director and assistant cantor in the Broder
Shul in Odessa, where Nison Blumenthal was chief cantor.
It was not until Pinchos Minkowsky became chief cantor,
however, that Nowakowsky had the opportunity to develop his talents as composer and conductor.

Only two of Nowakowsky's works exist in printed form,
published by himself; they are *Shire David* (Sabbath eve
music) and *Neilah* (concluding service for the Day of

Atonement). Many of his works remain in manuscript, and are in the possession of his son.

In Nowakowsky's music we find a deep sense of *nusach ha-tefillah* and a conscious striving toward a Jewish harmonic idiom. His *Adon Olam* in F (*Shire David*, p. 80), and *Tov L'hodot* in F (ibid., p. 30), show a fine sense of form, integration, and development of thematic material. An excellent example of the evolution of the melody in the *nusach* into a fugal theme, with development in Jewish style, can be found in his *V'shomru* in C minor (ibid., p. 57).

His oratorio, *Haazinu*, the farewell song of Moses, is still in manuscript, but on its merits David Nowakowsky may be ranked as the greatest of the nineteenth century synagogue composers.

He was also a distinguished conductor, and his musical performances on the Sabbath became known throughout Russia. Many gentiles could often be seen at the Sabbath services in Odessa's Broder *Shul*. Nowakowsky died in poverty, without the recognition his talents deserved, but he lives on in the hearts of all honest and sincere synagogue musicians.

IX. *Synagogue Music in the United States*

In 1756, the Jewish community of Charleston, South Carolina, engaged Isaac Da Costa as its first reader and cantor. He was later followed by Jacob De La Motta, Abraham Alexander, Emanuel Nunes Carvalho, and Abraham Azuby, who was cantor of Temple Beth Elohim in Charleston from 1785 to 1805.

It is not, however, until the early nineteenth century that we begin to hear of serious musical activity in the synagogue. In 1818, a chorus was organized by the Shearith

Israel congregation, the oldest in this country, for the dedication of its Mill Street Synagogue in New York. Synagogue choirs were gradually introduced in such synagogues as Anshe Chesed and Emanu-El, both in New
York. The developments taking place in European congregations were reflected in American synagogues as well.
In 1842 Leo Merzbacher, the cantor of Temple Emanu-El,
introduced a choir to lead congregational responses. According to procedure, the cantor gave the key for congregational singing. The works of Sulzer, Lewandowski, and
Naumbourg were in great demand in American synagogues.

When Leon Sternberger became cantor of Temple
Anshe Chesed in 1849, he sent for the music of Sulzer
and Lewandowski, requesting that it be delivered to
America post-haste. While organized choir singing encountered much opposition in this country, as it did in
Europe, special choral groups of men and women were
permitted to perform at dedications and other extra-synagogal activities. On such occasions they usually sang appropriate Psalms in Hebrew. In 1853, at a concert given
at Temple Emanu-El to raise funds for a new organ, Edward Weber prepared a program of religious music, which
was performed by chorus and orchestra.

Such cantors as Leo Merzbacher and G. M. Cohen of
Emanu-El, Jonas Hecht, Leon Sternberger and Ansel Leo
of Anshe Chesed, and Ignatius Ritterman and Judah
Kramer, of B'nai Jeshurun, were the early pioneers in the
development of synagogue music in our country, and were
therefore the logical forerunners of the Jewish musical
movement that was to come at the turn of the century.

The published music of that early period shows that the
Sulzer-Lewandowski Reform movement exerted a great
deal of influence on this side of the Atlantic. The American cantors of those days, whose music was sung in the
synagogues and who led the way in synagogue music,
were not of the highest musical caliber.

The Jewish women's section of the "Parliament of Religion," held in Chicago in 1893 in connection with the Columbian Exposition, issued a volume of Jewish music entitled *Principal Melodies of the Synagogue from Ancient Time to the Present*. This volume was edited by two of the outstanding cantors of that time, Alois Kaiser of Temple Ohev Sholom in Baltimore, and William Sparger of Temple Emanu-El in New York. It contained an attempt at a historical account of the development of Jewish music. In the music itself we find traditional modes and melodies for the Sabbath and holidays, hymns, and the works of contemporary composers of synagogue music, both American and European.

This volume, quite elaborately issued, bore the stamp of the Germanic influence of Sulzer and Lewandowski, with elimination of certain Jewish characteristics from melodies harmonized in the Western tonic-dominant manner. Nevertheless, it also showed the desire of the editors (which must have been shared by many others) to preserve the musical traditions of our people.

At first, synagogue choirs consisted only of volunteers. The sole reward offered was free synagogue membership for the men, and a suit of clothes for the boys. Later, in 1848, A. Hirshman, the choir leader at Temple Emanu-El, was paid seventy-five dollars for the year's services, while the choir singers received twenty-five dollars each for the same period. Married singers were given free tickets to the High Holiday services for their wives.

The Reform congregations in this country were founded in the nineteenth century by German and Bohemian Jews; the Polish and Russian Jews adhered to the Orthodox tradition. In the Orthodox synagogues they even retained the medieval musical trio—singer, bass, and cantor.

Jacob Fraenkel (1808-1887) became cantor of Temple Rodeph Sholom in Philadelphia in 1848. Alois Kaiser (1840-1908) became cantor of Temple Ohev Sholom in

1866. Samuel Welsh (1835-1901) became cantor of Congregation Ahavas Chesed in New York in 1865, but returned to Prague in 1880. Moritz Goldstein (1840-1906) became cantor of Temple B'nai Israel in Cincinnati in 1881.

After a series of brutal pogroms in Russia, starting in 1881, large numbers of East European Jews began to emigrate to America. With them, East European *hazzanut*, which had risen to great heights by this time, found its way into the new world.

In 1891, the great cantor and composer, Boruch Schorr of Lemberg, became involved in a conflict with his congregation. He had composed the music for a play, *Samson and Delilah*, which was presented in the newly emerging Yiddish theater. After the performance the composer came out to take a bow upon the stage. This angered the leaders of his congregation, and he was suspended from his duties as cantor for one month. He refused to submit to the punishment and left for America, where he accepted a post in the Attorney Street synagogue, Mogen Avrohom, on the Lower East Side of New York. After five years he returned to Lemberg and his old post at the request of his former congregation.

Another great cantor, Pinchos Minkowsky, of the Broder *Shul* in Odessa, came to New York in 1897 after he had also run into difficulties with his congregation. He accepted a post with the congregation Adath Jeshurun, on Eldridge Street, in New York's Lower East Side. A year after the returned to Odessa. He came to New York again after the First World War, but died soon afterwards, in 1924, in Boston.

Israel Cooper, cantor of the great Wilno Synagogue, also came to the United States in 1900, as a result of a dispute with his congregation. He had been censured for attending too many rehearsals and performances at the new Yiddish theater, thus neglecting his official duties. He became cantor of the large Kalvarier Synagogue on the Lower East Side in New York. He was the father of the boys who later formed the Empire City Quartet, a top-ranking vaudeville team in the first quarter of the present century.

Abraham Frachtenberg (1861-1927) came to this country in 1901 from Przemysl, Galicia. He was a pupil of the venerable Yeruchom Ha-koton, and was at one time the choir director of Nisi Belzer's choir, which was a considerable honor. He had a bass-baritone voice of light texture, but his great distinction lay in his talents as an improviser, composer, and choir conductor. He was a typical example of the nineteenth century cantor of the *chor-shul*.

Frachtenberg, like so many of his predecessors, knew very little about harmony, counterpoint, or form in composition. Sheer native talent enabled him to write a fine chorale and fugue. His compositions, rooted in the *nusach ha-tefillah*, were rich in melody and became very popular with congregations here and abroad.

Another gifted cantor of similar background was Zeidel Rovner (Jacob Samuel Margovsky, 1856-1946), who came to this country in 1912.

Composer-cantors rarely sang the works of others, depending solely on their own compositions. Most cantors did not conduct their choirs, but had special choir leaders for this task. The most distinguished of these musicians in the early part of the present century were Herman Wohl, Jacob Margulies, and Meyer Machtenberg.

In 1919 Cantor Jacob Beimel (d.1944) and this writer (as musical director) were engaged by the new Jewish Center on West 86th Street, New York, to work for a revival of congregational singing. That movement was initiated under the special sponsorship of Rabbi Mordecai M. Kaplan, who was then the rabbi of that congregation. While congregational singing has since flourished and spread throughout the country, in many ways, however, it has proved detrimental to the cause of choral singing in the synagogue.

Gustavus Poznanski, appointed temporary cantor of Temple Beth Elohim in Charleston in 1836 and elected to that post in 1838, introduced the organ into religious service in his synagogue—the first in this country to accept this reform. He also suggested discontinuance of the celebration of the second day of the Three Festivals. Penina Moise (1797-1880), the well-known Jewish poetess who lived in Charleston, wrote many religious hymns for that synagogue. Her hymns were sung in English. German hymn singing was also common among early American Reform congregations.

In 1848 the Har Sinai Reform Congregation was organized in Baltimore, Maryland. Three years earlier, in 1845, Temple Emanu-El was founded in New York. The only reform, however, that was instituted by Temple Emanu-El in 1845 was the introduction of the boys' and men's choir. In 1849, as we find in the minutes of this congregation, the cantor was required to chant in the ancient traditional style.

At first the traditional prayer-book was still used, with certain variations and omissions, and the music of Sulzer, Lewandowski, and Naumbourg was adapted to these changes. The appearance in 1894 of the first *Union Prayer Book*, with its many new prayers in English, and numerous abbreviations in the old Hebrew prayers, placed the Reform synagogue in a dilemma, since the old music was no longer suitable to the new prayers.

By this time, toward the end of the nineteenth century, gentile singers and gentile organists were providing the music at the Reform temple services. It was to these organists that the congregations turned for new music for the revised liturgy. Cantors Welsh in New York, Goldstein in Cincinnati, and Kaiser in Baltimore also composed some new settings.

In the hymnals edited by Otto Loeb in 1876, Simon Hecht in 1878, and Isaac S. Moses in 1894, and in the *Union Hymnal* (first edition, 1897; second edition, 1914), we find almost all of the hymn tunes—whether set to Jewish or non-Jewish texts—taken from Protestant hymnals or composed by non-Jews. Even those melodies that were written by Jews at the time were non-Jewish in character. It was not until the third edition of the *Union Hymnal*, (edited by the author of this article) appeared in 1932 that much of the non-Jewish material was eliminated and replaced by hymns translated from the *piyutim* and set to music of such Jewish composers as Achron, Alman, Binder, Beimel, Weinberg, and Heller. That *Hymnal* also included melodies from the liturgical works of Nowakowsky, Gerovitch, and others who worked within the Jewish musical tradition.

Sigmund Schlesinger (1835-1906), who became organist and choir-leader of Congregation Shaarei Shomayim in Mobile, Alabama, composed a complete musical liturgy for the first edition of the *Union Prayer Book*. His music, however, was almost totally devoid of any traditional elements, and more than any other, was responsible for the breakdown of the Jewish musical tradition in the Reform synagogue in this country.

Edward Stark (1863-1918), cantor of Temple Emanuel in San Francisco, was aware of the problem, and being the son of a cantor, proceeded to compose a musical liturgy for the *Union Prayer Book* which brought back some traditional elements into the service of the Reform synagogue. His was the first attempt in this direction. Not long afterward, in the nineteen-twenties, there appeared several other complete musical services by composers with a progressive outlook. Today such composers as Schalit, Fromm, Adler, Weinberg, Freed, Chajes, and many others are following in the footsteps of their nineteenth century predecessors.

In the early nineteen-twenties increasing numbers of

Jews began to agitate for the performance of the great synagogal musical literature in our American synagogues, and for the employment of Jewish choir personnel. This was practically unknown at the time in Reform synagogues. Soon many of the congregations in this country began to engage capable Jewish musicians to direct their musical services. This important step raised the musical standard of the synagogues and led to an improvement in the performances. Today many synagogues can be justly proud of employing Jewish musical directors who are excellent composers, first-rate musicians, and experienced choir conductors.

In the twenties many synagogues had begun to restore to their services the Jewish *nusach ha-tefillah* and Jewish melody. They sought a solution to the problem of Jewish harmony which had long engaged the attention of East European composers and to which the St. Petersburg Society for Jewish Folk Music was beginning to find an answer. Such composers as Ernest Bloch, Heinrich Schalit, Isadore Freed, Jacob Weinberg, Julius Chajes, Herbert Fromm, Hugo Adler, and others have since written services which have contributed much toward the development of a Jewish musical idiom, enriching the religious life of the American Jew. Some synagogue composers have also written complete services in oratorio form. The most significant and most successful attempt in this field was made by Ernest Bloch in his *Avodath Ha-kodesh*. Bloch's harmonic treatment of his Jewish material has influenced many Jewish composers throughout the world.

There is a healthy tendency among the contemporary composers of synagogue music to liberate the synagogue chant from the bar lines which have imprisoned it since the early nineteenth century. This has allowed the chant to regain some of its original character.

Joseph Yasser's theory that ancient Jewish music was pentatonic, and should therefore be harmonized with chords of the pentatonic scale, has also been of tremendous help in solving the harmonic problem. Many composers of synagogue music have turned to modal harmonizations and to harmonizations with fourths and fifths.

Unfortunately, some of the present-day composers of synagogue music have only a slight acquaintance with our musical tradition. This is to be deplored, for the *nusach ha-tefillah* is the product of centuries of Jewish musical experience. It should be held sacred and guarded jealously. It is our musical treasure, containing the essence of our originality as a musical people.

On the whole, the present state of synagogue music in our country is encouraging indeed. There is extensive evidence of a genuine desire to improve our musical service. Special services of music by individual composers are frequently held, and the annual Jewish Music Festival Month devotes a special Sabbath to synagogue music.

X. Modern Trends in Jewish Music in the United States

Three important factors contributed to the development of modern Jewish music here and abroad. The first was the Zionist movement, which began in 1881-1882 with the arrival of the first *Bilu* settlers in Palestine. This new phenomenon in Jewish life set off a tremendous wave of poetry and song. Some of the songs of that period are still remembered and sung today.

The second factor was the organization of the Yiddish theater by Abraham Goldfaden in 1876. People would come out of the theater after the performances singing such songs as *Rozhinkes Mit Mandlen, Flaker Faierl*, and many others which have since become folk songs. Goldfaden was succeeded in the Yiddish theater by such composers as Friedsell, Brody, Wohl, and Sandler. Such songs as *Dos Talisl, Dos Pintele Yid, Eili Eili* and others were first sung on the stage, and were later adopted by the Jewish people as part of their folk heritage.

The third and most important factor leading to the renaissance of Jewish music was the formation of the Society for Jewish Folk Music in St. Petersburg in 1908. The organization of the Society was preceded by intensive activity on the part of musicians and folklorists in collecting Yiddish folk songs. To the material that was already gathered and known they added the results of their own research. Out of this total mass of musical source material they began to shape longer compositions, often of high artistic merit, for piano, violin, voice, and chamber-music combinations. A Jewish musical style was thus beginning to be evolved, pointing the direction for Jewish music for decades to come. Joseph Achron's popular violin piece, "Hebrew Melody," was one of the products of this period.

Scores of concerts of Jewish music were given throughout Russia in those days. In 1912 Simeon Bellison, one of the outstanding clarinetists of our time, organized the Moscow Quintet for National Jewish Music, which toured the country, giving many concerts of Jewish music. Years later, in 1921, Bellison came to the United States with his *Zimroh* ensemble. This fine musical group appeared in New York and in numerous other cities throughout this country in concerts of Jewish music devoted solely to compositions by members of the St. Petersburg Society for Jewish Folk Music. Although the general public remained cool toward this new Jewish music, it gave warm inspiration to the younger Jewish composers, who at that time were a mere handful in this country. It opened for them a new world and new vistas into the future. The *Zimroh* concerts were important stimuli toward the development of serious Jewish music in America.

Jewish choral groups of mixed voices began to spring up in Russia at the end of the nineteenth century. Before that time, Orthodox tradition had not permitted men and women to sing together. Joseph Rumshinsky organized the first mixed choral society in Lodz in 1897, under the name of *Hazomir*. The chorus consisted of fifty voices. Its first concert, given at the State Theater, was a tremendous success, winning over all previous opponents and refuting their objections. Warsaw followed the example of Lodz and organized its own *Hazomir* under the direction of Leo Low. Before long the new immigrant population in America took up the idea and also began to organize choral groups.

During the first ten years of the present century a stocky man of medium height, with long hair, a flowing Windsor tie, and wearing a Prince Albert and a high hat, could be seen strolling up and down the streets of New York's East Side. His name was Platon Brounoff. He must be mentioned as one of the earliest pioneers in the field of Jewish music in New York City. He lectured on Jewish folk music at a time when such lectures were as yet unheard of, and was one of the first to include Jewish folk songs in his programs. In 1911 he organized the *Poale Zion* Singing Society, which he conducted for two years, and in 1911 he published a first collection here of Jewish folk songs with piano accompaniment. While Brounoff was not a musician of the highest caliber, his part in paving the way for Jewish music in this country cannot be overlooked. He was succeeded as conductor of the *Poale Zion* Singing Society by Henry Lefkowitch, later a publisher of Jewish music.

In 1916 this writer organized the Hadassah Choral Union under the auspices of the Hadassah. It was the first chorus in this country to specialize in the singing of Palestinian folk songs. Lazar Weiner, who founded the *Freiheit* Singing Society in 1923, has also helped to educate the broad masses to an appreciation of Jewish music.

Such groups as the Yiddish Culture Chorus, conducted by Vladimir Heifetz, the *Farband*-Labor Zionist Order

Chorus, conducted by Leo Low, and the choruses of the Jewish Music Alliance, until recently conducted by Max Helfman and Leo Kopf, have furthered the cause of Jewish music in New York, as have many other conductors and choruses in communities throughout the land.

In 1950 the Congress for Jewish Culture, through its music division, organized a competition for the best musical setting for mixed chorus of J. L. Peretz's poem, *Treist Mein Folk*. The competition was won by Cantor Leo Rosenbluth of Sweden. The new work was performed at a music festival arranged by the organization at Hunter College in New York, on March 26, 1950. The following Yiddish choruses participated: The Workmen's Circle Choruses of Philadelphia, Trenton and Newark, under the direction of Samuel Bugatch; the Workmen's Circle Chorus of New York, directed by Lazar Weiner; the *Farband-*Labor Zionist Order Chorus of New York, and the *Hazomir* of Waterbury, under the direction of Leo Low; the Yiddish Culture Chorus of New York and the Workmen's Circle Chorus of Patterson, under Vladimir Heifetz. Each unit performed by itself, and at the end of the program all combined in a joint performance (500 voices) of Rosenbluth's prize-winning work, under the direction of Lazar Weiner.

In 1940 Jacob Weinberg arranged the first of a series of annual Festivals of Jewish Art, in which he presented many works of great interest and value.

In 1910, the Bureau of Jewish Education was organized under the direction of Dr. Samson Benderly. One of the Bureau's goals was the furthering of a revival of Jewish music. The inclusion in the Hebrew school curriculum of Hebrew and Yiddish folk songs as well as liturgical responses, brought to our Jewish youth the knowledge that we possess a musical heritage of our own. The many thousands of youngsters who came under the influence of Samuel Goldfarb, the Bureau's music director, later became either members of Jewish choruses throughout the land or constituted audiences which patronized Jewish concerts.

Another important event in the development of Jewish music in this country was the arrival here of Ernest Bloch in 1916. Bloch won the interest of Artur Bodanzky, the German-Jewish conductor at the Metropolitan Opera in New York, who presented a concert of Bloch's Jewish orchestral compositions at Carnegie Hall in 1917. The program included his *Three Psalms* for baritone and orchestra, the *Three Jewish Poems*, and the first movement of his symphony, *Israel*. It showed the world that the Jews can produce a composer of the first rank, demonstrated to the younger generation of Jewish composers what the music of a Jewish composer could be like, and above all, it convinced many people that Jewish music of high quality could take its place in the concert hall on an equal footing with the music of other nations.

The arrival in this country of Joseph Achron (1886-1943), and his presence in New York for about ten years, was another great source of inspiration to Jewish composers. Joseph Yasser, noted musicologist, whose theories of Jewish music have helped many of the Jewish composers, has also exerted great influence. Solomon Rosowsky's activity in America from 1931 to 1933 advanced the cause of Jewish music to a considerable degree. With the cooperation of Mrs. Miriam Zunser and a group of Jewish musicians he organized *Mailamm* which did much for the cause of Jewish music in America while it was in existence. It was succeeded by the Jewish Music Forum, organized by this writer together with a small group of other musicians, in 1939.

Soon similar musical organizations began to spring up in Detroit, Chicago, Cleveland, and other cities. Jewish music had finally come of age. Firmly rooted, it was ready for further growth. The next step was the first Jewish Music

Festival, organized in 1944 by Dr. Bernard Carp, and held in May 1945 under the auspices of the National Jewish Welfare Board. The Festival has functioned successfully since then, and has continued to broaden its scope over the years.

When the time was felt to be ripe for the establishment of a school of Jewish music, it was undertaken by the Hebrew Union College and the Jewish Institute of Religion. The school was launched in October, 1948.

XI. Badchonim, Purim Players, Klezmer, and the Music of the Yiddish Theater.

The *badchon* is primarily a product of Jewish suffering and the Jewish sense of humor. At different times Jewish entertainers were variously termed *badchonim* (merrymakers), *letzim* (jesters or comedians), and *marshalks* or *marshaliks* (entertainers).

The *badchonim* already existed in the first centuries of the Common Era. Their method was at all times improvisation. This required talent and learning, for their extemporaneous verses were intermingled with quotations from the Bible and the *Talmud*. In the Middle Ages they formed small itinerant groups, patterning themselves after the troubadours. Their services were in especial demand at weddings.

Frequently *badchonim* had other sources of income, such as match-making. In a notebook belonging to the *badchon* Israel Kessler, who lived in Radziechow, Kowel and Tarnopol (in Galicia), we find entries, dated 1889, which deal with possible matches, dowries, *kest* (maintenance of bride and groom), and similar matters.

On *Purim*, songs, merrymaking and general rejoicing were often accompanied by folk plays called *purimspiel*. These comedies were primarily based on the Book of

Esther, and were performed on the day of *Purim* in the homes of the various householders of the community.

Operatic influence is discernible in the use of choral numbers as *entr'actes* and epilogues in *Dos Purim Lid Fun Yosef Ben Binyomin,* which is included in Eisik Walich's collection. The *Ashmedai Spiel* contains two interludes which were sung by the chorus of Solomon's attendants. *Shoshanat Yaakov,* the *Purim* liturgical hymn, was usually sung at the conclusion of all *Purim* plays. During the seventeenth and eighteenth centuries it was frequently arranged for solo and chorus, in the operatic style of the time.

Acta Esther (Prague, 1720), which, we are told, was read and approved by the famous Rabbi David Oppenheim and performed by his students, contains two songs in aria form and calls for the accompaniment of a variety of musical instruments. In *Hokmat Shlomo* we find a "Death March" for David, and trumpets for the crowning of Solomon. In the eighteenth century Jacob Dessauer, of Amsterdam, used music by various composers for his *Purim* play, *Mordecai and Esther: the Greatest of Jews.* Many popular melodies of the day must have been included in the performances.

The musical accompaniment for the plays was provided by the *klezmer* or *klezmorim* (instrumentalists), although in some cases, as in Bukowina, the *Purim* play was accompanied by gentile musicians. These *Purim* plays later evolved into the Yiddish theater.

The *badchonim* not only entertained at weddings, but also served as the voice of the people, comforting those who suffered in times of trouble, administering verbal chastisement when Israel went astray, and rejoicing on happy occasions; they were folk singers in the truest sense of the word. While most of their songs were improvised and soon forgotten, some of the *badchonim* published their verse. Among these we may mention Hershel Weinshenk-Tausig of Prague, who wrote a necrology on the *hazzan* Lippman Popper in 1655; Moses Steindal, who translated the Psalms into Yiddish verse in 1586; *hazzan* Jacob Koppel, who wrote an elegy in 1670 on the expulsion of the Jews from Vienna; Leib Walich, who composed a hymn in honor of King Charles (Prague, 1704); Wolf of Cracow, who wrote a song, *The Conduct of Life* (Prague, 1692); and Noah Abraham Altshul, who published wedding songs, as well as *Purim* and *Hanukkah* songs (Prague, 1676).

Badchonim disappeared in Central Europe toward the middle of the nineteenth century, but in Eastern Europe they survived far into the twentieth century. There were several outstanding *badchonim* in the nineteenth century. One of these was Berl Broder, who toured southwestern Russia with a troupe of *badchonim*. They became very popular, and were known as the "Broder Singers." Their theatrical performances, which antedated those of Abraham Goldfaden's theater, were given on a stage which was set merely with a table and two candles. Their acting and singing were unusually successful. Berl Broder published a collection of thirty songs in Yiddish (Lemberg, 1876).

Another outstanding *badchon*, Wolf Ehrenkranz, known as Velvel Zbarazher, was born in 1826(?) and died in 1883. Driven from his native town by irate compatriots who refused to tolerate his scoffing verses, he made his way to Rumania. At first he sang in inns and taverns. When his audiences and popularity grew, he was invited to entertain at rich homes and weddings. Velvel Zbarazher freed the Yiddish poem of its dependence on religious themes, and was a master of both Yiddish and Hebrew. His satire was especially bitter against the hasidic movement.

Eliakum Zunser (1840-1913) was born in Wilno. An unhappy fatherless childhood had not stifled his poetic gifts. His songs, for which he also composed the music, spread throughout Eastern Europe and enjoyed great popularity. He rapidly became one of the most famous *badchonim*, and was in great demand at wedding celebrations in rich homes. His songs, *Shivas Zion* and *Die Soche*, which he also translated into Hebrew, became the forerunners of the modern Israeli song. Zunser was a *badchon* who was able to write down the music of his songs. In 1889 he sailed for America, where he was welcomed with reverence and regarded as a great Jewish folk poet.

Klezmorim played an integral part in Jewish community life. In some Oriental communities, musicians accompanied the singing of special hymns during the intermediate days of *Pesach* and *Sukkot*. Later, in East European communities, town musicians accompanied the cantor and choir at the special concerts held during the ceremonial public kindling of *Hanukkah* lights. Jewish musicians also played at the *Kabbalat Shabbat* (Welcoming of the Sabbath) in the synagogues in Prague and in Holland in the eighteenth century.

In 1629, Jewish refugees from music-loving Mantua organized an orchestra in Venice, calling it *Be-zochrenu Et Zion* (When We Remember Zion). It was directed by Rabbi Leon of Modena (1571-1648). This group occasionally exchanged courtesies and compositions with non-Jewish musical groups.

During the Middle Ages music-making became an accepted profession among Jews, and every city and town had its own musicians. Frequently, Jewish musicians were preferred at gentile celebrations because of their sobriety and art. This eventually led various governments to impose numerous taxes and restrictions upon the Jewish musicians.

A typical Jewish band consisted of a violin, clarinet, bass, flute, trumpet, trombone, and both snare and bass drums. No Jewish wedding was complete without music. The musicians had a saying that a wedding without a band was like a funeral without tears.

Another instrument often used in Jewish bands was the *hackbrett*, or dulcimer. Michael Joseph Gusikow (1806-1837) became a master of this instrument. He toured Europe and even won the praise of Felix Mendelssohn.

Other noted *klezmer* were Podhotzer and his band, which included Yisroel Moshe Rabinovitch, fiddler (1807-1900), and Wolf Tcherniavsky (1841-1930), son-in-law of Yossel Drucker, who was nicknamed "Stempenyu."

Most of the *klezmer* could barely read music. Their playing was much like the improvised performance of the synagogue combination of singer, bass and cantor. However, what they lacked in musical knowledge, they made up in talent, for some of them were true *virtuosi* on their instruments.

At weddings, the clarinet was the principal instrument in the dance music, and the violin was used during *bedekens*, when the *badchon* entertained the bride just before the marriage ceremony. The violinist accompanied the *badchon* with improvised sentimental melodies and musical interludes.

Abraham Goldfaden, generally known as the father of the modern Jewish theater, was born in Starokonstantin, Volhynia, in 1840. In his work he consistently strove to lift the people's taste. His first plays were short sketches. Among the best known of these are *Shmendrik* and *Breindele Kosak*. Later, when he had established his regular theater, he wrote and presented a witty and beautiful full-length comedy, *The Two Kuni Lemels*, a satire on hasidic life and conduct, and a plea for the *haskalah* (Enlightenment).

It was his ambition to write operas on themes from Jewish history and legend in the style of Richard Wagner, who held musical sway throughout Europe at that time. His first attempts in this direction were the musical plays *Shulamith*, *Bar Kochba* and *Akedas Yitzhok*, for which he wrote both the librettos, usually in verse, and the music. However, although the music was sometimes original, most often was taken from oratorio, opera, and synagogue compositions. Yet many of Abraham Goldfaden's songs as original compositions soon gained such wide popularity that they virtually became folk songs. Goldfaden settled in New York in 1903. Here he produced an operetta, *Ben Ami*. He died in 1908.

The Yiddish theater continued to flourish with such composers as Herman Wohl, Sholom Perlmutter, Louis Friedsell, and Joseph Brody. Their music was, for the most part, in the folk manner, and was reminiscent of synagogue modes and melodies. Wohl and Brody were choir leaders in synagogues as well.

The modern Yiddish theater on Second Avenue in New York has produced a quartet of very able composers —Joseph Rumshinsky, Sholom Secunda, Abraham Ellstein, Alexander Olshanetzky. Their style has been completely different from that of the Perlmutter and Wohl days. While some of their music has folk characteristics, most of it is a Jewish imitation of Broadway jazz.

Rumshinsky and Secunda have produced some of their best work in incidental music to serious Yiddish plays presented by Maurice Schwartz in his Yiddish Art Theater. For his production of Sholom Asch's *Kiddush Ha-Shem* and *Di Tsen Gebot*, Maurice Schwartz invited Joseph Achron to compose the incidental music.

XII. *The Development of the Jewish Folk Song*

A. The Beginnings of Jewish Folk Poetry

If the theory that such Psalm titles as *Al Shoshanim, Al Neginot*, and *Al Yonathelem Rohokim* were the names of popular songs in Biblical days is correct, we have additional proof that secular folk songs existed at that time.

Ben Sira praises song at a wine banquet, but warns the people against association with female singers. The sages maintained (*Shir Ha-shirim Rabbah*) that songs of wine and lust cause destruction in the world, while Israel's sacred songs save the world. The Song of Songs is also assumed by many scholars to have been a series of popular songs incorporated in the Bible only after a religious interpretation was given to them.

Every people creates its own folk songs on its own soil. The Jews in Biblical times were no exception in this respect. They later took these songs with them into exile, just as they took their religion. Time and a succession of troubles all but obliterated them.

The oldest themes that have come down to us are found in the songs about Elijah, the Sabbath, and the holidays, in the group of songs called *zemirot*. There were also a great many songs for such occasions as weddings and circumcisions.

Robert Lachmann (*Jewish Cantillation and Song in the Isle of Djerba*; Jerusalem, 1940) points out that on the Isle of Djerba, which contains one of the oldest isolated Jewish communities in the world, the women's songs are always sung in Arabic. The texts give us a lively insight into the people's thought and feeling. We find here expressions of the desire to go to Jerusalem and longings for the coming of the Messiah. There is a song in praise of Moses and of Pharoah's daughter who found him on the river bank; there is a description of the Feast of Weeks which does not neglect the secular delights, especially those of eating and drinking; and finally, there is the favorite theme of the bridal period and the wedding. Similar themes are found in the secular songs for men.

After the expulsion from Spain in 1492, Spanish Jews migrated eastward, taking with them the Castilian *canciones* and romances of that period. Even today we find Jews in the Balkans and in North Africa who sing such

Ladino songs. In Greek, Turkish, and Arab surroundings these songs combined Judaeo-Spanish with local words and expressions that were added later. While there are both religious and secular songs, the former predominate. The melodies are Oriental in color, and vary somewhat according to locale.

B. The Yiddish Folk Song

Meanwhile, the Western European Jews of Germany and France created folk songs of their own, mostly religious in character, with melodies often borrowed from their region.

The oldest collection of Yiddish songs was made by Eisik Walich of Worms in 1595-1605. In 1727, in Fuerth, Elchanan Kirchan published the first collection of Yiddish songs with music under the title *Simchat Ha-nefesh.* The songs deal exclusively with religious themes, in particular with the Sabbath and Jewish holidays, and contain minute instructions as to their observance. This collection was republished in New York in 1926 with an introduction by Jacob Shatzky.

The characteristic Yiddish folk song originated in Eastern Europe, where the language of the Jews became predominantly Yiddish. Hence we occasionally encounter in it an admixture of Russian, Ukrainian, and other Slavic words.

The topics of these songs run the gamut of human life and emotions, from the cradle to the grave. The tunes are sometimes foreign, and sometimes of Jewish origin. The texts, for the most part, deal with Jewish life, but occasionally they are of foreign derivation, as *Der Rebbe Elimelech*, which is a Yiddish version of "Old King Cole."

The singing of folk songs was always frowned upon by the learned Jews. Their greatest concession in this direction was to sing a Hebrew folk song with Jewish content on *Simchat Torah*. The secular Yiddish folk songs were therefore confined mostly to the artisan classes, who sang them at their work.

Yiddish folk songs include numerous cradle songs, in which the mother prays not only for the child's health and happiness, but also that his heart be inclined toward the *Torah*. The melody of *Unter Dem Kinds Vigele*, for instance, is in the *Ahavah Rabbah* liturgical mode.

Jewish children were initiated into Jewish learning at the early age of three or four. The parents took pride in introducing the child to Jewish lore, and sang the song, *Gei Mein Kind In Heder*. Its melody is derived from the cantillation mode of *Akdamut*, a poem in Aramaic read on *Shavuot*, the Festival of the Giving of the Law, at which such introductions took place. This is a genuine Jewish folk song; both its text and melody are Jewish.

Although they spent most of their day studying in the *heder*, the Jewish ghetto children liked to play, like any other children. The great Jewish poet Bialik describes these Jewish boys with much tenderness in his beautiful poem, *Unter Di Grininke Boimelech*. The poem was set to music by Platon Brounoff and has become a folk song. It is in the *Ahavah Rabbah* mode, with a modulation to the major key on the fourth—a modulation frequently found in synagogue music.

A picture of little Jewish children being taught the alphabet by the *melamed* (teacher) is found in the song *Oifn Pripitchok* by Mark Warshawsky (1845-1907). The melody is based on the cantillation of the Prophets in the Ashkenazic tradition.

When the boy became nine or ten, and sometimes even earlier, he was initiated into the study of the *Talmud*. Later, when he was sent to the *yeshivah* in a larger city, he lived by "eating days" with various householders of the community. This was often depressing and humiliating. *Mai Ko Mashma Lon*, by Abraham Reisen, describes the lot of the *yeshivah bachur*. Its tune is derived from the melody used in studying the *Talmud*.

Were it not for the Jew's sense of humor, it is doubtful whether he could have weathered the storms of the exile. He laughed and often mocked at himself, his lot, and even his troubles.

Yiddish love songs are rare, for it was deemed improper for the Jewish maiden to express herself on the subject. Yet she wanted to get married as urgently as her parents wanted to see her married. In *Yome Yome* the maiden finally admits to her mother her wish to have a suitor. The melody is in the *Magen Avot* mode. The rhythm in the latter part of the melody suggests a Russian folk song.

A wedding was a great event in Jewish life. Relatives, rich and poor, gathered to celebrate it. Of no small importance were the musicians, whose task it was to add cheer to the occasion and give pleasure to the bride, the bridegroom, and the guests. In the song *Hatskele*, a poor aunt asks the musicians to play her a *kazatskele* (a wedding dance of Russian origin), even though she is poor and cannot pay for it. The first part of the melody is of Jewish origin, the latter part is Russian and in keeping with the character of the dance.

Wedding songs contributed a joyous element to the Jewish folk song. In *Di Mezinke Oisgegebn*, the parents who have married off their last child dance and sing to celebrate the long awaited event. The melody is Slavic in character.

Curiously enough, we find relatively little folk music in Yiddish dealing with the Sabbath. The reason for this is that folk songs came under the classification of *Shire Hol*, everyday songs, while on the Sabbath only the *Shire Kodesh*, or sacred songs, were sung in Hebrew. Whatever folk music developed about the Sabbath was sung either before Sabbath eve or after *Havdalah*, when the Sabbath was actually over. The only exception was the chant, *Got Fun*

Avrohom (God of Abraham), which the women recited or sang in Yiddish just before the *Havdalah*.

The song *Shreitzhe Yidn Shabbes* is a marvelous expression of the Jew's faith in the Sabbath; and *Melaveh Malkah* (Seeing Off the Sabbath Queen), attributed to the hasidic Rabbi Levi Yitzhok of Berditchev, is a picture of the Jew as he returns to his weekday routine. *A Chazendl Oif Shabbes* is a satire on the Jew who ran from one synagogue to another on the Sabbath to hear various cantors. The melodies of *Got Fun Avrohom* and *Shreitzhe Yidn Shabbes* are in the *Ahavah Rabbah* mode. *A Chazendl Oif Shabbes* is in the *Adonay Malach* mode. Both of these modes are frequently used in the Sabbath liturgy in the synagogue, and have influenced the folk song. These songs are excellent examples of genuine Jewish folk melodies.

Very few modern Hebrew poems about the Sabbath have been set to music, but among the best are two poems by Hayim Nahman Bialik—*Shabbat Ha-malkah* (The Queen Sabbath), and *Yesh Li Gan* (I Have a Garden), which have become popular folk songs. *Shabbat Ha-malkah* has even been adopted in some Jewish communities as part of the late Friday evening services; it is also sung at *Oneg Shabbat* gatherings, and has won a place among the regular *zemirot* in homes where these are still sung. The poem is really a paraphrase of the traditional *zemirah*—*Shalom Aleichem. Yesh Li Gan* is an idyllic love song which, strictly speaking, does not belong to the Sabbath. In this country it has become customary to sing appropriate new Israeli folk songs in Hebrew at Sabbath gatherings.

The Yiddish folk song also includes many national songs, holiday songs, and women's songs. There are, however, few nature songs, for Jews were confined to small towns and villages during the ghetto days, and rarely had the opportunity for close contact with nature and its beauty.

Efforts to collect Yiddish folk songs began on a small scale in the nineteenth century, but the serious work in this field came only at the end of the century, after the post-romantic movement in music had given way to nationalism. The Russian national school at this time was already in full flower, with the works of Glinka, Rimsky-Korsakov, Moussorgsky, and Tchaikovsky to its credit. In Norway, national music had such exponents as Grieg and Sinding, and the Bohemians had Dvorak and Smetana. The Jews also felt the impact of this new national movement. The first real effort at collecting the texts of Jewish folk songs was made by S. Ginsburg and P. Marek in St. Petersburg in 1901. Their collection contains the texts of 376 songs, without the music. Many similar collections have since appeared, and the work of collecting such materials continues into the present day.

The St. Petersburg Society for Jewish Folk Music, founded in 1908 by Joel Engel (1868-1927), set itself the task of collecting Yiddish folk songs and arranging piano accompaniments for them in a style that would reflect their true spirit and atmosphere. This Society, which counted among its members leading Jewish composers as Ephraim Skliar, Joseph Achron, Solomon Rosowsky, Moses Milner, Michael Gnessin, Alexander Krein, Lazare Saminsky, and Jacob Weinberg, not only collected and arranged, but also presented these songs at public concerts of Jewish music throughout Russia. Its members also began to develop Jewish art music, basing it on thematic material found in these songs, and seeking to evolve a truly Jewish musical style. These ideas came to even richer fruition two decades later, when some of the most active leaders of the movement migrated to America, and later found new inspiration when the land of Israel was reborn.

Here in America many Jewish musicians have busied themselves with arranging Jewish folk songs for concert performances. Among them have been Vladimir Heifetz, Henry Lefkowitch, Lazar Weiner, Jacob Weinberg, Pinhas Jassinowsky, Nicholas Saslavsky, and this writer.

These men have also contributed significantly to the development of the Yiddish art song.

The labor theme has always been present in the Yiddish folk song, but has received special attention in America, where many of the immigrants began their new life as artisans. David Edelstadt's *Der Arbeter* and *Mein Yingele*, to texts by the great Yiddish poet Morris Rosenfeld, are examples of this type of song. The melodies are in the *Ahavah Rabbah* mode. The Jews of the Soviet Union have also created songs that describe their crafts, occupations, professions, and loyalties.

The songs of the ghetto and concentration camps have been the newest addition to the Yiddish folk song. As always, our people gave voice to their suffering in poetry and song. Hundreds of poems were written during this terrifying period in Jewish history. Many were set to music —in most cases to well-known tunes or synagogue melodies. Occasionally a new melody was composed. The melodies often used, however, were inferior to the words.

These songs speak of courage and hope, of ghetto walls, of concentration camps, of longing for home and family, of bombings and the brutality of men. The partisan song *Zog Nit Keinmol*, the most popular and revered of those new songs (many Jewish audiences rise when this song is played) was composed by Hirsh Glick, who said, "These songs were written with blood, not with lead." The melody of *Zog Nit Keinmol* is a Russian folk melody. Another significant song from the concentration camps was *Ani Maamin*, which has become a cherished melody.

XIII. Hasidic Songs

The founder of hasidism, Yisroel Baal Shem Tov, or the *Besht*, as he was later called, was born about 1700 in the town of Okop, Ukraine. He spoke in easy parables which even the most lowly were able to understand. He taught that God could be found and approached not only by the learned scholars, but also by simple folk; that God was to be loved rather than feared; and, that God could be reached with prayer and song at all times and places.

The approach to God required preparation however. These preparations for the ultimate ecstasy of prayer led through three stages: *kavanah*, or complete absorption and concentration; *deveikut*, or a cleaving unto God in which the sense of separation from Him disappears; and *hitlahavut*, or that burning fire of devotion which follows complete surrender to prayer. In addition to these disciplines, men must "serve God in joy," for "God must be approached with joyous and singing heart."

Music, therefore, came to occupy an all-important place in hasidic life and practices. Hasidic rabbis, beginning with Yisroel Baal Shem Tov, propounded definite ideas and theories about the powers of melody. The *nigun*, the song without words, became the musical expression of hasidism. It was sung merely with a repeating syllable or a combination of syllables such as la, tra, bim, or bam.

Yisroel Baal Shem Tov, as folklore has it, was able to tell the character of a musician, as well as his life and his deeds, through his playing. He was also credited with the ability to discern words and meanings in the tones of a melody and to follow the thoughts of his *hasidim* as they poured their hearts out to him in a *nigun*.

Rabbi Shneur Zalman of Liadi (1747-1813) said, "Melody is the speech of the soul, but words interrupt the stream of emotion." A melody with words, he felt, was limited in time; with the end of the words, the melody also ceases. But a wordless tune can be repeated endlessly, allowing the singer to pour out his feelings through the *nigun* from the innermost recesses of his heart. This gave rise to the *ein sof nigun*, the melody without an end.

Rabbi Levi Yitzhok of Berditchev (1740-1810) was perhaps the most musically gifted of the hasidic rabbis. Music was an important medium of expression in his life. He taught his *hasidim* in song and prayed to God through song. He left us a number of songs with texts in which Hebrew and Yiddish intermingled. These songs are true gems of Jewish folk music.

Rabbi Nahman of Bratslav (1772-1811) also gave music an important place in hasidism. He regarded melody as the essence of all thought. "Every bit of wisdom in the world has its own melody," he declared. "All creation resolves into melody. Faith in God has its own melody, the most important of all, and affecting all others." He taught that there was music in the whole universe and in every man's soul. "Nature is replete with melody, heaven and earth are full of song. The man who hears it is purified and inspired to lead a new life, the more so if he also understands the dance, which brings complete harmony through its rhythm. Every limb of the body contains in itself a rhythm that corresponds to the rhythm of the melody. There is rhythm in the movements of the head and the feet, of the whole body and of every part of it, all in accord with the rhythm of the melody. And the melody is even more complete when it is invested with words, because the rhythm of the verses in consonance with the melody produces harmony. How splendid it is to hear it and to see it supplemented by dancing." Of all the *zaddikim*, or leaders of the *hasidim*, Rabbi Nahman was the greatest lover of melody, dancing, and song. He taught his followers, "There are gates in heaven which cannot be opened save by song and praise."

The *zaddik* of Ger, Yitzhok Meir, used to say to his *hasidim*, "Were I blessed with a sweet voice, I would sing you new hymns and songs every day, for as the world is created anew every day, new songs are created with it."

The melody without words, the *nigun*, became the most popular form of song among the *hasidim*. There were two types of *nigunim*: the meditative, expressing the moods of *kavanah* and *deveikut*, and the dance type, expressing moods of joy and supreme exaltation (*hitlahavut*).

Since the *zaddik* was regarded as a divine singer, the tunes he created were held to be holy and of heavenly inspiration. Several melodies attributed to *zaddikim* are still sung among *hasidim*. It is, however, uncertain whether these are original tunes or old melodies reshaped to suit the temperament and character of the *rebbe* and his "court." A melody attributed to a *rebbe* was called *dem rebbns nigun*.

When the *rebbe* himself was unable to lead his *hasidim* in song, one of his more musical followers would do so. In many "courts" there were special *hasidim* whose task it was to lead the singing and compose new melodies for holidays and festivals. Some of the "courts" developed unmistakable styles of their own, so that their melodies and the manner in which they were sung were immediately recognizable.

Individual *hasidim* were frequently associated in the "court" of the *rebbe* with certain tunes. When they were asked to sing, they were expected to sing a particular melody, and no other *hasid* could sing another's tune if its original "possessor" was present.

At their gatherings, the *hasidim* sang Psalms, songs with Hebrew and Yiddish texts, and songs without words. Many of their dance melodies were called *wolech* or *wolechish*, suggesting the musical style of the folk songs of Walachia, in Southeastern Europe.

At certain moments of religious exaltation, the *rebbe* or the *hasid* would introduce a melody, and its singing would fan the true hasidic fire. At those times the *hasidim* felt that their souls were united with that of the Creator, for in song they reached the heights of ecstasy. The cardinal element in singing was the joy it created. The melody was most important; the words were secondary.

While there was singing at all hasidic gatherings, the more fervent sessions took place at various hours on the Sabbath. The greatest intensity, however, was reached on the Three Festivals—*Pesach*, *Shavuot*, and *Sukkot*. Compared with these occasions, even the Sabbath celebrations seemed restrained, for the Jew was commanded, "And thou shalt rejoice in thy feast" (Deut. xvi, 14); and the *hasidim* took this command literally, especially on *Sukkot*.

On the second night of *Sukkot* the *hasidim* commemorated the Temple ceremony of the "water libation" with singing, dancing, and processions with candles. On the last two days of *Sukkot*, which ended with *Simchat Torah* (the Festival of Rejoicing in the Law), song and dance reigned supreme. The crowning moments came when the *rebbe* and the prominent householders danced with the *Torah*.

The *hasidim* found spiritual significance even in the hilarious celebration of *Purim*. Rabbi Levi Yitzhok of Berditchev danced as he chanted the first of the three benedictions preceding the reading of the *Megillah*.

Rabbi Abbush Meir of Sanz, who was extremely musical, composed a new melody for *Shoshanat Yaakov* every year. His *hasidim* would gather at the *Shalosh Seudot* (third meal) on the Sabbath preceding *Purim*, and he would teach them the new tune. It was then sung over and over again during the *Purim* celebration, and reappeared on the following Sabbath eve service in *L'cha Dodi*.

The night of *Purim* was a time of song and merry-making. The *Shoshanat Yaakov* held the center of attention. There were also songs, hasidic and others, in the vernacular. Often some *hasidim* entertained the *rebbe* and the other *hasidim* with a *purimspiel*, which was frequently accompanied by singing and even instrumental music.

On the following day, *Shushan Purim*, the rejoicing went on unabated, reaching a climax at the *Mincha* (afternoon) service, at which one of the *hasidim* acted as a cantor. He dressed in a *kittel* (a white shroud worn on the High Holy Days) and chanted the solemn prayers in melodies used on the High Holy Days, but parodying both melody and style.

Dancing, as we have seen, was an aid toward achieving a state of joyousness; but the dance in Jewish life was not an innovation brought in by the *hasidim*. The Bible often speaks of dancing. No less a person than King David himself danced before the Ark of the Covenant. In the Psalms, too, there are references to the dance (Psalm 150).

Among the great hasidic rabbis, Nahman of Bratslav was the most enthusiastic about dancing. He believed that dancing and the clapping of hands could move the judges on high to mercy. "Through joy we unite ourselves with God." Therefore the *hasidim* danced round dances on the High Holy Days, and the *zaddik* himself sometimes joined in. Life's realities were swept away, forgotten, as they danced round and round for hours, feeling no fatigue. Some of the more gifted rabbis and *hasidim* presented a pleasant sight as they danced, using their limbs and bodies with much grace. As a rule, these dances were for men only. A *hasid* would never be so bold as to dance with his wife except within the walls of his home, and even then infrequently. On the rare occasions when men danced with women, they did not join hands, but held on to the opposite ends of a handkerchief.

When the *Besht* brought hasidism to the Jews, it attracted mostly the simple and uneducated. After Ber of Mezhiritch (1710-1772), successor to the *Besht*, was won over to hasidism, his influence led many learned Jews to join the movement, for he himself was a great scholar. It was this wing of hasidism that produced the philosophical system known as *Habad*, which was founded by Shneur Zalman of Liadi, and won most of its adherents in Lithuania and White Russia. The *Besht* system drew most of its followers from Poland, Southern Russia, Rumania, and Hungary.

Habad derived its name from the initials of the three words designating the principles upon which it rested: *hokmah* (wisdom), *binah* (understanding), and *daat* (knowledge). This philosophy was permeated with the mysticism of Rabbi Isaac Luria; its goal was the attainment of divine bliss. This, its proponents taught, could not be achieved by leaping from extreme melancholy to extreme joy. It had to be approached gradually. The stages toward the elevation of the spirit consisted of: 1) *hishtapchut ha-nefesh*, or the outpouring of the soul and the effort to rise out of the mire of sin and the grip of the evil spirit; 2) *hitorerut*, or spiritual awakening; 3) *hitpaalut*, or the stage in which the seeker is possessed by his thought; 4) *deveikut*, or communion with God; 5) *hitlahavut*, the flaming ecstasy that precedes the highest stage; and 6) *hitpashtut ha-gashmiyut*, the ultimate stage where the soul casts off its garments of flesh and becomes a disembodied spirit. Born in 1544, Luria died in Jerusalem in 1572.

The *Habad hasidim* composed special melodies which embodied all of these stages, several of them, or only one. The founder of the *Habad* system himself composed a tune call *Dem Rebbns Nigun* to conform to his system.

The music of the two hasidic schools differed in their serious moods, but they shared the same tunes for joyous moods. On the whole, *Habad hasidim* preferred melodies of a mystical character and *zemirot* of the Lurianic period, which they sang to mystical tunes of their own.

The hasidic songs are characterized by Jewish melodic modes and idioms. Most of their melodies, however, are based on the synagogue prayer modes rather than on cantillation, since the *hasidim* were more familiar with the former. They even read the weekly portions of the *Torah* on the Sabbath in a melody which merely resembled cantillation, but did not follow the exact interpretation of the tropes. This was another of their innovations.

Their slow melodies are the most beautiful, and the songs attributed to Rabbi Levi Yitzhok of Berditchev are among the best of Jewish folk songs in their beauty and sincerity of feeling. However, in the *hitorerut* and *hitlahavut* melodies, the *hasidim* borrowed without reserve or discrimination from the peoples around them. We therefore find among these songs Oriental, Ukrainian, and Slavic tunes, as well as Cossack dances, military marches, polkas, and waltzes. Still, many of the dance tunes were based on synagogue modes.

The spirit of hasidism, with its beauty and wisdom, mysticism and fire, has given wings to the creative spirit of Jewish artists in every field. We shall not dwell on the extensive literature and poetry which came from the pens of both its adherents and critics at the height of the struggle against hasidism, but rather upon its influence on Jewish music.

Hasidism, as we have seen, has made an important contribution to Jewish folk music. The *nigunim* have a character all their own. Since so many of them served to express religious and mystical states, as in *Habad* hasidism, we have untold numbers of melodies consisting of up to seven sections—a form rarely found in the folk music of other peoples. Hasidism also left an indelible imprint on the cantorial art of the eighteenth and nineteenth centuries, and helped to develop the styles of many great cantors.

At the beginning of the twentieth century, hasidic songs began to appear, singly or in groups, in such collections of Jewish folk songs as those of M. Kipnis, J. L. Cahan, and F. M. Kaufman. A substantial collection of hasidic songs without words may be found in A. M. Bernstein's *Musikalisher Pinkas* and S. Rosowsky's *Mi-zimrat Haaretz*. Many hasidic songs arranged as art songs have been published by various Jewish composers.

The hasidic song in its many forms stimulated the musical imagination of numerous Jewish composers, who built upon this material a variety of musical works, both large and small. Outstanding among these works are the two suites drawn from Joel Engel's incidental music to *The Dybbuk*, which is arranged for a small ensemble and utilizes the various hasidic moods. Another fine example of this type of music is Solomon Rosowsky's *Fantastic Trio*, built upon *Habad nigunim*. Maurice Ravel's arrangement of *Mayerke* and Darius Milhaud's arrangement of hasidic songs are also noteworthy.

The moods, practices, and philosophies of hasidism have also inspired a number of composers. Works based on hasidism include Ernest Bloch's superb *Baal Shem Suite* for violin and piano, Aaron Copland's *Vitebsk Trio*, and this writer's *Two Hasidic Moods*, for string quartet. There are many other works for various musical combinations.

Since the beginning of the twentieth century, hasidism has also influenced the folk song of Palestine. In a great many songs that are being composed and sung in Israel today, we find closing sections consisting of melody alone, sung to such syllables as la or li, and reminiscent of the hasidic *nigun*. Most of the early *hora* melodies were hasidic dance *nigunim*. *Nigun Bialik*, very popular in the twenties of this century, was a hasidic melody.

In retrospect, this remarkable movement in Jewish life still retains validity for us primarily in the mystic spirit, the intimate love of God in nature, the spirit of fellowship which prevailed among the *hasidim*, and above all, in their faith in life. The *hasid* felt, in the face of all adversity, that God is kind and merciful, and loves his people with a love that is eternal. Hasidism has left for Jewish artists and musicians a heritage so rich that its influence will continue to inspire generation after generation in creating the Jewish art of the future.

XIV. Zemirot

Zemirot, or table songs, are known to have been sung as far back as the days of the Second Temple. It is believed that *Tsur Mi-shelo,* one of the *zeimirot* for the Sabbath eve, whose author is unknown, belongs to the early Tannaitic period, perhaps even before Yabneh. The poem is based on three benedictions—*Ha-zan, Al Ha-aretz,* and *Boneh.* It contains no reference to the Sabbath. Most of the *zemirot,* however, are products of a much later day.

The idea of making the Sabbath a day of delight and joy through music developed as time went on. Mounting persecution made the Jew's burden increasingly heavy. It became necessary to emphasize those elements in the Sabbath which could give him some respite from his troubled existence, some way of restoring his self-esteem. The Sabbath was to bring sweet peace and rest and remind him that he was a prince of God. It is, therefore, significant that the gayest *zemirot* were written at the darkest times in Jewish history.

The eleventh century witnessed the beginning of a great period in the history of Hebrew poetry, both sacred and secular. It was the fashion in those days to compose religious poetry to the rhythm and melody of popular secular songs, and to imitate their sound in Hebrew. At first the rabbis censured such practices, but ultimately the poets won. Many of the sacred poems became popular songs; some found their way into the liturgy; and a number became *zemirot* for the Sabbath.

Another factor in the development of the *zemirot* was the growth of the *Kabbala,* the mystic ideas of which became popularly associated with the Sabbath. Of particular significance was the mystical concept of a *neshamah yeterah,* a second or Sabbath soul, that descends upon those

who observe the Sabbath according to Law. Many believed that such a soul could be attained only through song
on the Sabbath. The Lurian kabbalists of the sixteenth century laid particular stress on the power of music. Isaac Luria
himself encouraged his disciple, Shelomo Alkabetz, to compose the famous poem *L'cha Dodi*. Together with the Song
of Songs, *Azamer Bi-shevahin*, and *An'im Zemirot*, it
forms the center of a group of love songs through which
the Jew expressed his love of God and the Sabbath. *L'cha
Dodi* quickly spread to all Jewish communities, and in
later centuries became a favorite text for composers of
synagogue music. Isaac Luria is also said to have composed
zemirot for each of the three Sabbath meals—*Azamer Bi-
shevahin*, *Asader Li-seudata*, and *Bene Hechala*.

Not only the words, but also the tunes of certain
zemirot are attributed to Isaac Luria and his kabbalist followers, including Israel Najara (1550-1620), the author
of the beautiful and popular poem, *Yah Ribbon*. He holds
a unique place among the poets of the *zemirot* period. In
later centuries hasidism, influenced by Lurianic mysticism,
contributed much to the music of the *zemirot*. Especially
characteristic of the hasidic manner of singing is the frequent interpolation of stretches of wordless song between
the phrases or verses of a poem.

Hasidic tunes for *zemirot* are almost always joyous and
rhythmic. Among the *Habad hasidim*, however, we find
melodies that reflect the mystic elements which colored
their beliefs. The most mystic melodies are those of the
Aramic *zemirot*, such as *Azamer Bi-shevahin* and *Yah
Ribbon*. This is probably due to the Lurianic origin of
these poems.

Both among *hasidim* and *mitnagdim*, *zemirot* served as a
bridge between table talk and religious discourses, between
the human and the divine, between the jocular and the
serious. It has frequently been said that a Jew must honor
God with the beauty of his soul and the beauty of his

throat. "While Israel feasts, he always sings in praise of God." The principal singers at the table were the father and the sons. Mother and daughters might join in the refrains or sing their own *zemirot*. These were the customs that developed as the singing of *zemirot* became more and more widespread during the Middle Ages, particularly in Germany and Italy.

There are *zemirot* for the three meals of the Sabbath, but the most important and colorful groups, from the point of view of both poetry and music, are those associated with the Friday evening and Saturday midday meals. At the Sabbath eve meal, the master of the home welcomes the Sabbath with the chanting of a group of prayers, beginning with *Shalom Aleichem*. The *Kiddush* follows. The actual *zemirot* are introduced with a meditative poem, *Kol Mekadesh* for Friday evening, and *Baruch Adonay Yom Yom* for Sabbath afternoon. The tunes are reminiscent of liturgical modes. *Kol Mekadesh* is sung in the *Magen Avot* mode of the Friday evening service, suggesting the "sweet peace and rest" of the Sabbath. *Baruch Adonay* is also sung in a Friday evening mode, that of *Adonay Malach*, suggesting Israel as the "prince of God."

Zemirot were sung not only at the Sabbath midday meal, but also at the *Shalosh Seudot*, the third meal, which usually took place after the Sabbath afternoon service, and almost always in the synagogue. The singing continued until sundown, and bore the character of a prelude to the departure of the Sabbath. It was followed by the evening service. After the *Havdalah*, which ushered in the secular days of the week, *zemirot* were sung again. Later in the evening, at the *Melaveh-Malkah* more *zemirot* were sung, as a fitting farewell to the Sabbath.

There are few parallels to the Jewish *zemirot* among the songs of other nations. Unlike the table songs of other peoples, they combine piety with good cheer and thankfulness. They reflect the material and the spiritual, tragedy and joy, changes of taste, and the progress of thought. Through all these elements, the general theme is the Sabbath.

XV. *Music in Israel*

With the modern rebuilding of Palestine, which began in the 1880's, the Jewish people developed new powers of growth. Along with these came a revival of song, which played an important role in our musical life.

The pioneering Jews felt the need of song as soon as they arrived in Palestine, as a part of the culture which they had set out to build. Indigenous and original folk songs do not spring up overnight, and so for thirty-five years the settlers experimented with the various types of songs they had known in the countries from which they had come. They sang their Yiddish folk songs translated into Hebrew, their liturgical songs brought out of the synagogue, and also Arabic and Yemenite songs which they had found in Palestine.

The period of 1881 to 1918 produced some popular songs, but few of them could truly be called Palestinian. While the resettlement went on with hope and enthusiasm throughout that time, it could not compare with the new burst of activity that began in 1918, following the issuance of the Balfour Declaration of 1917, and the end of the First World War. A wave of young men and women, *halutzim* and *halutzot* (pioneers) from all parts of Europe and from Eastern Europe in particular, streamed into the land in a determined effort to make use of the promise of a Jewish homeland held out by the Balfour Declaration. These *halutzim* and *halutzot* brought new energy to the growth and development of Palestine. They also brought with them a tremendous capacity for song and dance, an expression of their joy in being a part of the generation that was rebuilding Israel. The spirit of democracy which came with them pervades all the songs of this period. The people did not sing of kings and princes, but of their land, their work, their hope, their destiny, and themselves.

The modern Israeli song is characterized by constant experimentation with new rhythmic effects. This change of rhythmic design in Israeli songs is in keeping with the vital spirit one finds throughout the land. There is a great deal of syncopation, both simple and compound, reflecting the vibrant tempo of the new Israeli life.

The Palestinian song of the early period was a conglomeration of songs of the exile, songs of the various nations among which the Jews had lived, some Arabic and some Yemenite songs, and some excerpts from the Jewish liturgy. However, as time went on, there was a growing sense of musical inadequacy among the singing Palestinians. In the second period, beginning with 1918, they said, "It is true that we sing much, but our songs are not yet really Palestinian. These will come."

They did begin to come about ten years later, when the people struck deeper roots in the soil of the land. These new songs combined features of liturgical song with those of the Yemenite and Arabic song, emerging as an indigenous expression with a spirit entirely their own.

All of these bear kinship to various branches of Jewish music—the cantillation modes, the prayer modes, and the synagogue songs. Also encountered in the modern Israeli songs had been features of the cantorial art of the past centuries. The cantillation modes as traditionally used in reading the Bible have contributed much toward the evolution of the true Israeli song.

In its evolution toward originality the new Israeli song has taken on a number of characteristics which will in future years help to distinguish it among the folk songs of the various nations. There are, for instance, many musical folk figures commonly heard in Jewish exclamations, prayers, and study themes.

A melodic characteristic that frequently appears in Israeli song is the interchangeable accidental. Its effect is
extremely Oriental, lending a note of contemplation that
is typically Jewish. Many popular Israeli folk songs make
use of the interchanging accidental.

Another feature is the change of mode within a melody.
This type of modulating melody was frequently found in
the cantorial improvisations of the nineteenth century. The
patterns of these modulations are interesting, and will
probably play an important part in the Israeli song of the
future.

Modulation to a key a fourth above the original key has
always been characteristic of key changes in synagogue
music. As a matter of fact, the interval of a fourth up or
down is the strongest interval in ancient Jewish music. A
two-decker modulation to the fourth above occurs in some
new Israeli songs. Also, in a number of new Israeli folk
songs there are special effects which lend individuality to
the song and sometimes add to its humor.

"Let me write the ballads of my people, I care not who
makes its laws," said a wise man. It is a fortunate composer
who can write a simple melody which the people will adopt
as their own, making the song folk property; yet, few of
the great masters of music have succeeded in this direction.
In Israel a number of professional composers have tried to
write songs for the people. Although many of them were
sung for a time, few have attained the popularity of the
folk songs created by Israeli farmers and workers. Most of
the best songs of modern Palestine have come from the
agricultural settlements.

All the song writers in Israel are inspired with the high
goal of creating a true Israeli song, for Israel is trying to
develop a musical idiom characteristic of the land and expressive of the life of the people. There is full realization
that art music ultimately rests upon folk music, both of
which the people themselves are in the process of creating.

Among the early song writers from among the people there were many naturally gifted young Jews, such as Mordecai Zeira, Matthityahu Weiner, Shalom Postolsky, Nahum Nardi, Yedidya Gorochov, Yariv Ezrahi, David Zahavi, Gabriel Grad, Emanuel Pugatchov, Verdina Shlonsky, Zvi Kaplan, Emanuel Zamir, Sarah Levi, Menashe Ravina, Daniel Sambursky, and Moshe Bick.

Music schools have existed in Israel since 1910, when Shulamith Ruppin organized the Shulamith Music School in Tel Aviv. The Jerusalem School of Music was founded by the British Governor, Sir Ronald Storrs, in 1918, and was directed by Sidney Seal, a British pianist. Mademoiselle Dunia Weizman established a music school in Haifa in 1921.

The Palestine opera was organized in 1923 by Mordecai Golinkin. Since that time, it has presented almost all popular operas in Hebrew translation. Moshe Rudinow, former cantor of Temple Emanu-El in New York, and his wife, Ruth Leviash, were among the first members of that company. In recent years *Dan Ha-shomer* (Dan the Watchman), Israeli opera by Marc Lavry, has enjoyed great popularity.

In 1930 the Palestine Symphonic Ensemble, consisting of forty players, was organized by Zvi Kumpaneetz. It gave weekly concerts in Tel Aviv and Jerusalem.

The Palestine Philharmonic Orchestra was organized by Bronislaw Huberman, a famous violin virtuoso, in 1936. Its personnel consisted mainly of musicians who had fled from countries oppressed by Hitler. The first conductor was Arturo Toscanini; he was followed by Michael Taube, Joseph Rosenstock, Bernardino, Molinari, Charles Munch, Izler Solomon, Jascha Horenstein, William Steinberg, Issai Dobrowen, Leonard Bernstein, and Serge Koussevitzky. Now as the Israel Philharmonic Orchestra, it has truly become one of the most vital cultural forces in the Near East. The orchestra made its first American tour in 1951.

Music occupies an important part in the curriculum of the Israeli school system, and the Cultural Department of the *Histadrut* (Labor Federation of Israel) devotes a good deal of its efforts to the organization of choral bodies, which exist in large numbers throughout the land. The radio stations in Tel Aviv and Jerusalem also provide daily musical fare of good variety.

Jewish art music originated in the efforts of the St. Petersburg Society for Jewish Folk Music. Afterwards, most of the activity in the field was transferred to the United States. More Jewish music has since been composed, published, and performed in this country than in any other part of the world.

Jewish composers in America have produced works in all forms, from the shortest piano pieces to symphonies and operas. Among the more active of these composers have been Joseph Achron, Lazare Saminsky, Jacob Weinberg, Isadore Freed, Frederick Jacobi, Julius Chajes, Reuven Kosakoff, Chemjo Vinaver, and this author.

Internationally famed Jewish composers who have resided in the United States have from time to time written music on Jewish themes or to Jewish texts. Arnold Schoenberg (1874-1951) composed a work, *Kol Nidre*, as well as a cantata, *A Survivor From Warsaw*. His other works on Jewish themes are the Psalm *De Profundis*, an opera *Moses and Aaron*, and an unfinished oratorio *Die Jakobsleiter*. Darius Milhaud (b. 1892) has composed several artistic arrangements of hasidic folk songs and an elaborate setting of the Sabbath liturgy, which he called *Service Sacré*. His opera *Esther* has attained wide success. All of the music of Ernest Bloch (1880-1959) is considered Jewish, whether specifically designated or not. Aaron Copland has composed a trio *Vitebsk* and a choral setting on the theme of creation *In the Beginning*.

The composers of serious Jewish music in Israel include Marc Lavry, Frank Pelleg, Paul Ben-Haim, Verdina Shlonsky, Alexander Uriah Boscovich, Menahem Mahler-Kalkstein, Ben Zion Orgad, Oedoen Partos, Erich Walter Sternberg, and Joseph Kaminsky.

Composers both in and out of Israel are working toward the same goal—the development of a Jewish musical idiom. Israel is an inspiration for Jewish musicians. The Jewish music of the future will therefore not be the expression of any one particular segment of the Jewish people, but of *Klal Yisrael*—the entire world Jewish community.

BIBLIOGRAPHY

Ackermann, A., *Der synagogale Gesang in seiner historischen Entwicklung*, Trier, 1894.

Baer, Abraham, *Baal Tefillah (Der practische Vorbeter)*, 2nd ed. Frankfurt, 1883.

Berl, Heinrich, *Das Judentum in der Musik*, Berlin, 1926.

Binder, A. W., *New Palestinian Songs*, Vol. I, New York, 1926; Vol. II, 1933.

Ewen, David, *Hebrew Music*, New York, 1931.

Friedlander, Arthur M., *Facts and Theories Relating to Hebrew Music*, London, 1924.

Gradenwitz, Peter, *The Music of Israel*, New York, 1949.

Idelsohn, A. Z., *Jewish Music*, New York, 1929.

Kaufmann, F. M., *Die schönsten Lieder der Ostjuden*, Berlin, 1920.

Lachmann, Robert, *Jewish Cantillation and Song in the Isle of Djerba*, Jerusalem, 1940.

Landau, Anne I., *The Contribution of Jewish Composers to the Music of the Modern World*, Cincinnati, 1946.

Lang, Paul Henry, *Music in Western Civilization*, New York, 1946.

Reese, Gustave, *Music in the Middle Ages*, New York, 1940.

Reis, Claire, *Composers in America*, New York, 1947.

Rosowsky, Solomon, *The Music of the Pentateuch*, London, 1933-1934.

Sachs, Curt, *The History of Musical Instruments*, New York, 1940.

Saminsky, Lazare, *Music of the Ghetto and the Bible*, New York, 1934.

Sendrey, Alfred, *Bibliography of Jewish Music*, New York, 1951.

Werner, Eric, *The Doxology in Synagogue and Church*, Hebrew Union College Annual, 1946.

Wiley, Lulu Rumsey, *Bible Music*, New York, 1945.

Yasser, Joseph, *Mediaeval Quartal Harmony*, New York, 1938.

XII   ISRAEL'S CHORAL MUSIC

The early pioneers who came to Palestine after World War One brought a rich choral tradition with them. They began to organize all types of choral groups. Under the direction of Fordhaus Ben Zisi an oratorio society was founded in the early twenties. It began to perform such oratorios as *The Creation* and *Elijah* in Hebrew translations, the original tongue of the Bible upon which these texts had been based.

Today this choral tradition is stronger than ever in the young State of Israel. I was told during my recent visit to Israel that there are at least ninety large adult choruses throughout that tiny land, as well as innumerable children's choruses. They rehearse under very difficult conditions, but they come promptly and regularly because they love

(This article is based on the author's experiences during a trip to Israel. It appeared in the November 1952 issue of *Choral and Organ Guide.*)

choral singing. At one rehearsal in Jerusalem of the Kol Israel Chorus, which is a volunteer choral group of the Israeli Broadcasting Service, the rehearsal was held in the lobby of a school. It took place during early evening, and there was no heat, for fuel is expensive. There were about ten backless wooden benches lined up in rows. Upon these the men and women who gathered sat and rehearsed for one and a half hours, lovingly and interestedly.

At another rehearsal, which took place in an agricultural settlement, the chorus consisted of about eighty lusty voices, but very well balanced. Their rehearsal began in their dining room at about ten o'clock in the evening, after the tables were cleared and most people were through with their daily tasks. Many of them seemed worn and tired after a hard day's work in the fields, yet as time went on, their leader Shelomo Kaplan, a dynamic well-schooled and enthusiastic leader, had them singing in a vital and almost professional style. They rehearsed until midnight! I was told that several chorus members would have to be up at three in the morning for their duties on the farm and field.

In the Galilee there are three agricultural colonies which have three choruses under one leader. He rehearses them separately, and then brings them together for gala public performances. They rehearse under the same conditions as the chorus of Shelomo Kaplan—finishing late in the night and having very little sleep after that. I heard this triple chorus of Ain Hashofet, Ramat Hashofet, and Dahlia, at the music festival at Ein Gev, during the week of Passover. Ein Gev, on the Sea of Galilee, is a miniature Tanglewood. They sang a program of music which included a chorale by Bach, the final chorus from *The St. Matthew Passion* to a Hebrew text, some Jewish folk songs, some liturgical works, and choral music composed by Israeli composers.

The choral groups came to Ein Gev in not too comfortable buses, and did not return home until three in the morning. The love of music and of choral singing transcended any discomfort which might have been caused by such a strenuous pilgrimage.

The most important choral activity today is in Tel Aviv, Israel's chief metropolitan city. There are: the chorus affiliated with the Israeli Opera Company; the oratorio chorus of Fordhaus Ben Zisi, which recently presented the Brahms *Requiem* in Hebrew with the Israel Philharmonic Orchestra; and, the chamber chorus of Moshe Lustig, which performs old and new choral music. It was this latter chorus which presented Aaron Copland's *In The Beginning* during the composer's visit in early Spring.

A choral festival called a *Zimriyah* was arranged to be held in Israel during the early part of August. Jewish choruses from the United States, Canada, Great Britain, Belgium, Ireland, Italy, France, and Yugoslavia, as well as twenty-eight choruses from all parts of Israel participated. From the United States, five choruses of more than four hundred men and women joined in this festival. Each chorus was to present music of its own choosing, to include secular music, and especially the native music of the country from which the chorus came. All the choruses studied three pieces to be sung by the combined choruses at the final festival in Ramat Gan, near Tel Aviv. The three pieces were by Alexander and Nissimov, two Israelis, and also the performance of an Israeli song by Mordecai Zeira, which had been specially arranged for chorus by myself.

There were tremendous difficulties in transportation and other arrangements, but the great love of singing in chorus came through it all. To have heard the combined voices of two thousand singers sound forth in Ramat Gan surely gave one an inkling of what the great Levitical choirs sounded like during the days of King David, the sweet singer of Israel, and of the great Temple in the days of King Solomon.

XIII   THE MUSIC EDUCATION
OF ISRAELI CHILDREN

When one beholds the mixed population of Israel today,
one wonders how long it will take to weld the people into
a homogeneous nation. It is a common saying in Israel that
whereas the United States was called "a melting pot," Israel today must be "a pressure cooker," for there the
process of integration must be quicker. If the situation at
times may seem fraught with difficulties, one is alway asked
to behold the children, for there is the future of the Israeli
nation. When I questioned a Moroccan Jew about his
fluency in the Hebrew language, during my recent visit,
he answered: "I do not speak very well, but my daughter,
she speaks good!"

The Israelis see in the next generation the future and
hope of Israel. And it is for this reason that both in the

(This article was based upon the author's experiences on his trip to
Israel in 1952. It appeared in the December 1952 issue of *Israel: Life and
Letters*, published by the American Fund For Israel Institutions, now
the America-Israel Cultural Foundation.)

cities and on the land nothing is too good for the children. They are given every possibility to develop under the best conditions available. In the *kibbutzim*, in particular, one is struck by the modern equipment of the schools, bright rooms, comfortable desks, and everything which one would expect to find in America. The head of the educational department of the *kibbutz* Ain Hashofet (named in memory of Judge Brandeis) told me that the rich man's child in the United States could not hope for better primary education than that given there. All over Israel they are seeking to incorporate the most modern methods, and are constantly studying new trends in childhood education.

Music plays an important part in the education of the child. Instruction begins at an early age with Dalcroze eurhythmics and the playing of toy instruments. Musical instruments being scarce, the road to music is mostly through singing, yet somehow they manage, as they do in everything else. One finds pianos, though not often good ones, in the schools, as well as phonographs for the playing of records. The little recorder, which is easy to make and easy to play, has become very popular in Israel. Due to its flute-like tone, it is particularly suitable for the Oriental atmosphere and *melos* of Israel. A large literature for recorder, in combination with voices and other instruments, is gradually being created by the composers in Israel. It is also used as an accompanying instrument for dance. The Israeli composer, A. U. Boscovich, has written a charming group of pieces for two recorders and high and low voices. In them one finds the spirit of the new Israeli music idiom. The work is entitled *B'tupim Uvimcholot*.

The pedagogical aim is to provide children with a general musical education through the music of the classics, and a knowledge of Jewish music which includes liturgical music, folk music, and contemporary music of Israel.

I attended the *kinnusim*, or general assemblies of school choruses in Jerusalem and in Tel Aviv. At each *kinnus*, I heard twenty choruses—in all, forty. Their conductors are not always men and women who devote themselves entirely to music. In a great many cases, they are the regular teachers whose duties also include teaching music and leading a chorus. The results are not always most satisfactory from a musical point of view.

Each choir sang two or three pieces. The music ranged from the contrapuntal sixteenth century Pergolesi through Bach, Haydn, Mozart, Schubert, and Mendelssohn. In each group could be found at least one piece by a contemporary composer of Israeli folk songs. In the groups sung by children coming from Orthodox schools one could always find a liturgical selection by the German composer Lewandowski, or a liturgical work by an Israeli contemporary. One could also find folk songs of other nations, like French *bergerettes* and Negro-American spirituals such as "Go Down Moses," and "Nobody Knows the Trouble I've Seen." All the songs were sung in Hebrew.

The choruses, made up of boys and girls together, sang mostly unaccompanied. The children were well clad, orderly, and obedient to their teachers' orders. There were about eight hundred children assembled in Jerusalem in the auditorium of the YMCA, and a similar number in Tel Aviv's *Ohel Shem* hall. The children were both dark and light-skinned. Some of the boys wore skull caps, others did not, depending upon the type of the school from which they came.

The musical quality of the singing and performance itself varied according to the ability of the conductor. The tone of the groups in Jerusalem appeared to be better than that of the Tel Aviv choruses. In general, there seemed to be a lack of musical coloring such as contrast, loud and soft, crescendo and diminuendo, and all the nuances which go into any kind of musical performance. The thought occurred to me, and was later confirmed by others, that most of the teachers did not know how to train children's voices.

Most of the children produced their tone from the chest. Good children's tone can only be secured through head tones. That is the type of tone which one hears from good children's choirs in this country. The supervisors of the music departments—Emanuel Amiran and his assistant, Ben Zion Orgad—realize this shortcoming. They hope to remedy this problem by organizing supplementary music education courses in large cities for conductor-teachers.

Every parent in Israel wants his child to play a musical instrument. The music schools are therefore filled to capacity. I was told that there was a shortage of music teachers in Israel today. Just as years ago there were four teachers to every student, at present there are four students for each teacher. The *bona fide* music schools in Israel are on a high music level. There are many good teachers in Israel, and the results are very praiseworthy. Most children study either the violin or the piano. I believe that they would study the other instruments, too, if they had them. If they had cellos, there would be many a youngster who would be willing to study this instrument. The same is true of viola, bass, the woodwinds, and the brass instruments.

In the music schools in Tel Aviv and Jerusalem, a child takes an instrumental lesson as well as a theory or harmony lesson. It was interesting to note that their ear-training is done through modal melodies in the Israeli melodic style, which might seem strange to the ears of Occidental children and even adults. An American teacher was trying to explain the unfinished feeling of a modal melody, whereupon a student replied: "This does not seem unfinished. To us, it sounds quite complete."

The children do much of their singing outdoors, and that is perhaps another reason why it is so difficult for teachers to secure a soft, modulated tone. The overall fact, however, is that one recognizes immediately as one looks at them that the Israeli children are a happy lot. They are Israel's future.

XIV   THE JEWISH MUSIC
MOVEMENT IN AMERICA

In order to understand the history of the Jewish music movement in America, we shall have to go back to the first musical manifestations in the synagogues of seventeenth century Colonial America.

The Jews who migrated to America during the period from 1620 to 1800 came here for either of two reasons: for freedom of religion, or for adventure and profit. The first type of immigrant, mostly of Sephardic stock (Spanish origin), had sincere and genuine religious motives; but, many of the second type cared little one way or another. We find also that up to the beginning of the nineteenth century, no European cantor of substance or renown ventured to come to the United States.

(The material in this article was first presented as an address delivered at the Hebrew University in Jerusalem on March 20, 1952. It was subsequently revised for publication during the American Jewish Tercentenary Celebration in 1954, and for republication in 1963, by the National Jewish Music Council of the National Jewish Welfare Board.)

Isaac Da Costa, a cantor, came to this country from London about 1750, at the age of 29. He could not subsist completely on the earnings of his religious office, so over the years he engaged in various business enterprises, such as the sale of European and Indian goods, shipping, the sale of "Havana rum in pipe," and many other activities too numerous to mention. He died in Charleston in 1796.

When Jews who sought religious liberty arrived in America in the seventeenth century they immediately formed into a community. They built places of worship, provided Jewish instruction for their children, and founded the necessary beneficent institutions which their Jewish life required.

The modern Jewish music movement in America is generally taken to be about half a century old. Actually, there already were sporadic signs of it early in the nineteen century. We hear of a chorus which was organized in 1818 in the Shearith Israel Congregation for the dedication of its Mills Street synagogue in New York City, Synagogue choirs began gradually to appear in synagogues such as Anshe Chesed and Emanu-El in New York City during the early part of the nineteenth century. The introduction choir music into European congregations at that time was also making itself felt here in America. The works of Sulzer, Lewandowski, and Naumbourg—the musical reformers in Western Europe during the mid-years of the nineteenth century—were sought and used in American synagogues. While organized choir-singing encountered hard going in this country, as it did also in Europe, special choral groups of men and women were permitted to organize for dedications and other extra-synagogal activities. On such occasions they would sing various appropriate Psalms in Hebrew.

In 1843, at a concert given at Temple Emanu-El to raise funds to acquire a new organ, Edward Weber prepared a program of liturgical music which was performed by chorus and orchestra.

Such cantors as Leo Merzbacher and G. M. Cohen at Emanu-El; Jonas Hecht, Ezra Sternberger, and Ansel Leo at Anshe Chesed; Ignatius Ritterman and Judah Kramer at B'nai Jeshurun (all in New York City) were the early pioneers of synagogue music in our country. They were, therefore, the logical forerunners of the Jewish music movement which was to come at the turn of the century.

The published music of that period points up the fact that the influence of Sulzer and Lewandowski on German Reform held great sway on this side of the Atlantic, too. In those early days the American cantors who composed music which was sung in the synagogues, and who led the way in synagogue music, were not altogether of the highest musical calibre.

As a souvenir of the Jewish women's section of the Parliament of Religion, held in 1893 in Chicago in connection with the Columbian Exposition, a volume of Jewish music entitled: "Principal Melodies of the Synagogue from Ancient Times to the Present" was issued. It was edited by two of the leading cantors of that period—Alois Kaiser of Temple Ohev Sholom in Baltimore, and William Sparger of Temple Emanu-El in New York. In that volume there was an attempt at an historical account of Jewish music. One could find traditional modes and melodies for the Sabbath and holidays, hymns and synagogue compositions by composers of synagogue music both here and abroad.

Study of this volume reveals the Germanic influence of Sulzer and Lewandowski, with the nullification of some of the Jewish characteristics in a melody harmonized with Western tonic-dominant harmonies. This quite elaborately issued volume, nevertheless, shows a desire at that time on the part of the editors to adhere to the musical traditions of our people, traditions which form the basis not only of synagogue music, but also of our art music, which is a recent development.

There were three important factors which led to the modern Jewish music movement here and abroad. The first was the Zionist movement, which began in 1881 with the arrival of the first settlers in Palestine. This new phenomenon in Jewish life set off a tremendous wave of poetry and song. Some of the songs of that period are still remembered and sung. Among them are Eliakum Zunser's *Shivas Zion, Die Soche, Bemachrashti,* and *Die Blum.* These songs are the true forerunners of the modern popular Israeli songs.

The second factor was the organization of the Yiddish theatre by Abraham Goldfaden in 1878 in Eastern Europe. Our people came out of these performances singing such songs as *Rozhinkes mit Mandlen, Flaker Faierl, Yankele Geht in Shul Arein,* and many other of Goldfaden's songs which have become folk songs. Goldfaden settled in America in 1903 and continued his dramatic activities here. Successors to Goldfaden in the composition of music for the Yiddish theatre in America were such men as Friedsell, Brody, Wohl, and Sandler. In the plays for which they wrote the music they contributed such popular Yiddish songs as *Dos Talis'l, Pintele Yid,* and *Eili Eili.*

The third and most important factor in the renaissance of Jewish music was the organization of the Society for Jewish Folk Music in 1908 in St. Petersburg, Russia. This new movement proceeded with an intensive effort on the part of musicians and folklorists to collect Yiddish folk songs. A monumental collection of folk songs by Guinsburg and Marek was the most outstanding result. The leading spirit of this new Society was Joel Engel, who later went to Palestine, where he worked until his death in 1927. With him were associated such composers as: Michael Gnessin, Moses Milner, Alexander Krein, Solomon Rosowsky, Joseph Achron, Lazare Saminsky, and Jacob Weinberg.

To the material which was already gathered, these men added their own research and began to shape musical compositions in the larger art forms. This period produced many piano, violin, vocal, and chamber music works of high musical merit which pointed the way toward a Jewish musical style for Jewish composers of that decade, as well as decades to come. Joseph Achron's violin piece *Hebrew Melody*, was one of the popular products of that period.

Not being satisfied with just gathering and composing Jewish music, the group in Russia set out, through lectures and performances, to educate the Jewish people to appreciate this music. Many concerts of Jewish music were given throughout Russia in those days. In 1912 Simeon Bellison, an outstanding clarinetist, organized the Moscow Quintet for National Jewish Music, which gave many important concerts of Jewish music throughout Russia. Later, in 1921, Bellison came to the United States with his *Zimroh* ensemble. This gifted group appeared in New York and in many other cities in concerts of Jewish music comprised solely of the compositions created by the members of the Society for Jewish Folk Music. While the public was generally cool, this new Jewish music warmed the hearts of a handful of the younger generation of Jewish composers. To these American Jews it opened up a new world with wide vistas into the future. During the early days of the *Zimroh* ensemble's sojourn here, Bellison interested Serge Prokofiev, who was concertizing in America at that time, to compose a work for the group. He also gave Prokofiev the two folk themes which were later woven into that composer's *Overture on Hebrew Themes*, now a popular chamber work.

On the East Side of New York, during the early years of

this century, there strolled up and down the streets a stocky man of medium build, with long hair, flowing Windsor tie, in Prince Albert and high hat. He was Platon Brounoff, formerly a pupil of Rimsky-Korsakov and Anton Rubinstein. Brounoff must be mentioned as one of the earliest pioneers in the field of Jewish music in New York City. He lectured on Jewish folk music when such lectures were unheard of, and was one of the first to include Jewish folk music on his concert programs. In 1911, he organized the *Poale Zion* Singing Society which he conducted for two years; and, in the same year, he published the first collection of Jewish folk songs with piano accompaniment. Significantly, one of his four symphonies bears the title: "Return of the Jews to Palestine." While Brounoff was generally a musician with international interests, his part in making way for Jewish music in this country must be taken into account. He was succeeded as conductor of the *Poale Zion* Singing Society by Henry Lefkowitch, the Jewish music publisher.

In 1916 this writer organized the Hadassah Choral Union, under the auspices of the then new Hadassah organization. It was the first chorus in this country to specialize exclusively in the singing of Palestinian folk songs. Some Palestinians, who were in America at that time, sang these songs to me; I notated the melodies and then arranged them for female chorus. The members of this chorus consisted mostly of Jewish nurses, who later left to join the first medical unit going to Palestine. The guiding spirit of this organization was Mrs. Jacob Sobel, one of Henrietta Szold's close associates in the founding of Hadassah.

The Paterson, New Jersey, Singing Society was founded in 1918 by Henry Lefkowitch, and was later conducted by Jacob Beimel. Cantor Beimel then passed his leadership over to Leo Low, who had just arrived in America from Warsaw. Leo Low raised the level of performance of this organization and gave many important concerts of Jewish music with this chorus in New York and New Jersey. He was succeeded by Jacob Posner, Max Helfman, Samuel Bugatch, and Vladimir Heifetz.

This writer also founded in 1917 the New York 92nd Street "Y" Choral Society, which not only has given concerts of Jewish folk and art music, but has also given several premieres of large Jewish choral works. They include: Oscar Guttman's oratorio *B'reshit*; Jacob Weinberg's oratorio *Isaiah*; and my own choral poems *Israel Reborn* and *Requiem-Yiskor*.

Lazar Weiner, who founded the Workmen's Circle Chorus in 1925, has also helped to develop an appreciation for Jewish music among the people. In 1940 Jacob Weinberg gave the first of a series of annual festivals of Jewish art, in which he presented many Jewish works of great interest and value at Town Hall and Carnegie Hall concert stages in New York City. Other choruses, such as the Yiddish Culture Chorus conducted by Vladimir Heifetz, the National Worker's Alliance Chorus conducted by Leo Low, as well as others throughout the land, have helped to advance the cause of Jewish choral music.

In 1942, the Woodmere Choral and the Temple Israel Choral were combined as the United Temple Chorus under the direction of Isadore Freed. That chorus instituted an annual Ernest Bloch Award to stimulate the composition of Jewish works for female or mixed chorus, and also has aided many other causes in behalf of the advancement of Jewish music.

Large choruses devoting themselves to the performance of Jewish music may now be found in such major cities as: Chicago, Cleveland, Boston, Detroit, Philadelphia, Los Angeles, and San Francisco, as well as scores of smaller cities throughout the United States.

The repertoire of these choruses consists of choral arrangements of Yiddish and Hebrew folk songs, larger works on Jewish themes in the forms of oratorios and can-

tatas, many of which have been created in the United
States. Some choruses mix their repertoires with the classical choral works of Handel, Bach, Beethoven, Mendelssohn, and Brahms, and also with the moderns. Thus it seems
clear that the programs of the Jewish choruses in this country depend entirely on the education of the particular conductor and his musical tastes.

Concerts are given by these choruses in the largest audi-
toriums of the cities, where they perform before mixed
audiences of Jews and gentiles. In New York City, concerts of Jewish music are often given in Carnegie Hall and
Town Hall. In 1950 the Congress of Jewish Culture,
through its music division, instituted a competition for the
best musical setting for mixed chorus of J. L. Peretz' poem
Treist Mein Folk. The competition was won by Cantor
Leo Rosenbluth of Sweden. The new work was performed
at a music festival arranged by the Congress of Jewish Culture at Hunter College, New York, on March 26, 1950.
The following Yiddish choruses participated: the Workmen's Circle Choruses of Philadelphia and Trenton, under
the direction of Samuel Bugatch; the Workmen's Circle
Chorus of New York, under the direction of Lazar Weiner;
the Jewish National Workers' Alliance Chorus of New
York and the *Hazomir* of Waterbury, under the direction
of Leo Low; and the Yiddish Culture Chorus of New York
City and the Workmen's Circle Chorus of Paterson, under
the direction of Vladimir Heifetz. Each group performed
by itself. Then, at the end of the program, all 500 voices
performed jointly Rosenbluth's prize-winning work, under
the direction of Lazar Weiner.

In the meantime, Jewish music dealers on the East Side
of New York City, and book publishers, turned to the
publication of Jewish music, of which a negligible amount
was published up to 1900. Pioneers in this field were Joseph
P. Katz, Goldberg's Music Store, A. Teres, The Hebrew
Publishing Company, and the Bloch Publishing Company.

They were followed by the Metro Music Company, which in 1928 bought the copyrights of Jewish music held by Katz, Goldberg, and Teres. The Transcontinental Music Publishing Company was founded by Josef Freudenthal in 1936, and is now a leading publisher of Jewish music outside of Israel. In recent years the Mills Music Company, one of the larger publishers of popular music in America, has published a good deal of Jewish music of various types by some of the leading Jewish composers. Mills Music Company has also published many works by Israeli composers. Such leading publishing firms as G. Schirmer, Carl Fischer, and E. B. Marks have also published Jewish music, in a limited amount.

The early efforts in 1920 in the publication of Jewish music stimulated its performance throughout the country. We find Jewish singers including an occasional Jewish work in their programs. Sophie Braslau, at one time a leading contralto at the Metropolitan Opera House, used to sing *Eili Eili* at the Metropolitan's Sunday evening concerts; she also included this writer's *V'shomru*, a liturgical song, at her Carnegie Hall song recital in 1920. Increasingly, cantors and concert singers began to include songs of Jewish interest on their programs, and to give full concerts of Jewish music.

There are in this country three important publishers who issue Jewish music exclusively: the Bloch Publishing Company, which publishes for the most part synagogue music, as well as folk music and larger choral works; the Metro Music Company, which specializes in Yiddish theatre music, Yiddish folk and art songs in sheet music and collections; and the Transcontinental Music Company, which issues all types of Jewish music.

Recordings of synagogue music began to be made at the beginning of this century. Soon after the invention of the phonograph, virtuoso cantors such as Sirota of Warsaw and Kwartin of Vienna, were invited to record cantorial recitatives and synagogue choral works with male chorus accompaniment. This activity continued to a limited degree until after World War I. At that time, there were residing in New York four of the greatest cantors in the history of the cantorate: Joseph Rosenblatt, Zavel Kwartin, Mordecai Hershman, and David Roitman. Both the Columbia and the RCA recording companies vied for their recordings, and many records of synagogue music were made by them. As a result of the depression following 1929, these recordings suffered. Their sales fell off tremendously, and most of the original pressings were destroyed.

After World War II the recording business picked up again, and with the establishment of the State of Israel, the recordings of Israeli folk songs both here and abroad became big business. These recordings fall into three categories: Israeli folk and popular songs; songs for children; music recorded in Israel by small orchestras, to be used for folk dance purposes.

One of the pioneers in the presentation of Yiddish and Israeli folk songs on records in America has been the basso Sidor Belarsky. He has striven to present this music with all its charm and meaning. In recent years recording companies have recorded two Metropolitan Opera stars—Richard Tucker and Jan Peerce—in synagogue and Jewish folk music, with accompaniment by choirs and orchestras conducted by Sholom Secunda and Abraham Ellstein.

Unfortunately, little of Jewish art music for chamber groups and orchestra has been recorded either here or in Israel. Ernest Bloch's works, which are not only Jewish but also general in appeal, have been recorded most. His symphony *Israel*, and his cello rhapsody *Schelomo* enjoy popularity. His *Avodath Hakodesh* (Sacred Service) has been recorded twice, once conducted by Bloch himself, and more recently by Leonard Bernstein.

Darius Milhaud's *Service Sacré* (Sacred Service) has been recorded by Lazar Weiner conducting the Central

Synagogue Choir, with Cantor Frederick Lechner as soloist. This writer recorded *Songs and Prayers For the Sabbath*, with Dr. Stephen S. Wise reading the Sabbath liturgy (the only recording of his voice), accompanied by the Free Synagogue Choir, with music composed by myself.

A new phenomenon in the recording of Jewish music has appeared. Hasidic groups have taken to recording the songs and prayers which have become traditional and characteristic of their rabbis and their "courts." So now we have recorded music related to the Modzhitzer Rabbi, the Melitzer Rabbi, the Lubavitcher Rabbi, and others. This recording activity is unprecedented, and some of it provides valuable Jewish musicological material.

Today, the State of Israel is recording music of various Oriental groups which have migrated to Israel since its establishment. Their musical traditions are age-old. The government and private individuals feel that these musical traditions should be recorded before they are lost with the passing of this generation. Many of these recordings are available here. Actively engaged in this work are Edith Gerson-Kiwi of Jerusalem, who has worked for the government and for the Hebrew University, and Johanna Spector, who has done this work with private subsidy.

The greatest deficiency among the recordings of Jewish music is still the lack of recorded Jewish art music. Such recordings would give the public an idea of what is going on today in Jewish musical composition for solo instruments, chamber groups, symphony orchestras, larger choral works, and operas.

One of the developments coming from Samson Benderly's program of the New York Bureau of Jewish Education, organized in 1910, was the encouragement of Jewish music. The inclusion in Hebrew school curricular of Hebrew and Yiddish folk songs, as well as liturgical responses, brought to the attention of Jewish youth the fact that we possess a precious musical heritage of our own. The many

youngsters who came under the influence of Samuel Goldfarb, the Bureau's music director, later became members of
Jewish choruses as well as of Jewish audiences who patronized Jewish concerts throughout the country. Such music
education is now being carried forward and developed
under the auspices of the Jewish Education Committee of
New York and similar organizations in other cities in the
United States. Music was given an especial role in Jewish
education when Alexander Dushkin, himself a musician,
assumed the leadership of the Jewish Edcuation Committee.
Its current music director, Harry Coopersmith, has developed a curriculum of music for Jewish schools, whereby
children are taught the songs of the synagogue, Jewish
folk songs, and the choral singing of Jewish music of various styles.

The cantorial art, which has played such an important
part in the musical life of our people, and which is the
natural heritage of every Jew, is also being perpetuated
through classes in *hazzanut*. The text used is an excellent
volume of *hazzanut* for the Sabbath, edited by Harry
Coopersmith, and including music by two outstanding
cantors in America—Jacob Beimel and Gershon Ephros.
Classes for the training of Jewish music teachers are held,
and many of these teachers have gone to communities over
the entire country, bringing back, through the religious
school, the musical accompaniment to Jewish living, en-
hanced with poetry and beauty.

The Brandeis Arts Institute was established in 1945 in
Santa Susana, California, as an extension of the general
Brandeis Camp Institutes under Shlomo Bardin, executive
director. Max Helfman was its first musical director. The
threefold purpose of this special Institute was: to help foster,
orient, and channel the vast artistic potential of American
Jewish youth for the greater enrichment of Jewish life
here and abroad; to effect living contact with the contemporary artistic productivity of Israel; and, to establish the

proper instruments which can adequately bring these creative forces to the people, in order to vitalize them and be in turn revitalized.

Ernest Bloch arrived in this country in 1916. He succeeded in interesting Artur Bodanzky, the German-Jewish conductor at the Metropolitan Opera House, in presenting a concert of his Jewish orchestral works at Carnegie Hall in 1917. That program included Bloch's *Three Psalms* for baritone and orchestra, the *Three Jewish Poems*, the rhapsody for cello and orchestra *Schelomo*, and the symphony *Israel*. That concert showed the world for the first time that the Jews are capable of producing a composer of top rank. It showed the younger generation of Jewish composers in those days what the music of a Jewish composer working in larger forms could be. Above all, it showed us that if Jewish music is of high ranking quality, it can move into the concert hall and take its place alongside the music of other peoples.

The arrival in this country of Joseph Achron was of inspiration to other Jewish composers. Another influence on Jewish music has been Joseph Yasser, the noted musicologist, whose harmonic and melodic theories of Jewish music have helped almost all Jewish composers.

Solomon Rosowsky's sojourn in America from 1931 to 1933 advanced the cause of Jewish music in America organizationally. With the cooperation of Mrs. Miriam Zunser and a group of Jewish musicians he organized in New York a society called *Mailamm*. The aims were two-fold —to present monthly concerts of old and new Jewish music and to create an appreciation for that music; and to support the work in research into Biblical cantillation, which Rosowsky was then doing in Jerusalem. *Mailamm* did much for the cause of Jewish music in America.

At an international music contest on the occasion of the United States of America Sesquicentennial (1776-1926), a first prize was awarded to Jacob Weinberg for his three-

act opera *The Pioneers.* This first opera in the modern
Hebrew language was premiered in 1934 at the old New
York Mecca Auditorium. It was also published in America,
and was subsequently performed in Israel and Europe.

Efforts at Jewish musicology, in the form of the history
of Jewish music, date back to the middle of the nineteenth
century. In 1913 the Central Conference of American Rabbis issued a pamphlet by Rabbi Jacob Singer of Chicago,
entitled, *Jewish Music Historically Considered.* Later, in
the twenties, Abraham Zevi Idelsohn's excellent and au-
thoritative work, *Jewish Music in its Historical Development,* appeared. That volume was welcomed by both
Jews and gentiles, for it was the first scholarly work on
Jewish music to be given to the world. It especially meant
much to the Jewish musicians in America who were working in this field. New avenues for further investigation
were opened up, and waves of debate and discussion were
set off. At last there could be no more doubt that Jews had a
music of their own, that they gave the Western world its
musical foundations through their Biblical chant which influenced the Gregorian chant, and that they have contributed much to the development of the art of music in Western civilization.

The Jewish Music Forum, which was founded by this
writer in 1939, was essentially a Jewish musicological society. The purpose of this society was to present at each
meeting a scientific paper on some phase of Jewish music,
or a phase closely related to it, and new Jewish music. This
was followed by discussion and criticism. Much creativity
came out of these meetings, affecting all branches of Jewish music. The Jewish Music Forum functioned until 1962,
and then was reorganized in 1963 as the Jewish Liturgical
Music Society of America.

Over the years from 1939 to 1962, outstanding scholars
and musicians such as Curt Sachs, Joseph Yasser, Salo
Baron, Frederick Jacobi, Mario Castelnuovo-Tedesco,

Stefan Wolpe, Jacob Weinberg, Isadore Freed, Leonard
Bernstein, and a host of others, read papers, led discussions,
and performed their new Jewish works at the meetings of
the Jewish Music Forum. At the end of each season the
Forum sponsored symposia on various important subjects.
The symposium held in June 1940 on "The Status of Synagogue Music in America" resulted directly in improving
synagogue music, raising its level of performance, and
later, in the establishment of the School of Sacred Music
of the Hebrew Union College in New York City.

Eric Werner, Professor of Jewish Music at the Hebrew
Union College—Jewish Institute of Religion, has written
some very valuable articles in the Hebrew Union College
Annual on neglected by-ways in Jewish music of the Mid-
dle Ages. In 1959 he published his extremely important
work, *The Sacred Bridge*, which is a comparative study of
Jewish and Christian liturgy. Peter Gradenwitz's volume,
Music of Israel, was warmly welcomed here, as was also
Aron Marko Rothmueller's work, *The Music of the Jews*.

A volume of great interest entitled *Bibliography of Jewish Music* appeared in 1950. It is the work of Alfred
Sendrey, who was an orchestral conductor in Germany.
His hidden passion was Jewish music bibliography. When
he was exiled to America he came with several thousand
items already in his files. In America he developed this
materal, added to it, and received the encouragement and
help of members of the Jewish Music Forum. The bibliography as finally published in full by the Columbia
University Press was hailed as a significant work in this
field.

In 1952 the Composers' Committee for Israeli and American Jewish Music was founded by this writer with the
cooperation of outstanding Jewish composers here and in
Israel. The purpose of this group was to foster closer cooperation between Israeli and American Jewish composers
through mutual public performances and the exchange of

ideas. The full realization of this ideal has not yet been achieved.

Over the years the American Musicological Society has also invited Jewish musicologists to speak on various Jewish musical subjects at its monthly meetings. In 1950 the Society published in its journal an extensive article on "The Structure of the Synagogue Prayer Chant," by Baruch Joseph Cohon.

Branches of organizations like the Jewish Music Forum were established in Detroit, Chicago, Cleveland, Boston, and other cities. Jewish music was on the march; it had come of age. The first Jewish Music Week was held in 1945, organized by Bernard Carp, under the auspices of the then newly-formed National Jewish Music Council of the National Jewish Welfare Board. This has now been expanded and internationally observed as the annual Jewish Music Festival. Under such leadership as Ethel S. Cohen and Rabbi Emanuel Green, the National Jewish Music Council has continued to broaden its scope. Leah M. Jaffa, as its executive secretary from 1948 to 1963, contributed much toward its development and advancement.

When the first annual Jewish Music Festival was announced, a credo was set forth as follows: "Recognizing the importance of music in the culture of a people, the National Jewish Music Council aims to enrich American Jewish culture by highlighting its musical heritage. In elevating standards of Jewish music in content and performance, and by disseminating knowledge about it, the National Jewish Music Council endeavors to accord Jewish music dignity and status in Jewish and general culture in America."

The National Jewish Music Council, sponsored by the National Jewish Welfare Board, has grown since its founding in 1944 to approximately eighty affiliates representing national Jewish organizations, numerous local community

Jewish Music Councils, and a multitude of members-at-large.

From *Purim* to Passover each year, more than a thousand Jewish organizations, Jewish Community Centers, synagogues, youth councils, schools, Zionist bodies, women's organizations and fraternal groups schedule Jewish music events for the Festival. Included in these programs are symphonic, chamber and choral concerts featuring music by Bloch, Milhaud, Achron, Engel, Binder, Weinberg, Weiner, Freed, Jacobi, and others, along with the works of Israeli composers. There are also forums, exhibits, sermons, and special synagogue events, lectures, and radio and television programs. Many programs are planned at camps and veterans' hospitals by Jewish Welfare Board Armed Services workers and Jewish chaplains.

The Council has aided communities in sponsoring Festival observances and in conducting year-round music events. Finally, the Council has made available packets of reprints from Jewish Community Center Program Aids containing valuable program suggestions, music for Jewish groups, and a catalogue of audio-visual materials. In the "How a Song May Serve as a Project" program chairmen are advised how to correlate effectively singing, dancing, acting, music listening, and poetry-writing. The Jewish Music Council has also published an excellent annotated *Bibliography of Recorded Music*, edited by Eric Werner.

In 1963 and 1964, the themes for the National Jewish Music Month were "Bridging Israel and America Through Music," and "Honoring Four American Jewish Composers." To aid communities in carrying out these projects, an extensive bibliography of music by Israeli composers and by American Jewish composers whose work was inspired by Israel, was issued by the Council with the assistance of Issachar Miron and the America-Israel Cultural Foundation.

While Jewish Music Festival climaxes the work of the National Jewish Music Council, it is only part of a year-round plan whose aim is the stimulation of an interest in and appreciation of Jewish music and Jewish composers. Composed of national Jewish organizations, as well as noted scholars, musicologists, composers, teachers, rabbis, and communal leaders, the Council is a coalition of the musical interests of the Jewish community. In effect, it represents a cross section of those forces in American Jewry concerned with giving direction and impetus to a growing Jewish culture. It has by universal agreement become a significant factor in stimulating an abiding love of Jewish music and interest in Jewish composers. Through its *Jewish Music Notes*, a cultural supplement of the publication *JWB Circle*, the Council has introduced Jewish musical personalities to wider audiences and has reported musical events and new materials.

The National Jewish Music Council is striving to encourage community planning and group participation on local levels, and to offer information and advice concerning Jewish music, program planning for Jewish Music Festival and for year-round musical activities. It is concerned with stimulating composition, research and publication. Finally, it is trying to elevate standards of Jewish music in content, and to dignify the status of Jewish music. The advent of the Jewish Music Festival serves to focus attention on these objectives. It has therefore become an increasingly meaningful rallying point for all Jewish cultural forces among American Jewry. Its aims are simply stated in a brochure-catalogue issued by the National Jewish Music Council. The Festival has served to do more than promote performance and participation in Jewish music; it has brought varied segments of the Jewish community together on an inter-organizational basis, cooperating in the development of a cultural project of interest to all.

By 1956, it was felt that the time had come to intensify the focus upon new creativity. Art cannot stand still; above all it must be in a constant state of progress and evolution. The vitality and vibrancy of an art depends not only on its past and present, but most importantly on its future. Composers must be encouraged to create new works expressive of American Jewish life.

It is for this reason that the National Jewish Music Council then undertook a major long-range project of encouraging and stimulating national organizations and institutions, local Jewish Community Centers, synagogues, Jewish community groups, singly and collectively, to commission Jewish musical works. Each composition, the nature of which could be determined by the musical needs of the particular organization or community, would be written for a specific performer or performing group, and presented during the Jewish Music Festival by the artist or the group for which it was written. Where possible, the composer selected would be from the local community or from the region, depending on whether the sponsoring groups were local or regional in character.

Since 1957, over 150 new Jewish musical works have been commissioned all over the United States. They include four one-act operas, symphonic works, chamber music works, choral compositions, synagogue services, religious ballets, *Purim* and other holiday operettas, organ and piano pieces, and many other musical forms. There have also been some commissions for Israeli composers. Two Sabbath eve services, with music contributed by Israeli composers, were commissioned in 1961-1962 by Temple on the Heights in Cleveland, Ohio, through Cantor Saul Meisels, and Temple Beth El of Cedarhurst, Long Island, through Rabbi Edward T. Sandrow and Cantor Samuel T. Dubrow.

Some of the large and reputable orchestras in America such as, the New York Philharmonic, the Rochester Philharmonic, the Detroit Symphony Orchestra, the Baltimore Symphony Orchestra, and many smaller ensembles, as well as top-rate soloists, have included on their programs compositions of Jewish interest by American Jewish composers. Joseph Szigeti has featured Joseph Achron's *Stempenyu Suite* on his programs. Achron's *Hebrew Melody* has become a classic violin piece, and may also be heard frequently on radio networks when Jewish or Oriental atmosphere is sought. At its regular concerts and on a coast to coast network broadcast, the Detroit Symphony Orchestra played this writer's *Concertino for String Orchestra* and Jacob Weinberg's *Yemenite Rhapsody.* The *Symphony for Brass* by Isadore Freed was performed by the Philadelphia and San Francisco Symphony Orchestras.

Ernest Bloch's works are played most frequently. His cello rhapsody *Schelomo* is often heard in concert and on radio, and has become accepted as a classic by both Jew and non-Jew. His *Trois Poèmes Juifs* for orchestra is also frequently performed, as is his *Israel* symphony. His *Baal Shem Suite* is a popular selection in the violin repertoire.

The works of the gifted Israeli composer Paul Ben-Haim are frequently heard. On March 3, 1963, the Symphony Orchestra of the University of Miami, under the direction of Dr. Fabian Sevitsky, saluted the State of Israel with a performance of Ben-Haim's violin concerto; and in 1962, the Hartford Symphony Orchestra, under the direction of Fritz Mahler, performed his *Fanfare to Israel.* Arnold Schoenberg's *A Survivor From Warsaw,* for chorus and orchestra, was performed with great success by the New York Philharmonic in 1950.

Israeli folk songs are frequently heard all over the land, both in concert and informally. Thanks to the many excellent arrangements made by American Jewish composers, these melodies have been given a hearing on the large concert stages of America, bringing them before the public and making the names of their folk- and art-composers known in this country.

The Israel Philharmonic Orchestra and various choruses and dance groups have appeared in transcontinental tours, presenting for the most part general music and some works by Israeli composers. It may be said with pride that the musical standards of all these organizations have been uniformly high.

Soon the time was felt to be ripe for the organization of a school of Jewish sacred music. The Jewish Music Forum had aroused musicians, rabbis, and laity to the fact that, while we possess a tremendous literature of synagogue choral music, much of the music which was being sung in the synagogue was not synagogal in character. The extraneous musical influences which had nothing to do with our sacred *nusach ha-tefillah*—our Jewish musical tradition—had invaded this sacred domain. This was alienating our people from the synagogue.

Synagogues began to engage trained musicians to lead their music, and better singers were sought. It was found, however, that the cantor, who had to be trained for this calling, was largely the most deficient. With a few notable exceptions the cantorate in America had descended to very low standards. Congregations engaged cantors for their voices only, not taking into consideration their knowledge of the profession, their scholarship, or their piety. Many knew only the recitatives which they had learned by way of phonograph records, and for the most part, they were disappointed opera singers.

Thus the time had come for a cantorial school to be founded. There had been a great deal of discussion about such a school for a half century, but nothing concrete had ever been done; so, the Society for the Advancement of Jewish Liturgical Music was organized, and through its members headed by Eric Werner and this writer, con-

228

vinced the authorities of the Hebrew Union College to start a School of Sacred Music. The school was launched in 1948, and in June 1951 graduated its first class of eight students.

Courses offered in the school consist of: the history of Jewish music; *nusach ha-tefillah;* synagogue and folk music; music education; cantillation; choral ensemble and conducting; theory and harmony; sight-singing; analytical bibliography; and musical settings. Special courses are also offered to cantors in service who wish to improve their knowledge of the cantorate. A course for the training of organists was also initiated by Isadore Freed.

This cantorial school today has been heartily welcomed by the American Jewish community. Throughout the country, congregations seek trained cantors, just as Jewish communities throughout the ages have always sought trained rabbis with *s'micha.* Members of the school's graduating classes easily find posts awaiting them.

In 1952, through the efforts of Cantor David Putterman, the Jewish Theological Seminary of America opened the Cantors Institute and College of Jewish Music, and engaged Hugo Weisgall as its director. Its chief purpose is to train cantors for service in the many Conservative congregations in this country. The Yeshiva University, too, found it necessary to have its own school for cantors for the Orthodox congregations, and organized such a school in 1954.

And so, with members of the three faculties, three student bodies, and three cantorial alumnal organizations, the Jewish Liturgical Music Society of America was organized by this writer in 1963, with the aim of uniting the three groups of each school under a neutral canopy. The Society is dedicated to the advancement of synagogue music in America.

A significant forward step in synagogue music was instituted by Cantor David Putterman at the Park Avenue

Synagogue in New York City, when he organized his annual musical service dedicated to contemporary music for the synagogue. During these special services, Cantor Putterman has presented new music for the synagogue, composed especially for these occasions by many younger Jewish composers. The fruits of this worthwhile project are contained in a volume entitled *Synagogue Music by Contemporary Composers*, published by G. Schirmer.

Today we have two tremendous reservoirs of world Jewry—Israel and America—each with its own remarkable potentialities. In Israel, the land of our fathers, echoes of ancient Israel's Biblical song still resound, while the hopes and realizations of our people are re-echoed in new musical manifestations. Here in America Jews have striven for decades to hold fast to the faith of our fathers, and helped in the building and development of our country for three hundred years. We must not lose sight of the fact that after World War I, when many of the great Jewish creative musical spirits came to America, it devolved upon American Jewish musicians to carry forward the work. This they did. They helped to develop the Jewish musical art to the stage where it is today. In the last quarter of a century more Jewish music has been composed in the United States than in any other country in the world.

Jewish composers in and out of Israel are working toward the same goal, namely, the development of a Jewish musical idiom in a Jewish art music which will be recognized unmistakably as our own, and which will take its place alongside of the great music of other nations. Israel is the inspiration of all Jewish musicians. The true Jewish music of the future, however, will be the expression not of any particular segment of the Jewish people, but rather of all the Jews the world over.

XV NEW TRENDS IN
SYNAGOGUE MUSIC

To all those who have become accustomed to the synagogue music of Sigmund Schlesinger (1835-1906) and Edward Stark (1863-1918), the music which has come from the pens of the new generation of synagogue music composers such as Bloch, Freed, Weinberg, Schalit, Fromm, Chajes, myself, and others, must surely sound strange. Instead of operatic tunes, we now have melodies based on our musical tradition—*nusach ha-tefillah*. Instead of the tonic-dominant harmonies characteristic of the nineteenth century, new harmonic efforts are made to retain the character of the Jewish melody. Instead of secular rhythms, we have rhythms related to the Hebrew language.

The tremendous musical structure which our ancestors wrought in our round-the-year liturgy over a period of more than 2,000 years, consists of modes and melodies

(This article was published in the January 1955 issue of *The Journal of the Central Conference of American Rabbis*.)

divided into small motifs, each one designed to create the
atmosphere of a particular holiday, prayer, special occasion, or spiritual moment. If this musical tradition is wrong
or absent, a service loses its sacred and traditional spirit.
The sacred spirit of our people and its prayers are en-
shrined in our *nusach ha-tefillah.*

Melody: In the new synagogue music of our day we find
first of all a change in melodic materials. The musical material of Schlesinger was for the most part operatic in style;
he did not hesitate to take a complete operatic aria and set
it to an important prayer in the Day of Atonement liturgy.
A flagrant example of such misuse is found in *Ki Vayom*,
of the evening service for the Day of Atonement, where he
applies the melody of the famous aria by Donizetti, *Una
Furtiva Lagrima*. It is true that Schlesinger did make some
efforts at using traditional melodies in his works, but in the
harmonies he imposed upon them they lost their character
and spirit.

Edward Stark, a cantor in San Francisco, realized
Schlesinger's shortcomings and tried to effect a remedy. He
used more traditional material in his music, and sought to
adhere to the authenticity of modes. He also tried hard to
avoid the operatic style. He succeeded only partially because he was greatly handicapped by the lack of technical
musical equipment needed to deal with the harmonization
of a Jewish tune. At best, his music resembles the Germanic
style of Sulzer and Lewandowski, which planted synagogue
music in an alien harmonic soil in the nineteenth century.

Composers of present-day synagogue music have benefited from the results of fifty years of research and discussion on the nature of genuine synagogue music. It may be
that we have not arrived at the final answer as yet, but we
are much nearer to it than we were at the turn of the century. Our efforts during the past two decades indicate that
we are on the right track; our synagogue musical tradition
and the traditional melodies which have developed out of

our new approach are rooted in the cantillation modes of the Bible. These cantillation modes also were the foundations of the Byzantine chant of the Greek Orthodox Church and the Gregorian chant of the Roman Catholic Church. Both churches have guarded their musical traditions zealously.

Some of our modern composers will sometimes use a traditional tune *in toto*; others will compose an original tune in a traditional mode. An important step forward is the use of the correct mode and melody at the right time, thereby helping to create the right atmosphere and spirit of the occasion. Let us recall at this moment how the traditional *Rosh Hashanah* eve melody helps to establish immediately the spirit of the holiday in the synagogue; how the melody of *Kol Nidre* brings the spirit of the Day of Atonement to us; and how the soul of the Sabbath descends into the synagogue when *V'shomru* is sung in the *Magen Avot* mode, which is the correct modal tradition for this prayer.

I have endeavored over a period of two decades to bring back the beautiful cantillation of the Bible into the Reform service. Our young cantors and rabbis are now being trained to chant the *Torah* in such a way as to enhance the text and bring back musical beauty to our service. I have also tried to bring back the free chant into synagogue music, not only in solos, but also in choral passages, thus giving to the synagogue song a quality of authenticity and antiquity.

Harmony: In the synagogue music of the nineteenth century much of the true color of synagogue music was lost when the composers of that period attempted to harmonize our traditional music with the existing Western system of harmony. They did not go together. Toward the end of the nineteenth century serious synagogue music composers began to experiment with various methods of harmonizations. Their main goal was to harmonize the Jewish tune in such a way as to reflect its true beauty and characteristics. At the beginning of this century the composers in the Jewish Folk Music Society of St. Petersburg were active and most fruitful in this effort. Men like Achron, Milner, Rosowsky, and Weinberg understood the problem and tried to solve it. Soon such talented synagogue composers as Eliezer Gerovitch (1844-1913) and David Nowakowsky (1848-1921) began to follow them in their synagogue works. These two were the first to grapple with the important problem in this field, and it is for this reason that the works of Gerovitch and Nowakowsky remain useful for the modern service even in our own day.

Ernest Bloch (1880-1959), one of our greatest composers, and Joseph Achron (1886-1943), another gifted composer, both pointed the way for our contemporary musicians who are today writing synagogue music for the Reform synagogues. Joseph Yasser (born 1893) has developed harmonic theories in this direction which have also been very helpful. It must be said for posterity that it has been largely the Reform movement which has sponsored the new era in synagogue music during the past two decades. It was also the Reform movement in America which had the foresight and idealism to make music an important part of a rabbinical training curriculum. This now enables the student-rabbi to develop a knowledge not only of the text of the liturgy, but also of the music which should accompany it. With an appreciation of good synagogue music, the rabbi is able to plan an inspiring religious service. The School of Sacred Music, which is a surety for the perpetuation and development of Jewish music in America, is another of the notable musical accomplishments of the Reform movement in America.

Rhythm: In examining the many congregational tunes which are sung today, two significant facts emerge: 1) Most of the tunes are by Sulzer and Lewandowski; 2) Most of these tunes are in three-quarter (waltz) time. Sulzer and Lewandowski were contemporaries of Johann Strauss, the great waltz composer, and were undoubtedly influenced by him. Today it is felt that the composer must derive the rhythm for his melodic material from the rhythm of the text with which he is dealing. The Hebrew language has rhythmic individuality, and the synagogue composer must attune his ear to its pulse. In some cases measured rhythm is possible and even necessary; in others, the free chant will speak the true spirit of the liturgy. It is most important, however, to reveal through melody the accents of our ancient tongue.

Form: An important contribution which modern composers have made to synagogue music has been in the field of musical form. Form was sadly lacking in a good deal of our synagogue music literature of former days. Today we have services which are based on specific thematic material integrally woven throughout the work, as exemplified in Ernest Bloch's *Avodath Ha-kodesh*. Then, too, we have services where each individual piece is an integrated entity. Above all, it is satisfying to note that the new synagogue music, for the most part, is good music by all accepted standards in the art of music.

One of the primary reasons for the development of higher standards in the music of the Reform synagogue is attributed to the fact that our synagogues in the early twenties began to engage trained Jewish musicians to direct their music. Soon this small but able group was joined by others over the country, as well as by the musicians from Europe who sought haven here in the thirties, and whose contributions to the cause of good synagogue music in America should not be minimized.

The modern synagogue musician does not advocate the elimination of all old music and the substitution of the new; rather, he advocates a happy combination of both old and new, provided that both belong in the category of good music. He does not advocate that services by one composer be sung in their entirety, but rather that a musical program for a service be constructed and balanced like a fine concert program, with works by composers in various styles.

Special programs of new synagogue music and the production of new works are all part of the new trend in synagogue music. In preparation for such occasions—usually during *Hanukkah* and *Purim*, and for Jewish Music Month —the life and musical activity of the Jewish composer should be stressed, his work and aims described. The co-operation of all forces in the synagogue should be sought in order to make the occasion a cultural and spiritual success.

What are some of the goals of good synagogue music? The worshiper should be moved to deeper concentration upon prayer, and to more profound devotional feeling. Sacred music should help bring forth all that is good and tender in a human being. When the service is artistically performed, the worshiper undergoes a religio-musical experience unobtainable in any other manner. For this spiritual experience he will surely return!

XVI NEW JEWISH MUSIC
CREATIVITY

When Jewish Music Month was first instituted by the National Jewish Music Council of the National Jewish Welfare Board, it was a logical sequence to forty years of pioneering in the field of Jewish music in this country. Up to that time attempts to foster a Jewish musical art were made by various individuals and groups. The modern Jewish music movement in America may be said to have begun after World War I.

As a religious people, our greatest musical contribution has been through the medium of music for the synagogue. There have been early efforts here to bring good synagogue music into our religious service and to raise the level of performance, too. There were scattered performances of

(This article appeared in the November 30, 1956 issue of *The Reconstructionist*, volume XXII, published by the Jewish Reconstructionist Foundation. It was written in connection with the then-new project of encouraging the commissioning of Jewish musical works in America.)

Jewish folk songs in concerts of exclusively Jewish music, or Jewish mixed with other music given by Jewish choral societies and individuals who helped to keep alive the fact that we Jews had a folk music.

In 1917 Ernest Bloch presented his concert of original compositions at Carnegie Hall with the Metropolitan Opera Orchestra. Soon afterward the gifted Simeon Bellison arrived in this country with his *Zimroh* ensemble to concertize. Jewish music experienced a rebirth, for then, for the first time, Jewish musicians and Jewish audiences heard and began to understand what a Jewish musical art could be if it were fostered and developed. Such works as: Bloch's *Israel* symphony, his *Three Jewish Poems* for orchestra, and *Three Psalms* for baritone and orchestra, as well as the *Zimroh* performance of chamber music works by Jewish composers in the St. Petersburg Society For Jewish Folk Music, such as Achron, Engel, Krein, Milner, Rosowsky, stirred the emotions and imaginations of a small group of young Jewish composers in this country who became dedicated and determined to build a Jewish musical art. They aspired to carry on the musical ideals here which the St. Petersburg group began in Russia and which were destroyed by the USSR repressions.

Meanwhile, some of the leading Reform synagogues in America began to engage trained Jewish musicians to guide and lead their synagogue music. This resulted in better music and a higher level of performance. These musicians were Jewish composers as well, and so in the twenties of this century we witnessed the birth of an American literature of synagogue music. After about thirty-five years some of the composers represented in this literature are Bloch, Milhaud, Weinberg, Fromm, Chajes, Helfman, Jacobi, Saminsky and myself.

The first quality which any national music should have is that of good music by all musical standards. Our new synagogue musical literature has this quality. Furthermore, it reveals that each composer is striving toward a Jewish musical style in his own way, and that there is a definite trend toward the retention, purification, and development of our Jewish musical tradition—*nusach ha-tefillah*. It is, however, significant that almost all of this new liturgical music has been composed for the liturgy of the *Union Prayer Book*.

The Jewish musicians who came to this country after World War I and the native American-Jewish musicians began to create a literature of Jewish music in all musical categories and areas, ranging from the simplest piano piece to symphony and grand opera. It soon became apparent that this music had to be heard.

In 1931 Solomon Rosowsky, the Jewish composer and musicologist, came here from Palestine where he had settled earlier. Here he established, with Miriam Zunser and a group of Jewish musicians, an organization called *Mailamm*. The purpose of this organization was to support his research work in Biblical cantillation in Palestine, and to offer monthly concerts of Jewish music in New York City.

Subsequently, *Mailamm* was succeeded by the Jewish Music Forum, which was organized by this writer in 1939 with the express purpose of uniting all Jewish composers in America. It further sought to encourage research in all Jewish fields of musical endeavor, and to perform and discuss new Jewish music. The symposium on the "Status of Synagogue Music in America," sponsored by the Jewish Music Forum in 1940, had much to do with the creation of the Hebrew Union College School of Sacred Music in 1948, and the Jewish Theological Seminary Cantor's Institute two years later.

Above all, this varied musical activity was sufficient proof that the Jewish music movement in this country was alive and vibrant. The tremendous amount of Jewish music

which had been created up to that time, but which lay
dormant on the shelves of publishers and composers, had to
be heard. The Jewish community needed to hear this music,
and thus become conscious of the fact that as a people it
was our duty to help towards the development of Jewish
art in all its phases.

And so, in 1944, Bernard Carp, with the aid of a number
of Jewish musicians, organized the National Jewish Music
Council under the sponsorship of the Jewish Welfare
Board, which initiated the annual Jewish Music Festival
the first of which was held in 1945. The major task and
purpose was to secure performances of Jewish music by
Jews and non-Jews on a nation-wide scale. This task the
Jewish Music Council has eminently achieved during its
years of existence. Much Jewish music of all kinds has been
performed during this period all over the country in concert, radio, and televison, by artists of all categories and
faiths.

Art, as such, must not remain static. It must be in a constant state of evolution and revolution. The vitality of a
national art depends not only on its past, but, most important, on its future. I feel, therefore, that the National
Jewish Music Council has now reached the second stage of
its task. The first, as previously stated, was the *performance*
stage. The second, upon which it should now embark,
should be the *creative* stage. The time has now come for
the Council to lead the way toward new musical creativity.

How is this to be achieved? This year the Jewish Music
Council will proclaim to Jewish music groups throughout
the country, to its affiliated organizations, and to the general
Jewish community, that the theme for next year's Jewish
Music Month, and perhaps for years to come, will be
"Commission a New Jewish Musical Work." A Jewish
composer, or a composer who is a Jew, is to be selected in
a community or region for such a task and signal honor.

The nature of the work to be commissioned will be determined by the musical needs of the immediate Jewish community. These needs may be as follows:

In a community where there are chamber music groups, a string quartet, a piano trio or quintet in any form could be commissioned. A community may have a large chorus. In such a case, a large choral work should be commissioned, commensurate with the performance ability of the group. Hadassah may want works for two- and three-part female chorus for the many choruses extant in that organization. Many Community Centers have amateur orchestras. There is a dearth of easy Jewish music for such groups. Musical works of this type would be a real contribution to Jewish art.

Some communities with fine synagogue choirs may want to commission a new synagogue musical liturgy. Songs of a Jewish nature for children, and operettas for children and teen-agers are needed. They will have to be on Jewish themes and with new Jewish music. Many communities have dance groups which could choreograph special Jewish music written for Jewish dance. The larger Jewish communities may want to commission a symphonic work to be played by the local symphony orchestra, or even a one-act opera. These are only a few of the possibilities.

The composer of one of these projects should receive anywhere between twenty-five to one thousand dollars, depending on the form and length of the commissioned work, and a performance should be guaranteed. Where professional guidance is needed by an organization or a community, the national office of the Jewish Music Council will be ready to give assistance with all its facilities.

Jewish musical creativity ought to become our goal and task henceforth. It should be the goal and task of all Jews who are interested in the development of Jewish culture and Jewish music in particular. We should not be discouraged if, at first, this new idea does not catch fire;

rather, we should work step by step toward its achievement.

Strange indeed it is to observe that most Jews still consider Jewish musical art to be on the periphery of Jewish culture. They will accept music as an accompaniment to ceremony and prayer almost as one accepts dinner music. Yet, to place emphasis upon the important place which music should occupy in the circle of Jewish religion and culture is unthinkable! That is why we pay for everything in the synagogue but music. For that, the most specialized of all artistic areas, we often choose amateurs.

Our new commissioning project will help to place emphasis upon the importance of music in Jewish culture. The organization, too, of local councils of Jewish music throughout the country can thereby create a Jewish musical consciousness much needed among our people. Another benefit to be derived by commissioning new Jewish musical works will be the encouragement of Jewish composers who have dedicated their lives to the cause. It will also shepherd the large amount of composing talent among Jewish music students in the various music schools in the country into the fold of our Jewish musical art.

We are hoping that Jewish communities throughout the land will exchange performances of newly commissioned works, and that these new works will be valuable additions to the literature of Jewish music. Finally, we hope that other branches of Jewish art—such as painting, sculpture, and dance—will follow the example of their Jewish musical colleagues by uniting so as to give direction and goal to their artistic strivings.

This new project involves us all—sponsor, composer, performer, and audience. Let us all help to make it succeed. The soul of a people is embedded in its music.

XVII INTRODUCTION
TO CANTILLATION

In ancient days it was customary to study and recite poetry, prayers, and laws with the aid of melody, for through the medium of melody the meaning of the word became clearer, and the text itself was more easily remembered.

Moses admonishes the Children of Israel in Deut. xxxi: 19, "Write ye this song for you and teach it." All reading and study of the *Torah* among Jews, and later of the *Koran* among Mohammedans, was done with a speech melody known as cantillation. This cantillation is today read with the aid of ancient *neumes* or musically endowed signs known among Jews as: (a) *neginot*; (b) *t'a-amin*; (c) *t'ame haneginot neimot*,[1] as well as accents and tropes.

The evolution of our synagogal musical tradition may

(Prefatory essay for textbook on cantillation: *Biblical Chant*, written by A. W. Binder and published in 1959 by Philosophical Library— revised second edition published by Sacred Music Press in 1963.)

be said to have taken place as follows: First came the gradually shaped cantillation modes; out of these came the prayer modes or *nusach he-tefillah*; out of the prayer modes came the traditional melodies, such as *Kol Nidre* and *Musaf Kaddish* for the High Holy Days; and out of these foundations came the folk song, art song and art music.

The commandment to read the *Torah* in public appears for the first time in Deut. xxxi: 11,12, where Moses bids the Children of Israel to read the *Torah*, at a great convocation every seven years on the Feast of Tabernacles, at a time when all Israel will be gathered in Jerusalem.

The *Talmud* tells us that, "The Bible should be read in public, and made understood to its hearers in musical and sweet tones; and he who reads the *Torah* without tune shows disregard for it and its vital values and laws."[2] It further goes on to say that, "Whosoever intones the Holy Scriptures in the manner of secular song abuses the *Torah*."[3] These statements of the *Talmud* dating to the first century C.E. prove that the reading of the Bible in public in musical style was a long-established practice.[4]

Portions of the Bible were rendered musically in the early history of Israel in Palestine. We know, for example, that the Song of the Sea, the Ten Commandments, and certain Psalms were sung at the daily service in the Temple at Jerusalem.

Ezra, in 444 B.C.E., upon the return of Israel from Babylonian captivity, brought forth the *Torah* in solemn assembly and read it publicly—no doubt in a melodized fashion —in one of the open squares in Jerusalem, with observation of the proper syntactical stops, and possibly with interpretations.

The association of the *Torah* reading with melody becomes more evident from observation of the fact that only those books of the Bible which were obliged to be read in public were provided with tunes. These books are the Pentateuch, Prophets, Esther, Lamentations, Ruth, Ecclesiastes, Song of Songs, Psalms, and in some communities Job; whereas Proverbs, Ezra, Nehemiah and Chronicles have no tunes because they were not read at the public service.

The Book of Esther has been read since the time of the Maccabees, Lamentations at least since the destruction of the Second Temple, while the Song of Songs, Ruth, and Ecclesiastes were read as far back as the first century.[5]

This musical practice was perpetuated by tradition. It was for a long time remembered by ear, and was taught to children by special teachers who received a fee for such instruction.[6]

It is, however, interesting to note that before a system of graphic accents was devised and written down, a system of manual accents called *chironomy* was devised and even carried into the Middle Ages. We find it was practiced in Baghdad into the twelfth century. Rashi (eleventh century) observed in his day that this method was used by those Jews who came from Babylonia.[7] This system of chironomy was based upon the rise and fall of the finger or the stretching of the palm of the hand by an individual who was called *tomech* or helper. He stood at the right of the reader.

These signals served to remind the reader of the direction of the melody, and they were later incorporated into the various tropal signs posted above or below the scriptural text.

In time, scrolls were devised with a system of accents. At first only three signs were used: *kadma*, beginning of the sentence; *etnahta*, half stop; *sof pasuk*, period or full stop. These signs agreed with the early signs used by the Greeks, Hindus and Armenians.

The tradition of reading the *Torah* with tune was considered sacred, and therefore guarded and perpetuated. It developed, as time went on, up to the eighth century C.E. During that time a system of accents and their musical interpretation gradually came into being. This process was not an independent one. While it is a fact that the early Christian chant was a carry-over from the Hebrew Biblical chant, the *neume* system employed by the Jews was fashioned after the Greek and Syriac systems of interpunction. The crude musical notation which was being fashioned and perfected during the same period in the musical world at large also influenced Jewish musical efforts in that direction.

The Biblical trope agrees in outline with these foreign systems, but not in detail. The Hebraic accents had to be specifically adjusted to meet the meaning of the Biblical text. Hence it becomes clear that when the Jewish people lived as a nation in one land, their music influenced their neighbors. When the national independence of the Jews was destroyed, however, and they became scattered, the outside world influenced their musical efforts.

And so between the fifth and ninth centuries, when the Catholic Church was perfecting the Gregorian chant and its notation, and the musical world was devising its system of notation, the Jews were not idle. The family of Ben Asher in Tiberias, became particularly interested in accentuation and its systematic presentation. That interest culminated in the ninth century, when Aaron Ben Asher established the vocal punctuation in the Bible and provided the first scroll with such punctuation.

The musical interpretations of the tropes of the Bible are quite numerous. They include the Ashkenazic, Sephardic, Moroccan, Egyptian, Syrian, Baghdadian and Yemenite, some of these being still further subdivided into various geographic branches. Western Jewry uses the Ashkenazic system. Our interest is in the Ashkenazic system according to the East European tradition. There are many conspicuous similarities in the musical interpretation of the tropes of these various traditions, however, which proves that they all stem from a common origin.

The Ashkenazic system has gone through a long span of time and space. As it traveled through the many countries of the Diaspora, it acquired a modicum of diverse musical influences, yet the original Jewish outlines are discernible to those who are interested in searching for them.

When expertly chanted, the whole strikes one with its singular effectiveness in making clearer the meaning of the text and impressing it on the mind of the listener.[8] The most reliable specimens of traditional cantillation afford us a fair idea of the character of Jewish chanting in Biblical days.

In the Ashkenazic tradition there are six systems of musical interpretation of the tropes. For the Pentateuch, there are two with variations—one for the weekly reading, and one for the High Holydays. At the *Mincha* service on the Day of Atonement, the *Torah* is read with the Sabbath tropes. Variations occur when reading the Song of the Sea, Journeys, cadences on *Simchat Torah*, and when finishing each of the books of the Pentateuch. There is a special system for the Scroll of Esther read on *Purim*, the Scroll of Lamentations read on *Tisha B'av*, the Scroll of Ruth read on *Shavuot*, Song of Songs read during Passover, and Ecclesiastes read during the Festival of *Sukkot*. The Prophetical readings read on Sabbaths and holidays have a musical system of their own.

The style of Biblical chant is half-musical and half-declamatory, the reader always being mindful of the meaning of the text and welding it to the tropes. The musical element in the reading clearly predominates, however.

The rhythm of Biblical chant is of the irregular or asymmetrical brand. To place it behind rigidly spaced bar lines is to imprison its ancient and authentic character. Biblical chant is not influenced by any musical metric character of the tropes, but rather by the accentuation ingrained in the text which determines its musical flow.

The early church fathers were, and musical authorities

up to our time are, of the opinion that the Greek Orthodox chant and the Catholic Gregorian chant were derived from the Temple and Synagogue *melos* of ancient Israel. Musical history illustrates to us that early art music derived largely from the music of the church.

We can therefore conclude from these two historical facts that ancient Biblical chant served at least as one of the basic pillars of the art of music as we know it in our day.

FOOTNOTES

1. *Neginot,* from the word *nigun* meaning "tune"; *t'a-amin,* from the word *ta-am* meaning "sense" (revealing the sense of the word); *neimot,* from the word *ne-im* meaning "sweet" (adding sweetness to the words of the *Torah*). *Neimot* has also been traced to the Greek word *neume,* meaning musical sign.

2. B. *Megillah* 32A.

3. *Sanhedrin* 101A.

4. *Nedarim* 37B.

5. *Soferim* XIV:18.

6. *Nedarim* 1C.

7. "Look to the right for the signs of the *Torah*." *Berachot* 62A.

8. "All interpretations which are not according to the logic of the tropes do not follow or listen to them." Abraham Ibn Ezra: *Moznaim,* Offibach: 1791, page 4.

XVIII THE JEWISH LITURGICAL
MUSIC SOCIETY OF AMERICA

A little over a year ago, when the Jewish Music Forum, after more than twenty years of useful activity, was losing its purpose, we tried to find a reason why this was happening and what was the *present* need in this country in our chosen field. After a number of unsuccessful explorations, we came to the conclusion that the field of synagogue music was the area in which Jewish musicians in this country have contributed most and successfully. We have composed and published more synagogue music and are performing more music in our synagogues than any other Jewish communities in the world, including Israel.

Conditions are now quite different from what they were in 1939 when the Jewish Music Forum was organized. The

(With the presentation of this paper, the author opened the first meeting of the Society on February 4, 1963. The text was subsequently published in the first issue of the Society's annual *Bulletin* in September 1963.)

problem of performance is now well in the hands of the National Jewish Music Council, and the future of Jewish art music will develop with all other facets of the fine arts in Israel as well as America.

We here in America now have three cantorial schools from which we are graduating young men whom we are trying to school in what is best in synagogue music. When these men graduate, they are not finished. Just as a doctor or a lawyer must keep in touch with what is going on in his field, so do we all need a professional society where we can meet from time to time to discuss the past, the present, and the future of our chosen field. Students who graduate from a rabbinical or a cantorial school need to get together with their colleagues and their teachers for contact and knowledge. Therefore, we felt that the time had come for the formation of an organization which we shall call "The Jewish Liturgical Music Society of America." Its goals are as follows:

1. To raise the standards of music and performance in all synagogues.

2. To explore historical aspects of synagogue music during various epochs.

3. To establish closer relations with the synagogue musicians in Europe and Israel.

4. To perform and analyze old and new synagogue music.

5. To help preserve characteristic musical aspects of the practice of *hazzanut*, and encourage the improvisation techniques in the service.

6. To encourage the commissioning of new works for the synagogue.

7. To establish creative relationships with music committees of the synagogues.

8. To provide a forum for all synagogue musicians.

9. To publish a periodical on a regular basis in conjunction with the roster of membership, and make this also available to outsiders for subscription purchase. It is hoped

to publish texts or at least resumés of the papers and reports made at all the meetings of the Society.

These are some of the preliminary goals. Our aims and ambitions will grow as our Society develops. With the destruction of the great Jewish centers of Europe, it has become the responsibility of American Jewry, the largest Jewish community in the world, to preserve and stimulate the development of the Jewish liturgical heritage. In this new Society, we hope to unite in common dedication the creative and performing powers, the scholarly, and all those who have a genuine love for all aspects of the synagogue musical art.

XIX   HASIDISM

The founder of hasidism, Israel Baal Shem Tov, or the *Besht*, as he was later called, was born about 1700 in the town of Ukop, Ukraine. He spoke in easy parables which even the most lowly were able to understand. He taught that God could be found and approached not only by the learned scholar, but also by simple folk, that God was to be loved rather than feared, and that He could be reached with prayer and song at all times and places.

The rabbi gave his followers a God of love and mercy; he freed them from fasting, penance, weeping, lamentations, sorrow and distress. Thus did the *Besht* breathe new life into the dry bones of Israel in those days. Through his teachings and doctrines, he brought into Judaism of the eighteenth century a fervent stream of religious enthusiasm.

(This is the introduction to *Jewish Folk Songs in Hasidic Style*, a compilation of ten songs, edited and arranged by A. W. Binder, published in 1963 by Mills Music, Inc.)

But the approach to God was to be prepared; for the rabbi preached that the abode of kings was always approached through many corridors. Those preparations for real ecstatic prayer had to go through three stages: *kavannah*, complete absorption and concentration; *deveikut*, that cleaving unto God, in which the sense of separation from Him is lost; and *hitlahavut*, that burning fire of devotion which comes from complete abandon in prayer. But with it all, man must "serve God in joy." God must be approached with a joyous and singing heart.

Here is where music began to play an all-important part in hasidic life and was to become one of the cardinal principles of its beliefs and practices. With the importance which music was to occupy and the powers which were ascribed to it, hasidic rabbis, beginning with the *Besht*, pronounced theories, and definite ideas and principles about the power and potency of melody.

When the *Besht* brought hasidism upon the Jewish scene, it attracted, for the greater part, the simple and uneducated Jew. Dov Beer of Mezhiritch (1710-1772) was won over to hasidism. As the successor to the *Besht*, he attracted many learned Jews into the movement, being a scholar himself. Out of this wing in hasidism grew the *Habad* system, in contrast to the *Besht*. The *Habad* sect was founded by Shneur Zalman of Liadi, with adherents for the most part in Lithuania and White Russia. The *Besht* system drew its adherents from Poland, Southern Russia, Roumania, and Hungary.

Habad derived its name from the abbreviation of three principles upon which it was founded: *hochma*—wisdom; *bina*—understanding; and *daat*—knowledge. These philosophies were interwoven with the mysticism of sixteenth century Isaac Luria of Safed.

Hasidism gathered many thousands of Jews into its fold. In communities where Orthodox rabbinism held sway, serious struggles ensued when the followers of hasidism attempted to secure a foothold or to influence the community. These opponents to the movement of hasidism were henceforth known as *mitnagdim* (opponents).

What were their objections to hasidism? What were the changes in ritual and practice which the *hasidim* introduced: 1) their change of liturgy from the Ashkenazic ritual (German) to the Sephardic ritual (Spanish); 2) their omission of certain prayers, and the introduction of new hymns and prayers, with a disregard for the musical traditions in favor of some local catchy tunes; (Among the reasons for the issuance of an excommunication of hasidism in Cracow in 1786, was the accusation that the *hasidim* disregarded the traditional tunes.); 3) their scant attention to the prescribed hours of prayer, rather waiting for the arrival of the "proper mood" for prayer; 4) behavior during prayer. (Some *hasidim* in their zeal of devotion began to dance; others stood motionless; some prayed aloud and others in solemn silence.) The *mitnagdim* feared that hasidism was another disgraceful Sabbataism or Frankism. The rabbis and intellectuals fought hasidism through public arguments, books, pamphlets, and sermons; but the young people, particularly the *Yeshivah-bachurim* (Talmudical students), fought back in their own individual manner— through song.

Especially during the era of the Middle Ages, in the days of the troubadours and minnesingers, where there were no such things as newspapers in communities, individuals were lauded or chastised through the medium of song. The deed of an individual, good or bad, would be composed into a poem and then set to music. The song would circulate among the people, and they would sing it everywhere. In this way, the person involved got his due, good or bad. In later times, this happened particularly among the people in the mitnagdic communities. They fought hasidism with biting and often poisonous satirical songs, in which they ridiculed such matters as: the *zaddik*, his family, his hasidic followers, their blind faith in him. Of special targets were the wonders and miracles attributed to the hasidic rabbi, his ability to create something out of nothing, to "annihilate" space, his extraordinary "visits" to heaven, and many individual incidents.

In retrospect, as we evaluate the contributions of this remarkable movement in Jewish life, what seems to remain for us is far more beyond the then almost idolatrous worship of the *hasid* for his *zaddik*. What does remain encompasses such essences as the mystic spirit, the intimate love of God in nature, the atmosphere of fellowship which pervaded among the *hasidim*. Above all, there is that faith in life in the face of all misfortune, for to the *hasidim*, God is kind and merciful, and loves His people Israel with a love which is eternal. Hasidism has also left a heritage for artists and musicians so deep and so vast that its influence will continue to inpire generation after generation, and will continue to be an important part of the Jewish artistic heritage for future ages.

XX A HISTORY OF
AMERICAN-JEWISH HYMNODY

Poetic expression is to be found in the very early parts of the Bible. (Genesis : i:23; iii: 14, 19; iv: 6-7, 23-24.) The first great song of praise and thanksgiving is the "Song of the Sea" (Exodus xv: 1-18), sung by Moses and the Children of Israel when they were liberated from Egyptian bondage. It is really the first great song of freedom.

While the "Song of the Sea" is without rhyme or rhythm, parts of it, because of its beauty and meaningfulness, have been incorporated into the Jewish daily liturgy and have been set to music through the ages innumerable times. The "Song of the Sea" was part of the daily liturgy

(This article appeared in two parts for the October 1963 issue and the January 1964 issue of the quarterly *The Hymn*, published by The Hymn Society of America. It is based upon an address delivered by the author at the annual meeting of that Society held in May 1963. Subsequently this article was also included in the *Dictionary of American Hymnology*.)

in the Temple at Jerusalem, and was chanted by the Levites together with Psalms of the day.

If a hymn is a song of praise and adoration, then the Book of Psalms was the first hymn book of civilized mankind. Its deep religious feeling, its towering profession of faith, its manifold ways of praising God, made a deep impression on Jewish hymnody, which was to follow in later centuries, and upon the hymnody of Christianity.

Instrumental music was secondary to vocal music among the Jews in Biblical days. It was for this reason that the Jewish people, when they were exiled from their homeland, were able to accommodate themselves to vocal music exclusively and develop their liturgy and hymnody to such great proportions.

Justinian's religious persecution of the Jewish people during the fifth century, when he forbade every kind of Biblical exegesis or Talmudic interpretation offered in the synagogue, led to the development of a literature of new prayers and poetry. Through this medium the poets would in obscure and sometimes difficult language aim to deceive their Byzantine oppressors by interpreting the significance of special Sabbaths and holidays, and various parts of the Bible and *Talmud*. This new poetry gradually became part of the liturgy.

That period saw the beginnings of Jewish hymnody, which was not without the influence of Christian hymnody which at that time was just about beginning to flower. This new poetry was called *piyut*, and the composers were called *paytanim*. Many of these *paytanim* were also precentors. Among them were such great liturgical poets as Jose ben Jose (6th century), Yannai (8th century), who was the editor of *Mahzor Yannai* (a compilation of liturgy and *piyutim*), and Eliezer Kalir (8th century).

Because these poets were also precentors or *hazzanim* they frequently had to either compose melodies or adapt an already existing tune to their new creations. In the latter case they frequently used popular secular tunes of the day. This practice was to the great distaste of the rabbis, and was caustically censured by them. But the disputed tunes often won out.

In the eleventh and twelfth centuries Jehudah Halevi (ca. 1085-1145), Solomon Ibn Gabirol (1021-1069), Moses Ibn Ezra (ca. 1070-1138), and Abraham Ibn Ezra (1093-1168), were among the great giants in Hebrew poetry, devoting themselves to the composition of liturgical poems. Later, in his *Zemirot Yisrael* (Songs of Israel), the exceptionally gifted poet-liturgist Israel Najara (1550-1620) frequently gave the name of the then popular song with which his poem was to be sung.

Many hymns which were composed during the Spanish period in Jewish history are still sung on Sabbaths and festivals in the synagogue. These hymns may also be found in the *Hagadah*, which is the order of the *Seder* (Passover home service). They are also included in the *zemirot* group of songs which are sung around the Sabbath table, and in the liturgies of the minor festivals and fast days.

It was the vogue in those days not only to compose hymns to the rhythms of secular songs but also to begin a Hebrew poem with a Hebrew line which was the same in sound as the first line of a popular Spanish ballad. One poet composed a hymn to the melody of the Spanish song "*Muerame mi alma ai muerame*," with the similar sounding words in Hebrew—"*M'romi al mah am rav homah*." Others used the sound of *Senora* for *Shem Norah*, which in Hebrew means the Ineffable Name. Those practices were censured, of course, and looked upon with great disdain by the rabbis.

The influence of Arabic poetry was strongly felt during this period, and meters of various types were used in this new poetic literature. The acrostic, which was already known in the Bible, in Psalms, and in Lamentations, became a popular form. Frequently the poet's name was to be found in the first letters of the verses of his poetry. While rhyme is occasionally found in the Biblical poetry, the real poetic rhyme of at least one syllable of the last word's root seems to appear at about the sixth century. The Arabic system of syllabic accented meter and strophic structure became an accepted form in Hebrew poetic literature at that time.

Three hymns which were composed during the Middle Ages are still the most popular hymns in the Jewish liturgy, and are sung at Jewish services to this very day. They are 1) *Adon Olam* (The Lord of All) which was said to be the work of an unknown Spanish poet of the 12th century. 2) *Yigdal Elohim Hai*, the work of Daniel Ben Judah of Rome (early 14th century), which embodies the Jewish creed as formulated by Moses Maimonides (1135-1204). This was the hymn which was set to music by the English cantor Leon Singer after he was engaged as cantor of the Duke's Palace Synagogue in London. Thomas Olivers, a Welshman and a Wesleyan minister, once heard this tune at a synagogue service. He became enraptured with it and resolved to have it sung in Christian congregations. For this purpose he wrote the hymn "The God Of Abraham Praise," which is sung to the tune of *Yigdal*, which he named "Leoni" after Leon Singer's first name. It was published in 1772 and became so popular that it had to be published in eight editions in two years. It reached its thirtieth edition in 1799 (Idelsohn: *Jewish Music*, pp. 220-221). 3) *En Kelohenu*, which also stems from the Middle Ages. A tune for this poem, which was composed by Julius Freudenthal in 1841, is derived from German Christian hymnody of the eighteenth century. (Idelsohn: *Jewish Music*, p. 238.)

A brief survey of the origins of Reform Judaism in Germany and America are important in order to understand the foundations of American-Jewish hymnody, for it is the product of the American-Jewish Reform movement.

The Jews who came to this country in 1654 brought with them the Orthodox traditions which they had inherited from their forefathers. These were either Sephardic or Ashkenazic. The prayers and rituals were basically alike, except for a few variations, which did not change the fundamental forms and principles. It was not until the beginning of the nineteenth century, when Reform Judaism had just begun to develop in Germany, that ideas for change entered the minds of Jews in various American communities. Despite the time and distance which separated Europe from America in those days, new ideas such as the introduction of the boys' choir in ordered four-part fashion, and the new synagogue music which was composed by Salomon Sulzer (1804-1890) in Vienna, Louis Lewandowski (1821-1894) in Berlin, and Samuel Naumberg (1815-1880) in Paris, was known here on this side of the Atlantic Ocean almost at once.

In 1810, Israel Jacobson of Westphalia, Germany, founded a Reform temple in Seesen. His reforms consisted mainly in introducing the German sermon and hymn singing in German, after the style of the Lutheran Church. He eliminated most of the Oriental traces in the chanting of the liturgy, and also in the cantillation modes employed in reading the weekly Bible lesson in Hebrew. Instead, the Bible was just recited *parlando* style. These reforms stunned the Orthodox communities in Europe, as they later did those on this side of the ocean, too.

In 1818 a Reform temple was opened in Hamburg, with a modified and abridged prayer book, a mixed choir, and an organ. They also published a hymnal which contained Jewish poetry in German translations, and modified German Lutheran hymns set to music in the German chorale style. This hymnal was later to have an influence upon early Reform hymnody in America.

In 1824 the first Reform congregation in America was organized in Charleston, South Carolina. At first, services were held in the Masonic Hall of that city. Besides the abridged liturgy, the organ had been introduced into the service music, and the congregants sat with uncovered heads. These reforms divided the Jewish communities throughout the United States. In 1830 a slender volume was issued entitled: *The Sabbath Service and Miscellaneous Prayers Adopted For the Reform Society of Israelites.* It omitted all references to the return to Zion and to Temple rituals, but adhered closely to the traditional form and was filled with Jewish piety. It also contained twenty-eight hymns drawn from the Hamburg hymnal as well as from Protestant sources. Gustavus Poznanski (1805-1879) was elected cantor and rabbi in 1836. He was in favor of reforms, which included the introduction of the organ at the services.

The congregation published in 1843 its own hymnal entitled *Hymns Written For Beth Elohim Congregation.* This was largely the work of Penina Moise (1797-1880), who was one of the first American-Jewish hymnodists of artistic standing.

The first German-Jewish Reform Society (Reform *Verein*) was founded in Baltimore in 1845. That group used the Hamburg *Gebetbuch* (prayerbook) and the Hamburg hymnal. Despite the many objections and disputes which ensued in all cities where Jews attempted to organize Reform congregations, this movement took hold. Soon Reform congregations after the pattern of the Reform *Verein* were organized in New York, Philadelphia, and Chicago.

With the introduction of the mixed choir and the organ into the Reform service, the congregation seemed to feel that they were now shut out from the service and consequently demanded more congregational singing.

In 1873, Adolph Huebsch (1830-1894), rabbi of Temple Ahavas Chesed in New York City, published his own hymnal, which contained some of his own hymnal-poems.

These were in German; some were original and some had been adapted from Christian hymnody.

Simon Hecht of Evansville, Indiana, published a hymnal, *Jewish Hymns For Sabbath School and Families* in 1878. It contained forty-three hymns in English and nine in German. Twelve tunes were by Hecht, while the remainder were by M. Z. Timker, P. Esser, Christian Mathias, and C. C. Genung. The hymnal also included tunes which were adaptations from the works of Gluck, Mozart, and Mendelssohn.

Otto Loeb's hymnal, entitled *Hymnen Fuer Sabbath Und Festage*, was published in Chicago in 1876. It was designed for synagogue, school, and home use. The editor also hoped that it would be used at synagogue services for congregational singing. Some hymn-poems were borrowed from the Temple Emanu-El hymnal and also from the works of Rabbi Benjamin Szold and Rabbi Marcus Jastrow. The melodies employed were sometimes of traditional origin, but the general musical style was German.

A common practice in hymn-singing, in alternating tunes and texts, could be found in an interesting way in a hymnal which was edited by Landsberg-Wile, and published in Rochester in 1880. The music on each page appeared at the top, and the words of the hymn at the bottom. Each page was cut in half uniformly, so that one could adjust the music to the text of one page with that of another by fitting the pages together. Here, too, the texts were in German and English, with some liturgical responses by non-Jewish composers. The hymnal also included some traditional melodies associated with Jewish holidays.

At that time there seemed to have arisen some dissatisfaction with the non-Jewish character of Jewish hymnody as it was developing in America. Cantor Moritz Goldstein of Cincinnati, in the preface to his hymnal published in 1895, stated: "Music in the Reform synagogue is being taken from operatic and non-Jewish sources. Our musical tradition is being forsaken." He wished to restore it. For the tunes in his hymnal, Goldstein drew from the works of Sulzer and Lewandowski, and composed quite a few of his own. While one feels the Jewish spirit in his holiday tunes, the rest of his efforts did not, I think, fulfill his original purpose.

The Sacred Harp of Judah, by G. M. Cohen, was published in Cleveland, and contained elements of sight-singing in the preface. Cohen also considered the music of Sulzer and Lewandowski too difficult. He wished to have very simple music, for this work was to be for parents and religious schools, for home and synagogue. He also wanted more congregational participation. The work contained hymns in English and German, and a number of prayers from the liturgy set to music.

Judaism in America toward the middle of the nineteenth century was agitated by the small minority of Jews who wanted reforms. Isaac Mayer Wise (1819-1900) arrived in this country in 1846 and joined the ranks of those who championed Reform Judaism. He became rabbi of Temple Beth-El in Albany in the same year, and began to institute radical reforms such as family pews, sermons in English, mixed choir with organ, and confirmation for boys and girls, not necessarily at the age of thirteen, the traditional age of *bar mitzvah* for boys. These reforms had hard sailing in being accepted by the entire congregation in Albany, and so Wise went to Cincinnati, where he became rabbi of Temple B'nai Jeshurun in 1854. He subsequently was the author of an abridged prayer book which embodied his ideas for reforms. It was at first rejected, but later accepted by the Reform congregations in western and southern cities. Rabbi Isaac M. Wise constantly strove to unite all Jews, all factions, all communities in America. He proposed the idea of uniting all Hebrew congregations in 1848, but his dream was not completely realized until 1873 when the

Union of American Hebrew Congregations was organized in Cincinnati.

The rabbinate, too, was at a very low ebb in status during that time. Anyone with a bit of Hebrew knowledge and the ability to speak publicly became a leader in the newly formed Reform congregations. Wise also wanted a theological school in which to train students for the rabbinate. In 1855, he organized the Zionist Collegiate Association, but this effort did not meet with success. He did not give up his efforts for he felt that American Judaism needed qualified leaders in order to continue. Through his labors, the Hebrew Union College was organized and opened its doors to rabbinical students in 1875 in Cincinnati. With his new graduates and many other followers, Wise organized the Central Conference of American Rabbis in 1889, an organization which was to play an important part in modern American Jewish hymnody.

In 1868 Temple Emanu-El in New York City published a collection of forty hymns, thirty-six of which were translations from the German, by its rabbi, James K. Gutheim and by Felix Adler. Coincident with the Emanu-El collection were similar collections by Isaac M. Wise and Marcus Jastrow.

Rabbi Isaac S. Moses (1847-1926) of the Central Synagogue in New York published an elaborate hymnal in 1894. In 1914 its fourteenth edition was published. This collection contained 250 hymns in English, and four in Hebrew. There were some responses in Hebrew and English for the Sabbaths and holidays, for school and for small choirs. There were also sacred solos and traditional chants for prayers with organ accompaniment. Included were seven services for children, a Sabbath service for the home, a flower service, a national service, a *Hanukkah* and a *Purim* service. In studying this collection I have reached the conclusion that the character of the music is Western, and even when a traditional Jewish melody has been utilized, it becomes paralyzed by its alien harmonization. A system for harmonizing Jewish melody was just about beginning to flower at that time, but neither of his collaborators, his cantor Theodore Guinsburg and his organist Gideon Froelich, were aware of it. More than 50,000 copies of this hymnal had already been sold by the time the fourteenth edition appeared in 1914.

In 1918 the brothers Israel and Samuel Goldfarb published a little volume entitled *Friday Evening Melodies*. It contained a number of Hebrew hymns for the Sabbath, set to music by the editors, and a few Jewish hymns in English.

Abraham Zevi Idelsohn (1882-1938), the noted musicologist, published his *Jewish Songbook* in 1928. It included a complete musical service for the entire Jewish year, hymns for the synagogue, the school, and the home, based mainly on the synagogue musical tradition and on folk song. He utilized the traditional modes and chants of the Sabbath, festivals, and weekdays, not only for Hebrew texts but also for the English sections of the prayer book. A second and enlarged edition was issued in 1951, edited by A. Irma Cohon and her son Baruch Cohon. This edition added the cantillation modes of the various sections of the Bible, which are read in public on Sabbaths and holidays.

In 1950 the United Synagogue Commission on Jewish Education published a large and extensive volume, *The Songs We Sing*, edited by Harry Coopersmith. It contains many hymns in Hebrew harmonized by some of the leading Jewish composers, as well as a limited number of Jewish hymns in English. This volume is also devoted to Hebrew and Yiddish folk songs.

The Jewish hymnodists of the nineteenth and twentieth centuries may be divided into two groups. First we have the original poets, and then we have those who translated the great Hebrew poetry of the Middle Ages, and the German-Jewish poetry, into the English language. They were either English, American, or Americans of German-Jewish origin. Among the leading original hymnodists we find Felix Adler, Richard Gottheil, Isabella Hess, Marcus Jastrow, Emma Lazarus, Elma Levinger, David Levy, Alice Lucas, Harry Mayer, F. de Sola Mendes, Lily Weitzman, and Isaac M. Wise.

Among the translators were Isaac S. Moses, Israel Abrahams, H. M. Adler, Grace Aguilar, Solomon Solis Cohen, Arthur Davis, Elsie Davis, James K. Gutheim, Nina Salomon, and Israel Zangwill.

In 1877 the Union of American Hebrew Congregations offered a prize for a Jewish hymnal. The offer failed because there was only one entry by Simon Hecht, and that was not good enough. Simon Hecht later published his hymnal. The Central Conference of American Rabbis then decided to issue its own hymnal, to be called the *Union Hymnal*. The organization enlisted the cooperation of the Conference of American Cantors, with Cantor Alois Kaiser (1840-1908) of Baltimore as music editor. The result was a first effort which combined the prevalent features of preceding hymnals. It contained 117 hymns. Many of the texts were taken from non-Jewish sources, from the Gottheil and Hecht collections, and from the poetry of Penina Moise. There were also twelve liturgical responses taken from the works of Sulzer and Lewandowski, and many by Kaiser. The result was far from being a Jewish hymnal. It also contained twelve hymns for Sabbath schools, including the standard patriotic songs, and a section was devoted to anthem texts. This edition lasted for seventeen years, and was revised by a committee from the CCAR, headed by Rabbi Harry H. Mayer of Kansas City.

The second edition of the *Union Hymnal* contained 226 hymns in the hymnal section, exclusive of liturgical responses. The authors of the hymn texts were non-Jews as well as Jews. One hundred and forty of the tunes were of non-Jewish origin. Many were derived from various church hymnals, and some were marked "traditional," although their distinctive character was hardly recognizable after the Jewish chant had been placed behind bar lines and harmonized with a tonic-dominant harmonization. The committee evidently also tried to get some composers who were Jews to write Jewish hymn tunes, but in no case did these composers succeed. Even the cantors who were commissioned wrote melodies which were characteristicly German. Many melodies by Mozart, Beethoven, Schubert, Gluck, and Mendelssohn were adjusted to certain texts. This hymnal also had a section of children's services with simple responses, an innovation in Jewish hymnals at that time. It also had an anthem-text section, which was omitted in the third edition, that was to follow. While progress was made in this hymnal, it was still not enough.

So great was the dissatisfaction of the CCAR with the second edition of the *Union Hymnal* which appeared in 1914, that a committee for revision was appointed in 1917, with the mandate to create a Jewish hymnal based on the authentic Jewish musical tradition, and with hymn texts based on some of the great poetry of the Middle Ages. New hymn poetry by contemporary Jewish poets was to be commissioned. The same was to be done with the music. This committee was headed by Rabbi Louis Wolsey of Temple Rodeph Shalom of Philadelphia, who appointed me, then a young professional musician with already definite ideas about Jewish music, as its editor.

In my report as music editor to the CCAR in June 1930 at Newport, Rhode Island, I said among other things, that: "We set out to construct a Jewish hymnal, and this we think we have accomplished to a great extent. Many melodies are coming into the hymnal which have been tied to the musical traditions of our people. Passover poems have been set to Passover melodies, *Sukkot* poems to *Sukkot* tunes. . . ."

A good idea of the goal and scope of this hymnal may be culled from the preface to this third edition: "The Committee sought to meet the requirements of our congregations and religious schools by providing a revision which should ring true to the Jewish spirit. As against 226 hymns in the second edition, the present compilation has 266 hymns, many of which are entirely new. Considerable use was made of the second edition; many favorite hymns were retained, but many were eliminated because they did not answer the special needs of our congregations and religious schools; others were reharmonized or separated, or the language of the poetry revised so as to give more appropriate expression to the demands of Jewish theology. Jewish composers contributed melodies and settings that were inspired by traditional Jewish music.

"Many Jewish poems were introduced into our hymnody for the first time. The Committee on Revision was actuated by a desire to produce a hymn book which would stimulate congregational singing, inspire Jewish devotion, revive the value of Jewish melody, make use of neglected Jewish poetry, lean heavily where possible upon Jewish motifs, awaken in the children of our religious schools a love for Jewish poetry and song, encourage in the religious schools an earnest study of Jewish music, and finally contribute to the field of hymnody a publication which would be essentially Jewish in color, spirit, and purpose.

"One of the main purposes constantly in view was to make it as Jewish as possible, and thus meet one of the needs of our modern synagogal life, namely, the adaptation of Jewish traditional music to the usage and taste of our own days. This involves a two-fold question: what elements of synagogal melody best express our religious life in music employed by our congregations; and, how shall we clothe them in harmony that shall reveal their own peculiar modal character and melodic contours? We would not assert that we have solved these two problems. Not only in this hymnal, but also in our religious-musical life in general, they are still far from a solution. But we have made an earnest effort to proceed in this direction. We have called upon Jewish composers for aid. A considerable number of them have contributed compositions to this collection. Composers were urged to utilize some of the wealth of synagogal melody. This plea found a ready response. Even a superficial glance through the contents of this volume indicates how many of the hymns are based upon traditional melodies.

"The Committee, moreover, adopted a liberal attitude toward experiments in harmonization. Some of the hymns are not scored for four voices, but for one voice with accompaniment. Some are experiments, and attempt to make use of modern harmonic devices and to apply them to the original or synagogal melodies employed. But we recognize that the needs and tastes of our congregations are not one, but many. A number of old and new hymns have been included which are in the general tone, but which are not specifically Jewish. In the case of these, too, the Committee has exercised the utmost care. Although we must rely upon our own judgment and recognize our fallibility, we have tried to exclude all trivial and unworthy music. It has been our aim to combine Jewish and general musical values. Such a hymnal as this is not an end, but an advance on the road toward the achievement of a difficult goal. It is our ardent hope that it will help educate our congregations in the beauties of our musical heritage and lead them Godward 'on the wings of song.' "

At the time of this writing, that edition of the *Union Hymnal* has lasted thirty-two years. While there has been some criticism, the edition has served not only Reform Judaism in America, but also the Conservative and Orthodox Jewish communities. Some of its forward-looking hymns by Schalit and Achron are still to come into their own in years ahead. While music editor, I also contributed ninety-two hymns and harmonizations, which include my well-known "Come O Sabbath Day" Jewish hymn in English.

The CCAR felt that there was a growing need for children in the religious schools to have their own song book, and that the hymns in the regular *Union Hymnal* were not simple enough for Jewish youth. It therefore decided to formulate a *Union Songster*. This was issued in 1960 under the chairmanship of Rabbi Malcolm Stern of Norfolk, Virginia, and the music editorship of Eric Werner. Besides many songs based on Jewish folk materials, and hymns for various occasions in simple musical language, the songster also contains twenty-eight children's services for religious and American holidays.

And so it took more than a century of Jewish life in America to evolve a Jewish hymnody which would reflect the Jewish soul and the real spirit of the synagogue.

XXI A PERSPECTIVE
ON SYNAGOGUE MUSIC
IN AMERICA

The musical tradition of the synagogue goes back to the days of the Temple in Jerusalem, when the great choirs of Levites and instrumentalists intoned the Psalms of the day and the Song of the Sea. After the Temple was destroyed in 70 C.E. and sacrifices were abandoned, the synagogue service which replaced the Temple service consisted of the chanting of the liturgy and the Bible readings. These practices continue to this day. Over a period of two thousand years, however, the liturgy has vastly expanded and its music has also greatly developed.

The musical tradition of the synagogue consists of: 1) Cantillation modes for chanting the various portions of the Bible which are read in public; 2) Modes associated with the holidays, certain services, and special prayers and

(This article appeared in the January 1964 issue of *The Journal of Church Music*.)

phrases; 3) Melodies which have become associated with specific prayers and hymns; and, 4) Synagogue choral music which is the product of the nineteenth and twentieth centuries, although some beginnings were already made by Salomone Rossi in the sixteenth century in Mantua.

The first Jews who settled in America in 1654 brought with them the Orthodox Sephardic or Spaniolic, and the Ashkenazic or Western traditions from the Old World. However, when German Reform was introduced to European Jewry early in the nineteenth century, its ideas and effects were almost immediately felt here. Those reforms consisted of the following: certain alterations and eliminations in the liturgy; the introduction of the sermon in German; German hymn-singing; and, most significantly, the introduction of the boy choir with singing in four ordered and rehearsed parts.

The introduction of ordered choir singing experienced rough going in Europe as well as in America. Here, also, the controversial mixed choir was introduced into the synagogues which followed the reforms of the rabbi and cantor Gustavus Poznanski, when in 1836 he assumed the leadership of Congregation Beth Elohim in Charleston, the first Reform Congregation in America.

What choral music did those choirs sing? They sang the music of Salomon Sulzer of Vienna (1804-1890), Louis Lewandowski of Berlin (1821-1894), and of Samuel Naumbourg of Paris (1815-1880). They were all products of Western European ideas of Reform.

The actual Reform movement in America encountered many stumbling blocks and made slow headway until Isaac M. Wise arrived in this country in 1846 and assumed its leadership. The first edition of the *Union Prayer Book*, a creation of Isaac M. Wise, was issued by the Central Conference of American Rabbis in 1897. Many prayers and hymns had been eliminated, many of the remaining parts of the liturgy curtailed, and many new prayers in English substituted.

For this new liturgy there was no music. It was true that the synagogue music by Sulzer and Lewandowski could be adapted, but when that was done it sounded incomplete. Some cantors began to compose new music for the new prayer book, and non-Jewish organists and composers were also invited to do this. About that time, the end of the nineteenth century and the beginning of the twentieth, there were very few cantors of real musical stature and knowledge in this country. Consequently, the music which came out of this period had very little in it which was based upon the musical tradition, nor was its musical quality high.

Moreover, if cantors knew so little about the music of the synagogue, how much less did the non-Jewish organists know! Even Sigmund Schlesinger (1835-1906), an organist of the Jewish faith in Mobile, Alabama, who set the entire Reform liturgy to music, used very little traditional thematic material. He made unscrupulous use of operatic excerpts from Bellini, Donizetti, and Rossini. In general, Schlesinger produced music which was non-synagogal in spirit and atmosphere.

At the beginning of the twentieth century, Edward Stark (1863-1918), cantor of Temple Emanuel in San Francisco, realized the shortcomings of the synagogue music of that period and set to work to remedy it. He, too, set the entire Reform liturgy to music, utilizing much more of the musical tradition than had Schlesinger. Stark, however, was short of real musical tradition and training, harmonically and contrapuntally, and so while his ideas were lofty, his results were for the most part mediocre.

A real renaissance in synagogue music did not come about until the twenties of this century, when knowledgeable cantors began to appear on the synagogue scene. Trained Jewish organists and choir directors also were increasingly engaged by some of the leading Reform temples in the country.

The Free Synagogue in New York was formed in 1922 and engaged this writer as music director that same year. Thereafter, Temple Emanu-El of New York followed with Lazare Saminsky, Temple Keneseth Israel in Philadelphia with Isadore Freed, Central Synagogue in New York with Lazar Weiner, and Temple Israel in Boston with Herbert Fromm. These musicians started a new era in the music of the Reform synagogue in America. Their works were based on the musical characteristics of the tradition which has been developed and handed down over the period of two thousand years. They understood musical form, and above all they aimed to create a special harmonic scheme that would serve as suitable background for the Jewish melody, which is essentially Oriental in qualities. When earlier synagogue composers, such as Sulzer and Lewandowski, used musical material based on the traditions of the synagogue, the atmosphere of the music was all but destroyed, because it was harmonized with the Western tonic and dominant system. This was the wrong harmonic dress. Jewish composers started to realize this toward the turn of the century, and that quest for a suitable harmonic system for Jewish music still continues.

Many Jewish composers began to make use of the modal system of harmonization which was being used in twentieth century manner by such composers as Debussy and Ravel. This harmonic treatment seemed to suit the Jewish musical tradition, which was essentially modal. The new harmonic technique also seemed to express the various moods of the liturgy in prayer, praise, and supplication, and also to express the prophetic spirit of the Bible and the pain of persecution through the ages. Modal and contemporary harmonies, separate or together, are to be found in the works of such men as Bloch, Freed, Helfman, Chajes, Milhaud, Fromm, and myself.

Ernest Bloch, the great Jewish composer, came a long way in solving this problem in his music. He showed the way to composers of synagogue music, in particular, with his oratorio *Avodath Hakodesh* (Sacred Service) which he set to the liturgy of the *Union Prayer Book*.

Darius Milhaud, another fine Jewish composer, has also contributed a *Service Sacré* based on the liturgy of the Reform prayer book, in which he has utilized some synagogue melodies of the Sephardic tradition, which are essentially modal.

The newer harmonic styles of the twentieth century have also seemed to expressively reflect the various prayer moods of the liturgy. The great accomplishment of contemporary synagogue music is that it helps to establish a synagogal music atmosphere which had all but disappeared in the music sung earlier in this century. It is, after all, the supreme purpose of music in a house of worship to create the spiritual aura which the people seek there. For example, it should be the purpose of synagogue or church music on Saturday or Sunday to establish the spirit of the day of rest. A worshiper must feel in a house of prayer on that day that it is Saturday or Sunday, not Tuesday or Wednesday.

It is interesting to note that the Reform synagogue in America has made more progress in its music than the Conservative or the Orthodox branches. It is also significant that more synagogue music has been composed, published, and performed in America than in any other country of the world, including Israel.

The question may now be asked: "From where are to come the new listeners which this music requires?" It is difficult enough to present contemporary music in the concert hall. How much more difficult it is to present it in the church or synagogue! The answer is that we are today dealing with men and women who listen to good music all the time on radio or television, in concert or opera. No longer is the church or synagogue the only place where people come to hear music only once a week. They now come as conditioned listeners, and in many cases are truly conditioned to the contemporary musical idiom.

In New York City there are three cantorial schools: the School of Sacred Music of the Hebrew Union College-Jewish Institute of Religion, organized in 1948; the Cantors Institute of the Jewish Theological Seminary, organized in 1952; and, the School for Cantors of Yeshiva University, organized in 1954. The young cantors who graduate from these schools are trained in both the old and the new in synagogue music. For example, the bibliography course in sacred music at these schools aims to acquaint the students with the new music which has been created for the synagogue, to cultivate their appreciation for it, and to develop their skill to perform it.

The hope for bringing progress into the music of the modern synagogue lies with these young cantors, who are now conscientiously fulfilling it. All over the country, special services of contemporary music are given during Jewish Music Month. These annual music festival programs serve to acquaint congregants with what is going on in the music of the synagogue of our day. Some of this newer music eventually finds its way into the regular synagogue repertoire.

A society was organized in 1963 by the writer in order to unite the students, faculties, and alumni of the three cantorial schools. It is known as the Jewish Liturgical Music Society of America, and already boasts of a large membership which spans the continent. Its chief purposes are: to raise the standards of music and of musical performance in all synagogues; to explore the history of the music of the synagogue; and, to give hearings to new musical creativity in this field.

An exchange of ideas between church and synagogue musicians could go a long way towards advancing the cause of fine sacred music in this country. After all, the musical traditions of the church and the synagogue are derived from the same rich source.

XXII A REBIRTH OF
BIBLICAL CHANT

W̲hen Israel Jacobson (1768-1828) established his first
Reform temple in 1810 in Seesen, Germany, he instituted
the following reforms: he provided the temple with a bell
for calling the worshipers to prayer; he introduced German chorale tunes set to Hebrew and German texts; he
abolished the chanting of *Torah* cantillation as well as
synagogue prayer modes (*nusach ha-tefillah*), and with this
last change went the abolition of the *hazzan*. As rabbi,
Jacobson himself, read the service, and also the weekly
Bible reading without any chant, the way they were read
in a church service. Jacobson's program for Reform was
imitated by other German communities which wanted to
join in this movement.

Salomon Sulzer (1804-1890) began as a moderate when

(This article appeared in *The Cantorial Art*, edited by Irene Heskes,
which was published in March 1966 by the National Jewish Music
Council of the National Jewish Welfare Board.)

he became the cantor of the temple on the *Seitenstatten Gasse* in Vienna in 1826. He shifted his position later to stronger reforms when he recommended to the synods at Leipzig and Augsburg, in 1869-70, the abolition of the cantillation of the Pentateuch on the Sabbath and Holy Days. It is interesting to observe that the Hamburg Reform temple, which was the model at first for the Reform movement, decided in 1879 to bring back the cantillation of the *Torah* and the *hazzan*.

The Reform movement in Western Europe found an echo here in the United States almost as soon as it was born in Germany. In 1836, the first Reform congregation to be established in Charleston, South Carolina, took Gustavus Poznanski as its rabbi and leader. Reform grew among the German Jews of America, leading to the development of Reform groups in Baltimore; and then in New York, Philadelphia, and Chicago, groups followed for the most part the pattern of Baltimore, as did the Jews in Germany follow that of the community in Hamburg.

It was not until Isaac M. Wise arrived in America in 1846 that Reform Judaism felt the impact of a leader who was to prove to be the champion of the movement in this country. Wise was a man with musical knowledge. His acquaintance with Salomon Sulzer during a sojourn in Vienna made him feel, as Sulzer did, the importance of music in this new movement. Shortly after becoming rabbi of Temple Beth-El in Albany, New York, he abolished the office of cantor and substituted the plain reading of the liturgy, eliminating the cantillation of the *Torah* and the *Haftarah*.

Without cantor or musical tradition (*nusach ha-tefillah*), of which cantillation is such an important part, the atmosphere of the Reform temples was soon barren of Jewishness. Then Protestant hymns were introduced, and the synagogue music was composed and sung by non-Jews.

This made it difficult to recognize the true musical spirit and atmosphere of the synagogue.

In 1921 the Jewish Institute of Religion was founded in New York by Stephen S. Wise, a great artist as well as a great rabbi. He understood what an important part genuine liturgical music could play in the American synagogue, and he realized that very little of the music that was being sung at that time in synagogues (including his own) had anything to do with true synagogue music. He wanted the young rabbis who were being trained at the Institute to have a Jewish musical education which they could apply when going to their various religious posts. In 1921 Rabbi Wise invited me to found and direct the department of music at this new rabbinical school.

The first courses offered were *Synagogue Music* and *Folk Music*. I began to feel very strongly at that time that rabbis ought to know the musical meanings of the tropes which punctuate the Biblical texts. It was important for a rabbi to know how to chant the *Torah* beautifully on the Sabbath and Holydays, and to be able to read a *Haftarah* when called upon.

I further felt that Jewish boys at thirteen should not be deprived of the privilege of chanting from the *Torah* and *Haftarah* at *bar mitzvah*, a privilege which countless generations of Jewish youths had experienced. At that time we began to bring back the *bar mitzvah* ceremony at the Free Synagogue in New York City, the congregation of Rabbi Wise.

The introduction of a course in *Cantillation* was eagerly welcomed by the rabbinical students, who realized the importance of attaining that knowledge for many reasons, not the least of them being the avoidance of certain embarrassment in the future. Gradually, cantillation found its way back into the Reform synagogue.

As early as 1518, in Johann Reuchlin's *Grammar*, an

attempt was made to notate the Biblical tropes in musical notation. Other attempts were made later by Salomon Sulzer of Vienna in 1838, by Samuel Naumbourg of Paris in 1864, by Abraham Baer of Gothenberg in 1877 and more recently, by Solomon Rosowsky in a major work on cantillation published in 1957. It must also be mentioned that the various editions of the Pentateuch published over the years frequently have included musical tables of the tropes, but these have been carelessly interpreted and notated. In those tables only the bare musical interpretation of the trope has been given, without combining it with other tropes in varied groupings. No intimations have been given of exceptions to the rule, nor of special musical detours, such as we find in the *Shirat Hayam*, in the various cadences at the end of each book of the *Torah*, and for *Simchat Torah*.

The reading of the Pentateuch on the Sabbath and Holy Days was usually entrusted to an educated layman, sometimes to the beadle (or *Shamash*), and rarely to the cantor. When the beadle or the layman was musically sensitive and endowed with a good musical memory, one could depend on a more or less authentic musical reading. However, when the musicality of the reader was in doubt, many inaccuracies were heard. Some of these inaccuracies, occurring with even a reasonably musical reader, gradually found their way into the interpretations of the tropes.

The greatest musical disfiguration occurred in the *Haftarah* trope, which was sometimes taught by anyone who, though he may have had just a smattering of it, still wanted to make a little extra fee by teaching it to *bar mitzvah* boys. They could only tell that *pashta* goes up and *darga* goes down. How far up or how far down, they couldn't say.

There was need for a comprehensive notation of the tropes in all their combinations, complete with their variations and exceptions. Solomon Rosowsky made an auspicious beginning with his *Music of the Pentateuch*. There were however still five other systems which had to be written down: the tropes of the *Haftarah*, the High Holy Day trope, *Echah, Megillat Esther*, and *Shir Hashirim*.

A practical textbook and a method of teaching the tropes to students of all ages was greatly needed if cantillation was to survive inspite of the phonograph records and the inept *bar mitzvah* teachers.

The musical conclusions which I reached in my book, *Biblical Chant*, published in 1959, were based on a lifetime association with the chant in its various versions, critical comparisons between various versions both written and oral, and an intimate involvement with the musical tradition of the synagogue. My notations of the various systems of the tropes seem to be logically correct. The more I studied the tropes, the more I realized that they follow a logical form of musical development such as one finds today in the development of a musical motif in the works of the great masters.

I have taught over four generations of rabbis at the Jewish Institute of Religion-Hebrew Union College, and two generations of cantors who have graduated from the School of Sacred Music of the Hebrew Union College since 1949. They, in turn, have helped to bring back the beauty of cantillation to their synagogues and to restore some of the original musical contours of the trope which during an earlier era had become almost obscured by time and neglect. My prime purpose was to bring about a re-birth of cantillation in order that it might resume its rightful place in the service of the synagogue.

XXIII SALOMON SULZER'S LEGACY TO THE CANTORATE

It is hardly realized that Salomon Sulzer's music and influences extend even today into the synagogues of all groups of Judaism. His music for the responses *Barchu*, *Shema*, the *Kedusha*, and *Hodu Al Eretz* are known to millions of Jews, and are sung at all services. While his synagogue choral works are not as popular as they once were, this music did set the pattern which was followed by almost all subsequent composers of synagogue music in the nineteenth century, and also influenced the music of the early Reform synagogue in America.

Salomon Sulzer was born on March 30, 1804 in Hohenems, a little town in Voralberg, an Austrian province between the Tyrol and Switzerland. As a child, he was rescued from a frightful accident. It was then that his

(This article was written on the occasion of the seventy-fifth *Yahrzeit* of Sulzer in 1964. It was published posthumously in the February 1967 issue of the annual *Bulletin* of the Jewish Liturgical Music Society of America.)

mother vowed him to the service of God and dressed the
boy in white. After receiving his Jewish training at the
Yeshiva in Endingen, Switzerland, and his musical training
in Karlesruhe, Baden, Sulzer decided to become a *hazzan*.

He was elected *hazzan* in his home town at the age of
fourteen, and became a pupil of the well-known Salomon
Eichberg (1786-1880), who in turn was a former pupil
of Israel Lovy (1773-1832). Both Lovy and Eichberg were
two of the most renowned *hazzanim* of their day.

When the Vienna Jewish community sought the services
of a *hazzan* for their newly built temple in 1826, they engaged young Salomon Sulzer for this post, and appointed
Isaac Noah Mannheimer as their chief rabbi. These two
men were to make noteworthy contributions, each in his
own field, and importantly as a combination were able to
prevent serious internal schisms among Central European
Jewry.

When Sulzer came upon the cantorial scene in Vienna,
the music in European synagogues was in a chaotic state.
True, Israel Lovy in Paris had begun to bring some order
out of this chaos, but it needed the talent, perseverance,
and the personality of Salomon Sulzer to establish this
order on a firm and musical basis.

Synagogue music in that day was carried on by "the
group of three": *hazzan*, boy's voice, and bass (if the *hazzan*
was a tenor, or vice versa). They improvised their harmonizations and sometimes their tunes. All singing was
done from memory. One never knew whether what happened at a rehearsal would also take place at the service.
The musical tradition (*nusach ha-tefillah*) became distorted and in many cases it was completely discarded in
favor of popular tunes and musical styles of the day. Often
it was so distorted as to become unrecognizable. The services were noisy, without decorum, a particular aspect which
early reformers set out to rectify.

At the start, Salomon Sulzer was more concerned with

the reconstruction of the *nusach ha-tefillah*. He strove to cleanse it of the impurities which had penetrated it over the years.

In the preface he wrote for the first volume of his *Shir Zion*, published in 1840, he articulated the principles which had guided him up to that time: "The institution of the regular four-part choir in the synagogue proved to be a sacred and fruitful one and has become a well-established general practice. . . . Yet, this institution is still young, and needs sympathetic support and aid on the part of the communities."

He continued, "I made it my duty to give maximal consideration to those tunes which have come down from antiquity and to restore their archaic flavor in its original purity, cleansed from later flourishes of dubious and tasteless character. This restoration was more easily achieved with chants for the High Holy Days than in the Sabbatical chants."

While early German Reform eliminated the *hazzan*, the chanting of the *Torah*, and even the musical tradition of the synagogue with its particular Jewish character, the Vienna community and its distinguished Rabbi Mannheimer were won over to Sulzer's ideas and ideals, as were many other communities. The Vienna service became the pattern not only for most synagogues in Central Europe, but for those in Eastern Europe as well. Hundreds of cantors came to study with Sulzer, and thousands of people came to hear him, among them the great composers of the day, including Franz Schubert (who became his close friend) and Franz Liszt. In writing of his experience on hearing Sulzer at a Sabbath eve service, Liszt said, "Only once were we given the opportunity to hear what a true Judaic art could be. We have seldom been moved as deeply as we were that evening: so stirred that our soul was entirely immersed in meditation and participation in the service." Sulzer also became one of the outstanding interpreters of

Schubert's *lieder*. Evidence of their friendship is Schubert's contribution of the Psalm 92 (*Tov L'hodot*), a musical setting of the original Hebrew text which was included in Sulzer's first volume of *Shir Zion*.

The Jewish community in Vienna also commissioned Beethoven to compose a cantata for the dedication of their new temple in 1826. Beethoven considered this idea for a while, but later declined. The task was accomplished by the composer Seyfried, a pupil of Beethoven. It may very well be while Beethoven was considering this commission that he busied himself with the study of Jewish thematic material, and that *Kol Nidre* was brought to his attention. We find the theme of *Kol Nidre* woven through Beethoven's C♯ minor string quartet, opus 131, composed during that period.

Though Sulzer's intentions were laudable for his time, when they are examined from our point of view, they fall short of complete realization. Both volumes of *Shir Zion*, one for the Sabbath and the other for Holy Days, are divided into cantorial recitatives and choral pieces, the latter being sometimes brief and at other times extended. Cantors owe a debt of gratitude to Sulzer for having written down the musical tradition of the synagogue for almost all of the chants of the synagogue year. Sulzer sometimes wrote those recitatives with bar lines, and at other times without them. Our tradition is asymmetrical in style and when imprisoned behind bar lines loses its personality and freedom.

In paring off unnecessary musical accumulations on the cantorial chant, which Sulzer set as one of his most important tasks, he sometimes cut down to the bone and even into the marrow. (See volume two *Shir Zion*, published in 1866: *Ashre Ha-am* #342, and *Shema Yisrael* #336.)

It was not until he came into close contact with many East European cantors who came to study with him that Sulzer really got to know the real *nusach* of the traditional synagogue. It was at that time that he wrote his second volume of *Shir Zion*, which contains some of his best work. Excellent examples are *B'rosh Hashanah* #354, which is full of deep feeling, *Meloch* #381, and *Veteerav* #391, which are of his best. The brief choral responses in the preliminary prayers to *Maariv* after *Kol Nidre* are examples of Sulzer's more Jewish choral writing.

Sulzer was, however, least strong in a Jewish way when writing in the choral medium. He rarely struck the Jewish chord. He did not know, nor did any of his contemporaries, how to treat and harmonize the *Ahavah Rabbah* mode. In his cadence to *Mi Chamocha* #75 in his Sabbath morning service, the penultimate chord, before going to G *Ahavah Rabbah* is d-f♯-a-c, instead of d-f-a♭-c, later inserted by his son Joseph. The latter chord gives us the Sabbath morning atmosphere, but the first does not. He similarly did not know how to harmonize the cadence at the end of *Shema* #369, in volume two.

Sulzer sometimes indulged in changing the *nusach* from minor to major, thus destroying its musical purpose at a certain high point. He did this in the *Barchu* #25 in his Friday evening service, volume one. When this response is returned to minor, one feels the sanctity of the Sabbath again. He made the same change from minor to major in *Hamelech* ♯339, volume two.

This was the style of that day. The purpose of early Reform was to eliminate Oriental *melos* and everything that sounded "too Jewish." The soul of the synagogue went out with this change. It was for this reason that people who know the musical tradition of the synagogue have called Sulzer's music "un-Jewish."

Sulzer frequently followed an exquisite cantorial recitative with a choral response in Western style, which was incongruous. He did not achieve the ability to develop a Jewish tune or mode. In his *Yigdal* #296, volume two, he began with a beautiful traditional tune, repeated it several times, and instead of developing it, went off at *shefa* into a German-sounding chorus, returning at *gomel* to the original tune. He should have further developed his theme or followed it by a new section in the High Holy Day style.

Sulzer's problem, and that of his contemporaries, including Lewandowski, was to find the correct harmonization for the synagogue musical tradition. Here he was confronted with a *melos* which was Eastern and Oriental, and he tried to harmonize it with the Western tonic-dominant system of that period. The two just did not mix. In many of Sulzer's and Lewandowski's works there is the attempt to harmonize a traditional melody in that form, thus destroying the character of the piece. (See *Avinu Malkenu* #462, volume two, and Lewandowski's *Avot*, volume two.)

Sulzer's critics admired and emulated his institution of the four-part choir, as well as his dignified and devotional style while chanting the service. Of notable importance, however, was the addition by others of the Jewish spirit, achieved by applying Sulzer's process of combination with the *nusach ha-tefillah*, but with an effort to find its proper harmonization. Among the cantors of his day who went one step further than Sulzer in this direction were Eliezer Gerovitch of Rostov, Hirsch Weintraub of Koenigsberg, Samuel Naumbourg of Paris (in a limited sense), and later, David Nowakowsky of Odessa.

In Sulzer's most exalted moments (and there were many) he expressed himself with true dignity and deep religious feeling. At times it was Jewish, and at times Protestant, as for example in his recitatives in his C major *Tov L'hodot* #18, volume one, and in the cantorial solos of his various versions of *Adon Olam* #52. He evidently did not object to the Protestant style, for he included in his *Shir Zion* the works of Seyfried, Schubert, and Fischoff, who were non-Jews.

Many of Sulzer's tunes, especially those in volume one, which include tunes commonly sung at our services today, are in three-quarter time or waltz time. Living in Vienna at the very time when Johann Strauss, the waltz king, held sway, made it difficult to escape uninfluenced by the waltz rhythm. No less a master than Johannes Brahms was one of the victims. Sulzer really went into waltz time at the end of the E flat *Adon Olam* #49, which most likely delighted the hearts of the Viennese.

The ability to develop a Jewish theme and to harmonize the Jewish modes with a suitable harmonic background had to wait until the turn of the century. Then, Jewish composers such as Achron, Milner, Engel, and later Bloch, Freed, Fromm, Chajes, and this writer, began to evolve a harmonic background for our musical tradition and to give musical forms to our synagogue music which were lacking in a good deal of our nineteenth century music literature.

Whatever our criticism of Salomon Sulzer may be today, he must be viewed historically. He was the product of a particular period which demanded change, and he gave it his imprint. It took courage and talent to accomplish the changes which he instituted. He left to cantors of all times an example to emulate. His complete dedication to his profession, the sanctity and dignity which he brought to it, made everyone in and out of the synagogue respect him and his office.

Sulzer was a great singer with a beautiful light baritone voice, a fine synagogue composer and community organizer, and for these qualities he truly earned the title of "Father of Modern Synagogue Music." It was he who first called his office "cantor," after the manner of Bach. When Sulzer received the title of *Morenu*, Rabbi Leopold Loew wrote, comparing him to another Salomon:

> "Truly the masters of song he led.
> The Holy in word and tune he wed."

XXIV   ISAAC OFFENBACH:
HIS LIFE, WORK AND
MANUSCRIPT COLLECTION

His Life (1779-1850)[1]

Isaac Judah Eberst was the father of Jacques Offenbach,[2] the famous opera composer of France. Isaac was born on October 26, 1779. He left his home town of Offenbach at the age of 20, and went to seek his fortune in other towns along the Rhine. While learning bookbinding, he had a master who occasionally played the violin. One day Eberst found enough courage to ask his employer whether he would allow him just to draw the bow over the strings. He

(Late in his own life, Binder renewed his interest in the life and work of Isaac Eberst-Offenbach as a significant synagogue musician. Binder passed away shortly after he sent off this manuscript, which considerably amplified his treatment of the same materials presented in a short article published in the March 28, 1930 issue of *The Jewish Tribune*. This posthumously published essay appeared in the *Year Book XIV* of the Leo Baeck Institute, London, in 1969.)

succeeded to some extent in making a pleasant sound on the instrument, and, from that day on, was allowed to use the violin during his spare time. He persisted and, self-taught, soon became proficient on the instrument. Later, in his own bookbinding shop, Isaac engaged two men to do the work, while he devoted himself to teaching the violin, in addition to managing the business.

Isaac Eberst also possessed a beautiful tenor voice. This, together with a sound knowledge of Hebrew, qualified him in 1803 for the position of cantor in Deutz, where shortly thereafter he married Marianne Rindskopf, daughter of one of the families residing there. In 1816 he was called to become cantor of the community of Cologne, a position which he held with honor and dignity until his death in 1850. In his latter years, he combined this position with that of acting rabbi for the same congregation. The charm of his personality, his wit and humor, made him many friends and earned for him admission into the select circles of society, where he soon became known as "the Offenbacher." This nickname became so well known that he finally discarded the name Eberst.

When Isaac Eberst first arrived in Deutz in 1803, the political situation as it affected Jews was in a state of flux. The era of enlightenment, which came to the Duchy of Cologne from France, manifested itself in the establishment of a new college in Bonn in 1777, where Jews were permitted to study but could not obtain a degree. When the French occupied the left bank of the Rhine, which included Cologne (they entered on October 6, 1794), the Jews of the Rhenish Department became citizens of France.[3] This implied full equality before the law. In Autumn 1797, the poll tax (*Koerpersteuer*) for Jews on that bank of the Rhine was abolished.[4] Under the leadership of the rabbi of Bonn seventeen families formed themselves into a Jewish community in Cologne on October 12, 1801. When the consistorial system was decreed on March 17,

1808, Cologne, where the Jews began to settle in 1798, was joined with Krefeld, with Leo Carlsberg as rabbi. On the same day, Napoleon's *décret infâme* was proclaimed in France, gravely affecting the position of the Jews.

After Napoleon's defeat, the Prussians occupied the territory. Their Edict of March 11, 1812, granted the Jews of Prussia almost complete equality, but the French Decree of 1808, which had discriminated against Jews in the conduct of trade, was not to expire until the end of 1818. This made it exceedingly difficult for Jews to engage in trade and commerce without special certificates which were not easily secured.

It was probably because the securing of a permit to conduct business had become too difficult that an educated man like Isaac Offenbach (Eberst), with business experience and an engaging personality, chose the cantorate as a profession. He, therefore, like many another talented young man of that period with a good voice and Jewish knowledge, became a cantor in spite of the poor salary offered. He came to Cologne in 1816 to improve his opportunities to support a growing family.

The Cologne community had been part of the Bonn Consistory, since 1817, so the rabbi could only preach periodically in his various communities. The cantors of the communities were therefore often asked to preach and to perform certain rabbinical functions. Isaac Offenbach officiated in the capacity of both rabbi and cantor throughout his life.[5] His sermons showed depth and poetic feeling and a comprehensive command of Biblical literature.

Offenbach's salary was rather modest. In 1843, after about 20 years of service as cantor, he received only 43 *thaler* for that year.[6] So he applied for an increase of a fixed salary of 80 *thaler* and 10 measures of cereal and Passover flour. From this income he had to support a family of a wife and 10 children. True, the cantor also received some fees for serving at weddings and funerals, and from

the sale of synagogue seats, and special gifts from congregants on the High Holy Days.[7] Furthermore, a cantor's
wife supervised the ritual bath for women which yielded
some additional income.[8]

Of the ten children in the Isaac Offenbach family, seven
were daughters and three sons. Two of them, Jakob (later
known as Jacques) and Julius (later called Jules) were
destined for fame in the world of music. To Jakob, his seventh child, the father presented a violin when he was six
years old. The boy learned quickly; at the age of eight he
was already playing violin concertos and composing little
songs. When Isaac Offenbach realized that his son Jacques
showed extraordinary talent for the cello, which later he
preferred to the violin, he was not content to leave him
with his teachers in Cologne, but took him and his brother
Jules to the Paris Conservatory, of which Luigi Cherubini
was then the head. It was then one of the chief musical
centers in Europe. Jacques studied cello and composition,
while Jules studied violin.

Jacques and Jules returned occasionally to Cologne for
a vacation. Their home there was a source of inspiration
to them, inasmuch as both father and mother were musical and in sympathy with their sons and what they were
studying. Isaac Offenbach chose to send his sons to the
Paris Conservatory for their advanced musical studies
rather than to Berlin, because the political situation for
Jews was easier in France than in Germany. In Germany
it was very difficult for a Jew to rise to a high position in the
world of music without embracing Christianity. This was
not necessary in France; nevertheless, for marriage and
society, his son Jacques did convert to Catholicism.

Isaac Offenbach's personal charm brought him many
friends among the leading musical personalities in Cologne.
His home was the meeting place of artists, writers, lawyers,
and people of high standing in German society. He was a

member of the Cologne Musical Society, which had been established in 1812. In later decades many other Jews were active in this Society. In 1852 Wilhelm Hertz was its conductor, and in 1875 Anselm Cohen was among the leaders of the *Sing-Akademie* and also director of the Men's Chorus. Ferdinand Hiller (1811-1885) was in charge of the musical life of Cologne for three decades. Hard-working and self-sacrificing, he did much to raise the level of musical life there. Among his works are a musical setting of the 137th Psalm and an oratorio, *The Destruction of Jerusalem*. He too later converted to Christianity.[9]

A noted contemporary of Isaac Offenbach was the artist David Levy Elkan, distinguished not only in his profession, but also by his enthusiastic interest in Jewish communal affairs. Among his works with a Jewish theme are a Scroll of Esther and lithographic illustrations of the *Hagadah*.

Due to the fame which the young Jacques Offenbach was gradually acquiring in Paris, Jacques Fromenthal Halévy, the French-Jewish composer, began a correspondence with Isaac, with whom he had many things in common. Halévy was very much interested in the music of the synagogue, having composed some settings for Hebrew liturgy; those compositions are to be found in the synagogue collections of Samuel Naumbourg, who at that time was chief cantor in Paris.

Between Isaac Offenbach and his son Jacques we find a strong resemblance in many respects. In some of the sprightly tunes to be found so abundantly in Jacques' work, we can see the father's influence.

Isaac Offenbach was considered one of the leading cantors of his day. But his talents were not confined only to his great abilities as cantor and rabbi. He also wrote plays and beautiful poetry. His rabbinic sermons, poetic and profound, showed a great knowledge of the Bible and of

Hebrew literature. With these traits, he filled with honor the post of rabbi and cantor in Cologne for nearly thirty years.

Jacques was the particular favorite of the family, and his mother always brooded over his absence. She became sickly. At a critical stage in her final illness, a physician, who was a friend of the family, suggested that the presence of Jacques might improve the condition of his mother. His wit and humor, which he had inherited from his father, together with his loving personality, might prove as always of great comfort to her.

The younger brother Jules at that time was *Chef d'Orchestre* at the opera at Bordeaux, and Jacques was then concertizing on the cello. Nevertheless, the two of them left their work to return to their home in Cologne. The mother rallied, but her condition was already too serious. She passed away within a few months, on November 17, 1840. The family was greatly stricken by this loss. In a letter subsequently written to Jacques and Jules, their father Isaac penned the following poem:

> *Weinend betrat Ihr euer eltern Haus,*
> *Weil euern jungern Ihr nicht mehr fand!*
> *Weinend geht Ihr heute nun wieder hinaus*
> *Weil der Himmel euch eure Mutter entwandt!*
> *Auch meine thranen fliessen mit den euern,*
> *Denn die, so Ihr beweint, waren auch meine theuern.*
> *Weinet Sohne weinet nur,*
> *Das Herz wird euch dann leicht*
> *Und ist verlischt der Thranern spur*
> *Die Herzen trost ersteigt.*
> *Und lindering wird die Zeit uns bringen,*
> *Und wird in freud, uns einst umschlingen.*
>> Mourn for the house of your parents,
>> Your dear one is no more.
>> As mourners depart ye from here,
>> For Heaven has taken your mother.

My tears shall be coupled with yours,
For she was also my dearest.
   Tears, dear sons, tears,
   Can only lighten your hearts,
   And when the last will flow,
   Comfort will fill your hearts.
   For time alone will bring
   Healing and joy again.

Isaac was particularly attached to his son Jacques, as was this son to his father. One time after his mother's death, Jacques left his busy Parisian life and came with his wife and children to stay with his lonely father and comfort him. After that visit in 1848, Jacques returned to Paris, and the family wrote "the house became very quiet." Father and son never saw each other again. Isaac Judah Offenbach died on April 26, 1850. He had been considered one of the leading cantors of his day.[10]

His Music

The struggle over Reform, which at the beginning of the nineteenth century shattered European Jewry, had an impact also on its synagogue music. In 1810 Israel Jacobson of Westphalia had organized a synagogue service without a cantor, introducing the organ and a mixed choir as well as the singing of Hebrew texts[11] to the tunes of German chorales and hymns. In their efforts to achieve emancipation, many Jews sought to discard some of the traditional Jewish practices and the Oriental character of their synagogue music. Getting away from the minor modes in the liturgy was considered an important element in early German Reform. The elimination of orientalisms had widespread effects, not only in the Western European countries, but also in the East. The synagogue musicians of the latter part of the nineteenth century and of the twentieth century, however, systematically brought back the original style, realizing the danger of losing the musical tradition in which the synagogue service truly is embedded.[12]

During the first half of the nineteenth century the community of Cologne was Orthodox, according to the Ashkenazi tradition, and had adopted the rite of the neighboring city of Deutz.[13] There was no talk of Reform[14] until Rabbi Israel Schwarz became permanent rabbi in 1859. The music of Isaac Offenbach, therefore, mainly followed the Orthodox tradition, though we find among his manuscripts some already scored for male chorus, dated Cologne 1848,[15] as well as many prayers set to original tunes in waltz, minuet and polka rhythms.[16]

Synagogue music forms the bulk of the Isaac Offenbach Manuscript Collection. As a cantor, he was well versed in the style and traditional melodies of the synagogue. He was, however, also a contemporary of the three great musical masters of that period—Mozart, Haydn and Beethoven—and there is evidence in Offenbach's music that these three composers had influenced him.

Offenbach's loyalty to the synagogue as well as his passion for general musical composition led him to divide his synagogal work (which, in his mature life, became his only means of musical expression) into two sections: a) compositions based on the traditional prayer motives and melodies; b) synagogue music in the style of the minuet, gavotte, polka, etc., bearing the stamp of the style of his contemporaries. Thus, while the major part of his works, like *Unetaneh Tokef*, *Mechalkel Chaim*, *Kol Nidre*, and *Kaddish Lemusaf*, are based upon the traditional modes and melodies known to Western Jews, many other of his compositions are in the elegant style of Mozart and Haydn. It was customary at that time for concert performers to improvise on the popular tunes of the day. This was probably also done in the synagogue by improvising a minuet or a polka melody to some of the lighter portions of the liturgy such as, for example: *Melech Elyon, Ki Anu Amcha, L'cha Dodi.* We are made aware of the fact that Jews also came to the synagogue to be entertained by their cantors, for this was the only way most Jews could satisfy their hunger for music. This was also one of the reasons for the popularity of the virtuoso cantor who dominated the synagogue scene throughout the nineteenth and part of the twentieth centuries.[17]

Isaac Offenbach was constantly in the process of composition, as his works indicate. He would quite suddenly think of a new version to the *nusach* of a certain prayer, or an entirely different tune, as late even as the day before Holy Day, jot it down, and probably sing it the next day at the service. In Offenbach's High Holy Day music we find the old style with which prayers, such as *Kaddish, Barchu, Kol Nidre,* and others were introduced on the High Holy Days. Usually, a long and florid wordless improvisation would be intoned by the cantor with the help of his musical assistants (most frequently a bass and a boy soprano), and this would finally culminate with the words of *Barchu, Yitgadal,* or *Kol Nidre.*

Most of the synagogue music of Offenbach is scored for the old combination prevalent in those days, namely cantor, discant, and bass. Yet, when choral music began to take root in the Austrian and German synagogues. Isaac Offenbach was not unmindful of it. It evidently took him a long time, probably fifteen or twenty years, to convince his congregation of the change, for his manuscripts do not show four-part writing until 1846. This we find in a complete Friday evening service, scored for male chorus, with cantor soloist.

When Salomon Sulzer introduced his music which simplified and often eliminated the florid portions of the *nusach ha-tefillah,* Isaac Offenbach followed suit with his own revised versions of this music.[18] Thus we find in his *Nigunim Leyamim Noraim*[19] an early version of the High

Holy Day *Kaddish* before *Musaf*, and later in the volume a simplified version showing the influence of the time. Offenbach did not go as far as Sulzer, who may have seemed too modern for his congregants in Cologne.

Many of Offenbach's chants, for example *Unetaneh Tokef* from the *Musaf* High Holy Day liturgy,[20] which ordinarily would be chanted in minor, are in a major key, again showing the influence of Salomon Sulzer and also of the ideas of Reform. Sulzer and the emerging fame of Lewandowski[21] had a tremendous impact on synagogue music in the East and West. In the place of improvised, unorganized singing, the ordered four-part choir became more and more the norm as the century progressed.

In the big cities, large choirs were employed and choral singing was firmly entrenched by the mid-nineteenth century in Paris, Berlin, Vienna and other substantial European communities. The three great synagogue composers of the day were Sulzer in Vienna, Lewandowski in Berlin, and Naumbourg in Paris. By the end of the century, almost every city had a *Chor-Shul*, and the output of the composers of choral music increased by leaps and bounds, bringing forth a choral literature which stands as a monument to the preferences of European Jewry of the past.

Isaac Offenbach was a forerunner who, in his own way, succeeded in making his congregants aware of the new movement in synagogue music which began to stir when he began his cantorial career in Deutz in 1803, and which was in full bloom at the time of his death in 1850.

His Manuscript Collection[22]

When one approaches the manuscript collection of Isaac Judah Offenbach, one becomes aware of his former vocation, namely bookbinding, which seemed to manifest itself in later life as an avocation. Consequently, we find that most of his manuscripts are neatly bound and titled, always clearly and legibly written—*Nigunim Leyamim Noraim,* Sermons, Addresses, Poems and Plays. This makes the study of them easy and pleasurable.

Violin Obligati to Sabbath Eve Service: Dated Cronberg, 1799-1800. Title pages show Isaac Judah Eberst, von Offenbach; containing violin obligati to several versions of *L'cha Dodi* in the following forms: *alla polacco,* minuet, and *siciliano;* all spirited in style, rhythmic and joyous. The violin was one of the instruments used as accompaniment to the *Kabbalat Shabbat* service in those days. Isaac Judah Eberst held at this early time the position of discant, as well as violinist.

For Guitar(re) (Published): Volumes II-III of a series entitled *Douze Sonatines Pour La Guitar (re),* containing practice pieces in the old dance forms, as for example, march, rondo, polonaise and waltz; Volume XIII of a series entitled *Uebungs-Stuecke,* containing pieces for practice purposes, also in dance forms. All show a gift of melody and rhythmic inventiveness, but bear witness of the strong influence of Mozart and Haydn.

Purim and Passover: Dated January 29, 1833, a pamphlet (mss.) containing humorous poems for *Purim,* written in Yiddish, some of them set to music; music for the Passover *Hagadah* (published Cologne 1838), containing: traditional melodies such as *Echad Mi Yodea* and *Adir Hu,* an original melody for *Chad Gadya* which has become quite well known, and melodies for *Hodu, Chasal Siddur Pesach,* and a German hymn for the Passover festival; a volume dated 1829, entitled *Nigunim Le-pesach,* containing Holy Day versions of the liturgy, including such compositions as *Tal, Hallel,* and various *piyutim.*

High Holy Day Music: Two volumes entitled *Nigunim Leyamin Noraim.* The first, dated 1828-1829, contains almost all the liturgy to be sung by the cantor and his helpers. There are recitatives, chants, and set-pieces.

Another volume, entitled as above, but dated 1842, is a collection of many revised and completely changed versions of the pieces found in the former volume. This, surely, was the personal copy which Isaac Offenbach used at the service. There are also helpers' parts.

Pieces Composed By Singers: It was the custom at that time for a singer or choir leader, when applying for a position, to bring an original composition to the cantor. This composition was intended to show the musical abilities of the applicant. In the collection we find a piece by Simcha Hakoton which contains nuances such as forte, crescendo, written in Hebrew characters. Another piece, by Abraham Alexander, shows style and imagination, and Haydnesque influence. And, there is a collection of High Holy Day chants of Shemuel Hakoton.

Sabbath Music: A score very neatly bound, dated Cologne 1848, for male quartet, contains the entire *Kabbalat Shabbat*. It is the only volume which shows the use of the four-part choir. The arrangements prove a thorough knowledge and understanding of four-part writing.

Miscellaneous: A volume containing various versions of the *Shabbat Mevarchim Ha-chodesh* liturgy, according to the Holy Day or festival which it precedes; boy soprano and discant parts of Sabbath and Holy Days services; various chants for various parts of the year; *zemirot* (home songs); pencil sketches and the musical notation of the chanting of *Akdamut*, an Aramaic poem chanted on *Shavuot*.

Jacques' Composition: The collection contains a composition entitled "Confession for the Day of Atonement Service." It bears a felicitous inscription by his father, which reads in translation as follows:

"Confession" by my son, Jacques (may he live). Composed during the penitential days in the year 5602.

He and his brother, my son Jules (may he live) sang in the synagogue, and assisted me in the *musaf* service, for the honor of God, and my honor. May the Lord prolong their days and years, and give them blessing and success in all the works of their hands. Amen.

(signed) Hakoton Itzik Offenbach

The work is in F minor, scored for three parts, three-quarter time, melodious and full of feeling. Isaac Offenbach evidently sang this work at the service during the rest of his career as cantor, for we find this version of *Ana Tova* repeated in his other volumes of High Holy Day compositions. This composition, dated 1842, at a time when Jacques was twenty-three years of age, reveals the fact that the boys came to assist their father as choristers even after they were already known as accomplished musicians. Jacques' own biography tells us that in 1841 he already gave a series of concerts of his own compositions in Paris.

Jules' Composition: A cradle song, setting of a German poem entitled *Wiegenlied* (lullaby) for medium voice, and piano accompaniment. The melody is in the German *lieder* style above a rocking accompaniment.

Sermons, Prayers, and Other Addresses: Neatly bound and titled, as well as neatly and very patiently written is a sermon on a quotation from Psalm 34, delivered on November 2, 1836. In this group we also find *bar mitzvah* sermons, wedding addresses, and prayers for various occasions.

Calendar and Music Chart: A very ingeniously thought-out calendar indicating holidays and seasons from 1860 to 2000; and a music chart indicating note values, rests, accidentals, evidently used in training choir boys in sight-singing.

Personal: A biography of her family, dated November 1902, by Julie Offenbach-Grunwald (Isaac's daughter), written while in the United States, in her own handwriting. She was eighty years old at that time. It is written in German, with a great deal of feeling, sentiment, and pride of family.

A Prayer: Written by Isaac Offenbach for his deceased wife whom he loved so very dearly. In this prayer he speaks to his children of their great and irreplaceable loss. Attached is a list of dates from 1843 to 1862, indicating the anniversaries of her death.

FOOTNOTES

1. According to the manuscript biography written by Julie Offenbach-Grunwald, daughter of Isaac Offenbach.
2. There is a great deal of confusion in available books of reference as to the real name of Jacques Offenbach's father. The *Oxford Companion to Music*, 8th ed., 1950, gives the name of Wiener, on the basis of information supplied by a granddaughter of Offenbach's to the *Radio Times* (January 29, 1932). Still more variants are to be found in other musical dictionaries. Most German or Jewish works of reference give Eberst or Ebersht; one anti-semitic publication has Ebersucht.
3. Adolph Kober, *History of the Jews in Cologne.* Jewish Publication Society of America, Philadelphia, p. 180.
4. *Ibid.,* p. 181.
5. See MSS biography of Julie Offenbach-Grunwald.
6. Equivalent to $.
7. Kober, *op. cit.,* p. 320.
8. *Ibid.,* p. 236.
9. *Ibid.,* p. 311.
10. His talents were many-sided. Besides his ability as cantor and rabbi, he also wrote plays and poetry.
11. A. Z. Idelsohn, *Jewish Music,* New York, p. 232.
12. A. W. Binder, "Cantorial Art in the Nineteenth Century," in *The Jewish People-Past and Present,* Vol. III, p. 336.
13. Kober, *op. cit.,* p. 252.
14. The elimination of the *piyutim,* for example, was not discussed until 1862.
15. The manuscripts are to be found in the Library of the Hebrew Union College-Jewish Institute of Religion, New York City.
16. See description of manuscripts in this article.
17. Binder, *op. cit.,* p. 336.
18. Idelsohn, *op. cit.,* p. 246.
19. Cf. note 15.
20. Cf. note 15.
21. Idelsohn, *op. cit.,* p. 269.

22. This complete collection of manuscripts was presented to the Library of the Hebrew Union College-Jewish Institute of Religion in New York City in 1923 by two granddaughters of Isaac Offenbach: Miss Isabella Grunwald and Mrs. S. Redlich, both residing in New York City. The gift was made through the kindness of George Alexander Kohut, at that time.

XXV MY IDEAS
AND THEORIES IN MY
SYNAGOGUE COMPOSITIONS

I was born in New York City into an Orthodox household. My father was a wonderful *baal tefillah*, a learned Jew, who knew the *nusach ha-tefillah* very well but read no music. I was told by my father that my grandfather in Galicia had been a fine *sheliach tsibbur* with a beautiful voice and a good knowledge of the tradition.

When I was four years old, I began to sing in my father's musical trio: *hazzan, meshorer,* and *zinger*—myself, the boy soprano. Father accepted compensation only for his High Holy Day services. We rehearsed almost every night about a month before the Holydays. By the age of six, I was already singing solos and helping in the harmonization in thirds. It all fascinated me, and I began to play *shul,* picturing myself as the *hazzan.* Later I dreamed of

(This lecture was delivered by the author at a meeting of the Jewish Liturgical Music Society of America on March 12, 1964. It has not been previously published.)

some miracle which would make a choir of singers appear magically, and I would then lead them in the manner that I saw in the large synagogues on the East Side.

My father soon recognized that there was some talent in his little seven-year-old son, and so he took me to the then-just-arrived cantor from Galatz, Roumania, Abraham Frachtenberg. I sang with Frachtenberg until I was fourteen, having during those years developed a sturdy boy's voice. I was the alto soloist, and was told that people enjoyed hearing me sing the prayers. Frachtenberg had been a *meshorer* in Yeruchom Hakoton's choir in Berditchev. His contemporaries in this choir were such illustrious future cantors as Boruch Schorr and Jacob Bachman. Frachtenberg, himself, had a very light bass-baritone voice with an agile coloratura in falsetto. He conducted his own choir, and had no choir leader like the other *hazzanim*. It was in choir training and conducting that he excelled. Frachtenberg's choir was well-known and his synagogue compositions were admired. It was during these years with Frachtenberg, that I became steeped in the "Yeruchom tradition," and learned the technique of choir training. Then, when my voice changed at the age of fourteen, I became the choir director of the Kamenitzer *Shul* on Attorney Street, with Abraham Singer as the cantor.

The background of *nusach ha-tefillah*, which I inherited from my father and from Abraham Frachtenberg, was to stand me in good stead later on in my career as a synagogue musician. At the age of sixteen, I became organist and choir director successively in two small temples for several years. It was then that I began to realize how sterile was the music of Schlesinger and Stark, which was widely sung in those days and I daresay even today. In 1922, when Rabbi Stephen Wise called me to become music director of the Free Synagogue, which at that time held its services in Carnegie Hall, I felt that it was my duty to do something about letting Reform Jews hear some of the works by synagogue masters of the nineteenth century: Sulzer, Lewandowski, Naumbourg, and Nowakowsky. The Reform services had become saturated with music composed for the *Union Prayer Book* by non-Jews.

I soon realized that all was not *kosher* with Sulzer and Lewandowski, either. Somehow, to me, their music did not always create the synagogal atmosphere that I knew. There was what Idelsohn called in their music something *galchish*. I knew the reason for this was that there was so little genuine *nusach ha-tefillah* in their music. Even when *nusach* was used, it was put behind bars and harmonized with Western tonic-dominant harmonies. To say that I knew all the answers in 1923 would be an error. I am not sure whether I do today, either.

In this brief exposition, I shall confine myself solely to the ideas and theories embodied in my four Sabbath services and four responses for the Sabbath eve. At a future time, I plan to discuss my particular musical ideas in other of my liturgical works such as: evening service for the New Year; morning service for the New Year; afternoon service for the Day of Atonement; *Neilah* service; and my recently published musical liturgy for the Three Festivals.

I felt very strongly that in most synagogues on *Shabbat* you did not feel that it was *Shabbat*. On *Pesach*, you did not feel that it was festive, and, on *Rosh Hashanah* and *Yom Kippur*, there was a secular atmosphere. Some of the warmth and beauty which those holy days brought with them had almost completely disappeared from the synagogue. There were many reasons. However, one very important reason was that the traditional *nusach ha-tefillah* for each of those Holy Days either had disappeared conpletely or else was unrecognizable when presented. In my first Sabbath service, *Hibbat Shabbat*, published in 1929, there were intimations of things to come in my later services.

For instance, in my first service I introduced the pure

nusach in the *Tov L'hodot*, especially in the cantorial recitative *Mah Gadlu*. I had not learned yet how to sustain it, for it goes off into strange fields. The same is also true in *Mi Chamocha* in the same service. In *Malchut'cha*, I introduce the *Maariv nusach*, but do not sustain it here either. These were small changes in the melodic aspects.

I consider my most important contribution to synagogue music to be the return to the *nusach ha-tefillah*, which is our rich musical tradition of the synagogue, and the efforts to purify and perpetuate it. I use the *nusach ha-tefillah* not for its own sake, but for what it has meant to our forefathers. What it did for the service in the past, it can do for the synagogue service today.

I have always said that it is not what thematic material is used by a composer, but what he does with it, which really counts. It matters how he develops it—melodically, harmonically, and rhythmically. In my harmonic treatment of the *nusach*, I have used modal harmonization which suits the special modal character of the *nusach*. For instance, in my evening service for the New Year, I have used quartal harmonization in fourths and fifths. I have also made use of such modern harmonic devices as polytonality, and at times the twelve-tone technique.

There are many fine features in the traditional *nusach* which are gradually disappearing and being forgotten. I refer, for example, to the *nusach* for the phrase *Adonay Elohenu Attah Anisam* in the *Kabbalat Shabbat*. Very few of the contemporary cantors use it, or even know it. To the Jew of the past, it meant an expression of faith which was strengthened on the Sabbath. In the *Union Prayer Book*, we do not have the Psalm 99 where this phrase occurs; and so I use it in my *Rinat Shabbat* for *Mi Chamocha* in a unison chant, and later in *Adonay Yimloch*, harmonized for chorus. I do not interfere with the *nusach* for *Malchut'cha*; that remains. I have made it a point never to change the *nusach* which is associated traditionally with a certain prayer. New ideas are introduced in prayers which do not have a musical tradition.

In *Shema Yisrael*, I introduce the cantorial *melisma* and have it repeated in unison by the choir. It is difficult to do, but beautiful and ancient in effect. The revised *Union Prayer Book*, which appeared in 1940, brought back many of the *Kabbalat Shabbat* Psalms, but they are not recited on one Friday evening. They are distributed over five Sabbaths. That revised prayer book also introduced a *Torah* service for Friday eve with a new liturgy, and a *Hanukkah* service. I was the first to set it to music. I determined that I was going to try here to bring back the *nusach ha-tefillah* and the spirit of the Sabbath, which had all but disappeared from the Reform synagogue. Thus, the blessing over the Sabbath lights introduces the *Magen Avot* mode and the Sabbath spirit. A motive from this piece runs through the new sections of the entire service work.

Setting the *Torah* service with its new liturgy presented a problem. For *Lo Yare'u*, which comes from the Prophet Isaiah, I use the cantillation mode of the Prophets, which, of course, belongs to the Sabbath. For the *Shema*, I use the *Magen Avot* mode, and for *Emet Elohey Olam*, a familiar *zemirot* melody. The *Hine Mah Tov* is a Palestinian folk song; *Or Zarua* is the *nusach*; and, *Yimloch* is based on the *Adonay Malach nusach* with a *Halleluyah* resembling the tune of *Hatikvah*. It was at that time (1929) that I was having a fight with the Hymnal Committee about getting *Hatikvah* into the new edition of the *Union Hymnal*. I felt that if the "Hatikvahites" lost, then the Reform Jews would be getting the melody through this piece.

My four responses for the Sabbath eve represent an all-out effort to return the *Magen Avot nusach* to the modern service. The *Barchu* and *Shema* are based on the *El Chai V'kayom nusach*. The *May the Words* has all the features of the *Magen Avot nusach* as found in *V'shomru*: the characteristic modulation to the fourth in major, the switch at that point to minor, and the return to the *Magen Avot* mode which brings back the "sweet peace and rest" of the Sabbath.

I composed my *Sabbath For Israel,* a Friday evening musical liturgy, in 1952 after my third visit to Israel. I have always felt that in the future the musical idiom which we have come to know as "Israeli," will make itself felt also in the synagogue. Hence, I set out with the idea of combining elements found in the Israeli song with the *nusach hatefillah* of the *Shabbat* eve. I decided to maintain the *nusach* for those parts of the liturgy which have a musical tradition, and to utilize the Israeli musical idiom for those sections which do not have a set tradition. At no time did I use an Israeli tune. All thematic material is original, but in the Israeli style.

For example, the *L'cha Dodi* is in Yemenite style. I also wrote it in 2/4 rhythm, instead of the tiresome 3/4 tempo in which thousands of settings for this poem have been made. I also tried to adhere to the rhythm of the Hebrew. In *Shiru Ladonay,* I experiment with the unison free chant for choir. I do not feel that the chant ought be limited to the solo voice only; rather, an archaic effect is achieved when the chorus chants freely in unison, and when the chant is not overharmonized. This effect is also achieved in the chanting of *Lema-an Tizkeru* to the *Torah* trope which is also found in this Israeli service volume.

In *L'chu N'ran'nah,* I have combined the *Adonay Elohenu* theme with the *L'chu N'ran'nah nusach. Barchu* is in the *Magen Avot* mode, but the ending is Israeli. Since the *Shema* has no set *nusach* on Friday evening, it is here that the Israeli style is utilized. *Mi Chamocha* is conceived as a *hora,* composed without a solo. I visualized Miriam joining with the women of Israel in the *Shirat Hayam,* not only singing but dancing to this great and majestic text.

Yismechu is in the *Magen Avot* mode instead of the *Ahavah Rabbah,* in which it is usually sung and rightly so, for it belongs to the Sabbath morning liturgy. However, when sung on Friday evening, I think that it ought to be sung in the *Magen Avot* mode. For the *Beracha* before *Magen Avot*, I use the beautiful tradition associated with this prayer, with all its special characteristics. In *Magen Avot* I go into a theme in Israeli character, but the piece definitely ends in the *Magen Avot* mode, despite its musical meanderings.

The *Kiddush* is an Israeli one. However, before I launch into the Israeli section, I pay homage to the *nusach* of *Asher Kideshanu*. After all, it is the Sabbath and we should not forget that fact. The *Adoration* is again, for the most part, a unison chant for choir in the dorian mode, a mode often used in Israeli folk songs. The theme for *Adon Olam* is again in Yemenite style, developed and manipulated to a climax and the close of the service.

I have tried to outline here some of my ideas and theories embodied in my synagogue music. My own musical efforts have been towards bringing back the *nusach ha-tefillah* to the American synagogue by: its full embodiment into the liturgy; its combination with the Israeli idiom; the liberation of the chant from behind the nineteenth century bar lines; and, the search for the proper harmonic background for our synagogue modes. These have been some of my goals during my career as a synagogue musician. They are my credo.

BIBLIOGRAPHY OF WORKS
BY A. W. BINDER

Compiled by Lewis Appleton

(This listing was originally prepared by Lewis Appleton in August 1964, as a special program resource for the 21st annual Jewish Music Festival. It was subsequently included in the tribute manual: *The Life and Work of A. W. Binder*, published by the National Jewish Music Council of the National Jewish Welfare Board, and edited by Irene Heskes. Additions have been made to complete the list.)

TITLE	TEXT	PUBLISHER	COMMENT

I. SACRED MUSIC

A. Sabbath Services

TITLE	TEXT	PUBLISHER	COMMENT
Kabbalat Shabbat (Welcoming the Sabbath)	T		Sabbath Eve Music, Torah Service, and Hanukkah Service. Cantor, SATB, organ

TITLE	TEXT	PUBLISHER	COMMENT
Hibbat Shabbat (Love of the Sabbath)		T	Sabbath Eve. Cantor, SATB, organ
Sabbath for Israel (A Musical Liturgy)		T	Sabbath Eve. Cantor, SATB, organ
Rinnat Shabbat (Joy of the Sabbath)		B	Sabbath Eve. Cantor, SATB, organ

B. Three Festival Service

Three Festival Musical Liturgy		T	Cantor, SATB, organ

C. High Holy Days

Evening Services for the New Year and the Day of Atonement (Arvit L'rosh Hashanah V'yom Kippur)		T	Cantor, SATB, organ
Morning Service for the New Year		T	Cantor, SATB, organ
Afternoon Service for the Day of Atonement		T	Cantor, SATB, organ
Neilah Service		T	Cantor, SATB, organ
Requiem-Yizkor (Complete Memorial Service)		T	Cantor (Baritone), Contralto, SATB, organ

TITLE	TEXT	PUBLISHER	COMMENT
D. Mixed Chorus			
Four Sabbath Responses	H.E.	T	Cantor (Baritone) SATB
V'shomru	H.E.	CF	Solo, SATB
V'shomru	H.	GS	Cantor (Tenor or Baritone) SATB
Introductory Songs for the Sabbath morning	H.E.	SHP	Solo or Unison Choir
Kedusha	H.	T	Cantor (Baritone) SATB
Tov L'hodot	H.	T	Cantor (Baritone) SATB
Neilah Kaddish	H.	T	Cantor (Baritone) SATB
Etz Chayim	H.	T	SATB
Uvashofar Gadol (The Great Trumpet)	H.	MMI	Cantor (Tenor or Baritone) SATB
Festival Song (Shirat Chag)	H.E.	T	SATB
Halleluyah	H.	T	SATB
Halleluyah (of Trees and Brooks)	E.	PMC	SATB
Sing Unto The Lord	H.E.	GS	Baritone Solo, SATB
Lord Do Thou Guide Me	E.	T	SATB and High voice
Song of Penitence	E.	PMC	SATB

All with organ (piano) accompaniment.

TITLE	TEXT	PUBLISHER	COMMENT
	E. Solo Voice		
Lord Do Thou Guide Me	E.	T	Medium and High (Also for Weddings)
Prayer and Supplication (Based on Psalms 119, 169, 175)		SMP	Medium voice (f-F)
Rochel M'vakoh Al Boneho (Roitman, Arr.)	H.	M	(F-f)
Hashkivenu	H.	B	(A-e flat)
Song Of Dedication	E.	T	Medium voice
A Prayer For Hanukkah	E.	T	Medium voice
The Lord Is My Shepherd	H.E.	T	High or Medium voice
Let My Prayer	E.	GS	High voice
Lord, Do Thou Consider Me (Wedding Song)	E.	BH	High and Low voice

II. WORKS INCLUDED IN COLLECTIONS AND ANTHOLOGIES

A. Ephros' Cantorial Anthology	B	
Vol. I, Adonay, Adonay, p. 14		SATB—Rosh Hashanah Morning Service

TITLE	TEXT	PUBLISHER	COMMENT
Vol. II, Zochrenu, p. 300			SATB—Neilah Service
Vol. III, B'tset Yisrael, p. 176			SATB—Three Festival Morning Service
Vol. IV, L'chu N'ran'nah, p. 21			Cantor (Medium voice) SATB Sabbath Eve Service
Vol. V, M'hera #2, p. 272			Cantor and SATB Wedding Service
B. Special Songster			
Adon Olam, p. 2		SMP	Congregational Singing
C. Synagogue Music by Contemporary Composers (Anthology for Sabbath Eve) Kiddush, p. 304		GS	Cantor (Medium voice) SATB
D. The Jewish Year In Song		GS	A collection of songs, hymns, prayers and folk melodies in English, Hebrew and Yiddish for synagogue, school and home.
E. Jewish Publication Society Holiday Anthologies			

TITLE	TEXT	PUBLISHER	COMMENT
Music in "Hanukkah Book"	H.E.Y.	JPS	Anthology edited by Emily Solis-Cohen
Music in "The Purim Anthology"	H.E.Y.	JPS	Anthology edited by Philip Goodman
Music in "The Sabbath Book"	H.E.Y.	JPS	Anthology edited by Abraham E. Millgram

III. ART SONGS

Solo Voice

Eliyahu Hanavi (Peretz) A Song Story (Elijah, The Prophet)	Y.E.	MMI	Mezzo or Baritone
Chavatzelet Hasharon (Rose of Sharon)	H.	M	(D-a)
In Eretz Yisrael	Y.	M	(E-f)
Shabbes Bam Shalos Seudos (Atah Echad)	Y.	M	(d-g)
A Tefillah—A Prayer	Y.	M	(D-e)
Zing, Neshome! Zing	Y.	M	(D-F)
Shomer Yisrael	Y.	M	Range High
Rochel M'vakoh Al Boneho (Rachel Weeps for her Children (David Roitman)	H.	M	

TITLE	TEXT	PUBLISHER	COMMENT
Two Prayers of Kierkegaard: 1. Thou Hast Loved Us First 2. Thy Loving Care	E.	MR	Medium voice

All with piano accompaniment.

IV. JEWISH FOLK MUSIC IN YIDDISH

A. Solo Voice

Az Ich Volt Gevehn Der Boireh Ho-oylom	Y.	M	Hasidic Folk Song (D-d)
Gesang Fun'm Berditchever	Y.	M	Hasidic Folk Song (G-d)
A Chazend'l Oif	Y.	TBH	Medium voice

B. Mixed Chorus

Az Der Rebbe Geht	Y.	T	SATB
Ematay (When)	Y.H.R.	T	SATB
L'kovod Dem Heiligem Shabbes	Y.	B	SATB
Oy Vey Rebbenu	Y.	B	SATB
Vig Lied	Y.	T	SATB
Du Zolst Nit Zogn	Y.E.	MMI	Songs of the Jewish Partisans—SATB

TITLE	TEXT	PUBLISHER	COMMENT

V. HEBREW FOLK SONGS
AND SONGS IN FOLK STYLE
(Including Songs of Israel)

A. Solo Voice

TITLE	TEXT	PUBLISHER	COMMENT
Music in "Sabbath Day of Delight"		JPS	Book on the Sabbath by Abraham E. Millgram
Ani Maamin (I Believe)	H.E.	ZOA	(A-B)
Artsa Alinu	H.	ZOA	(D-E)
Shir Nekama (Song of Revenge)	H.	ZOA	(A-D)
Zemer, Zemer Lach (A Song of My Land)	H.	ZOA	(C-D)
Rad Halaylah (The Night Descends)	H.	ZOA	(E-D)
Shir Haligyonot (Song of the Legionnaires by Zeira)	H.	ZOA	(C-F)
The Jewish Year in Song	H.E.Y.	GS	Collection
Pioneer Songs of Israel	H.E.	EBM	Collection
Songs Israel Sings	H.	M	Collection
New Palestinian Folk Songs			
Book I	H.	T	Collection
Book II	H.	B	Collection

TITLE	TEXT	PUBLISHER	COMMENT
Jewish Folk Songs in Hasidic Style	H.E.	MMI	Collection Medium voice
Palestinian Song Suite	H.E.	B	Collection Medium voice
Shivas Zion (The Return to Zion by E. Zunser)	H.E.	B	Collection Medium voice

B. Mixed Chorus

TITLE	TEXT	PUBLISHER	COMMENT
Shir Ha-emek (Song of the Emek)	H.E.	MMI	SATB and TTBB
Ani Ma-amin (Song of Faith)	H.E.Y.	MMI	SATB and TTBB
Four Israeli Songs			
1. Kacha, Kach	H.E.	EBM	SATB
2. Ayn Charod	H.E.	EBM	SATB
3. Ba-ah Menucha	H.E.	EBM	SATB
4. Laila Seleh	H.E.	EBM	SATB
Avatichim (Watermelons)	H.	T	SATB
Na-aleh L'artsenu (On to Our Land)	H.	T	SATB
Nigun Bialik (Song Without Words)		T	SATB
Pakad Adonay (The Lord Remembered)	H.	T	SATB
Polka Halutzit (Halutz Polka)	H.	T	SATB
Shirat Hashomer (Song of the Watchman)	H.	T	SATB

TITLE	TEXT	PUBLISHER	COMMENT
Shirat Hechalil (Song of the Flute)	H.	T	SATB
Yiboneh Hamikdosh (May the Temple be Rebuilt)	H.	T	SATB
Mi Y'mallel (Israel's Heroes) Hanukkah Round	H.	T	SATB
Halleluyah		T	SATB
Festival Song (Shirat Chag)	H.E.	T	SATB

With piano accompaniment.

VI. MUSICO-DRAMATIC WORKS

A. *Cantatas, Oratorios, Musical Narratives, Choral Ballet, Opera*

Israel Reborn	E.	B	Choral Poem with Narration. Baritone, SATB, piano or organ
The Heart of America	E.	T	Choral Poem. SATB, p or o. (Orchestral acc. available)
Amos On Times Square	E.Y.	B	Cantata. Tenor, SATB. p or o acc.
Hanukkah Of The Maccabees	E.	T	Musical Narrative for Rabbi, Soli, Mixed Chorus, Congregational Reading. p or o acc.

TITLE	TEXT	PUBLISHER	COMMENT
Esther, Queen Of Persia	E.	T	Musical Narrative for Rabbi, Soli, SATB and Congregational Reading. p or o acc.
Passover To Freedom	E.	T	Musical Narrative for Rabbi, Soli, SATB and Congregational Reading
The Legend Of The "Ari"	E.	LG	Oratorio for Tenor, Baritone, Soli, SATB, p or o acc. (Orchestral version available)
A Goat In Chelm	E.	T	Opera. Story by Sholom Aleichem. 3 Female, 4 Male voices with piano or Orchestra acc. (30 min.)
Hora V'hodayah	H.E.	IMP/L	Choral Ballet. Nine Horas on Biblical and Liturgical Texts for Soprano, Alto, Tenor Soli, SATB and Choreography. p or o acc. (Orchestral version available)

B. Bible Lessons With Music

B'shalach: Exodus xiii: 17-22	H.E.	SMP	Reader, Cantor, Soprano, Mixed Chorus, Tambourine, p or o acc.

TITLE	TEXT	PUBLISHER	COMMENT
Akedat Yitzhak (Sacrifice of Isaac)	H.E.	SMP	Reader, Cantor, Tenor, Contralto, Mixed Chorus, p or o acc.

VII. TEXT BOOK

Biblical Chant		SMP	A richly illustrated textbook making it possible to study Cantillation by way of modern music notation.

VIII. SECULAR AMERICAN MUSIC

A. Solo Voice

All The Pretty Little Horses (Negro Lullaby)	E.	EVC	Arr. for High and Low voice
The Banjo Player	E.	EVC	Medium voice

B. Mixed Chorus

Five American Folk Songs			
This Train	E.	TP	SATB with piano
Cowboy Lament	E.	TP	SATB—a capella
All The Pretty Little Horses	E.	TP	Alto & SATB with piano
Adam in the Garden Pinin' Leaves	E.	TP	SATB with piano
Little Black Train	E.	TP	SATB with piano

TITLE	TEXT	PUBLISHER	COMMENT

IX. MUSIC FOR CHILDREN

TITLE	TEXT	PUBLISHER	COMMENT
Hanukkah Songster	H.E.	B	Unison Children's Chorus and piano
A Purim Songster	H.E.	B	Unison Children's Chorus and piano
Judas Maccabeus	E.	B	Oratorio for Children 2-p. Chorus, Soli and piano
Seder Melodies	H.E.	B	

X. SACRED MUSIC WORKS INCLUDED IN COLLECTIONS & ANTHOLOGIES
(Including Music for both Solo Voice and Mixed Chorus)

A. Union Hymnal
—Volumes 1
and 11

CCAR   *Numbers*

5, 11, 15, 16, 27,
46, 52, 62, 63, 64,
69, 74, 77, 80, 83,
85, 86, 91, 94, 95,
100, 106, 107, 108,
118, 122, 132, 142,
152, 153, 155, 157,
159, 164, 171, 176,
178, 194, 205, 206,
211, 243, 247, 248,
258, 260, 267, 273,
277, 279, 280, 283,
288, 290, 293, 297,
300, 301, 303, 304,
305, 307, 308, 309,
311, 314, 315, 322,
325, 327, 330.

TITLE	TEXT	PUBLISHER	COMMENT
B. Union Songster		CCAR	*Numbers* 4, 12, 13, 22, 24, 26, 27, 32, 41, 46, 110, 113, 114, 115, 116, 118, 124, 151, 152, 154, 158, 159, 196, 197, 200, 204, 248, 258, 262, 270, 271, 290, 295A, 325, 369, 384, 386, 388, 393, 396, 425.

XI. INSTRUMENTAL MUSIC—SOLOS

A. Piano

Three Winter Scenes		GS	Easy
Variations on a Yemenite Theme		L	Medium difficulty
The Lily of Sharon (Suite) 1. Toccata 2. Lily of Sharon 3. Dance with Variations		IMP/L	Medium difficulty
Three Piano Pieces Flowers in the Wind Boatsong at Dusk Hora		TP	Easy
Sonata (Ruth and Boaz)		T	Advanced
Sonatina #1		T	Medium difficulty
Sonatina #2		T	Medium difficulty

TITLE	TEXT	PUBLISHER	COMMENT
Two Pieces For Piano a) Moonlight on "The Wall" b) Moishelach und Shloimelach		T	Medium difficulty

B. Organ

TITLE	TEXT	PUBLISHER	COMMENT
Sabbath Rest (See also Evening Service for the New Year and Sabbath for Israel)		T	
Two Organ Pieces in "Organ Music for Worship" 1. Rinnat Shabbat 2. Fantasy		WM	Medium difficulty

C. Violin

TITLE	TEXT	PUBLISHER	COMMENT
Minuetto for Violin and Piano		GS	Easy
Hora for Violin and Piano		MMI	Medium difficulty

D. Cello

TITLE	TEXT	PUBLISHER	COMMENT
Pastorale and Dance for Cello and Piano		MMI	Medium difficulty

XII. INSTRUMENTAL MUSIC ENSEMBLES

A. Chamber Music

TITLE	TEXT	PUBLISHER	COMMENT
First Trio: For Violin, Cello and Piano		MMI	

TITLE	TEXT	PUBLISHER	COMMENT
Second Trio: For Violin, Cello and Piano		MMI	
String Quartet		MMI	
Two Hasidic Moods For String Quartet a) Meditation b) Dance		MMI	
Dybbuk Suite For String Quartet, Clarinet and Piano (Chamber Orch.) Beggars' Dance Shir Hashirim Wedding March Leah's Dance		MMI	

B. Orchestral and Chamber Music in Rental Library
of
Mills Music Inc.

Concertante for String Orchestra			
Concertino for String Orchestra			
Night Music (for String Orchestra)			
King David (Rhapsody for Piano and Orchestra)			Picc. 2 fl. 2 ob. 2 cl. 2 bas. 4 hrns, 2 tr. 4 trb, perc. Strings.
Israeli Suite (for Full Orchestra)			Same Orch. as above
Lament (for Orchestra) In Memory of the Warsaw Ghetto			Same Orch. as above

TITLE	TEXT	PUBLISHER	COMMENT
Poem of Freedom (for Full Orchestra)			Same Orch. as above
Overture "Hechalutzim"			Same Orch. as above
Theodore Herzl (Overture-Fantasy for Full Orchestra)			Same Orch. as above
Dybbuk Suite (4 sections) Chamber Orchestra and Full Orchestral version			Same Orch. as above
Piano Trio No. 1 (Violin, Cello and Piano)			
Piano Trio No. 2 (Violin, Cello and Piano)			
String Quartet			
Two Hasidic Moods (for String Quartet)			
Pastorale and Dance (for Cello and Piano)			
Hora (for Violin and Piano)			

PUBLISHERS INDEX

SYMBOL	NAME	CITY
B	Bloch Publishing Company, Inc.	New York
BH	Behrman House	New York
CCAR	Central Conference of American Rabbis	New York
CF	Carl Fischer, Inc.	New York
EBM	Edward B. Marks Music Company	New York
EVC	Elkan-Vogel Company, Inc.	Philadelphia, Pa.
GS	G. Schirmer and Company	New York
IMP/L	Israel Music Publications (Agency for U.S.: Leeds Music Co.)	Tel Aviv, Israel
JPS	Jewish Publication Society	Philadelphia, Pa.
L	Leeds Music Company	New York
LG	Lawson-Gould Music Publishers (G. Schirmers)	New York
M	Metro Music Company	New York
MMI	Mills Music Inc.	New York
MR	McLaughlin and Reilly Company	Boston, Mass.
PMC	Plymouth Music Company	New York
SMP	Sacred Music Press (Hebrew Union College— Jewish Institute of Religion)	New York
T	Transcontinental Music Publications	New York

SYMBOL	NAME	CITY
TBH	T. B. Harms Company	New York
TP	Theodore Presser Company	Bryn Mawr, Pa.
WM	Wallen Music, Inc.	New York
ZOA	Zionist Organization of America	New York

Key to letters indicating language of text:

E   English
H   Hebrew
R   Russian
Y   Yiddish

Other abbreviations:

p-Piano
o-Organ
acc.-accompaniment
S-Soprano
A-Alto
T-Tenor
B-Bass or Baritone
Orch.-Orchestra

INDEX

Aaron ben Moshe ben Asher (fl. 10th cent.), masoretic scholar, 93, 245

Abbush Meir of Sanz, (fl. 19th cent.), hasidic rabbi, *hazzan*, 123, 186

Abraham Ibn Ezra (1093-1168), Spanish Hebrew poet, scholar, 257

Abrahams, Israel (1858-1925), English scholar, Hebraist, 265

Achron, Joseph (1886-1943), Russian-born American Jewish composer and violinist, 26, 27, 163, 166, 169, 181, 198, 211, 219, 223, 226, 233, 237, 268, 288

Acta Esther (*Purim* play), 121, 171

Adler, Felix A., (1851-1933), German-born American rabbi, founder of Ethical Culture movement and hymnodist, 263, 265

Adler, Herman A., (1839-1911), German-born English rabbi, author and hymnodist, 265

Adler, Hugo C. (1894-1955), German-born American cantor, composer, 163, 164

Admon-Gorochov, Yedidya, Russian-born Israeli, composer, 197

Adon Olam (Heb. "Lord of the World"), liturgical hymn, 258

Adon Olam (Bloch), 33

Adon Olam in F (Nowakowsky), 155

Adon Olam (Sulzer), 287, 288

Adonay Malach prayer mode, 102, 106, 114, 137, 180, 193

Aeolian minor mode, 114

Aguilar, Grace (1816-1847), English-born Jewish poet, author, 265

Ahasuerus (Goldfaden), 125

Ahasuerus, King, 119, 124

Ahavah Rabbah prayer mode, 106, 107, 137, 138, 178, 180, 182, 286

Ahavas Chesed Synagogue, New York, 160, 260

Akedas Yitzhok (Goldfaden), 174

Akiba ben Joseph (c. 40-c. 135), Tanna, founder of rabbinic Judaism, 139

Albeniz, Isaac (1860-1909), Spanish composer, 8

Albert, Eugen d' (D'Albert) (1864-1932), German pianist and composer of French descent and Scottish birth, 127

Alexander, Haim (Heinz), Berlin-born Israeli composer, 202

Al Hanisim (Heb. "For the Miracles"), *Hanukkah* hymn, 66

Alkabetz, Shelomo ben Moses Halevi (c. 1505-c. 1580), Hebrew poet and kabbalist, 100, 192

331

Leon, Meir (*cont.*)
lish-born cantor, composer, opera singer, 258
Leon of Modena (Jehudah Arieh Leone) (1571-1648), Italian rabbi, writer, musician, 147-148, 173
"Leoni," see Leon, Meir
Letzim (Yid. from Heb. *letzon*, "jester"), 122, 170
Levi-Tanai, Sarah, Israeli composer, 197
Leviash, Ruth, Jewish concert singer, 197
Levinger (Ehrlich), Elma, author, poet, hymnodist, 69, 265
Levine, Maurice, American Jewish conductor, 40, 41, 44
Levitzki, Mischa (1898-1941), Russian-born American Jewish pianist, 77
Levi Yitzhok of Berditchev (1740-1809), hasidic rabbi, 123, 180, 183-184, 186, 189
Levy, David, hymnodist, 265
Lewandowski, Louis (1821-1894), Poznan-born, Berlin composer, conductor of synagogue music, 12, 23, 26, 55-56, 64, 80, 95, 107, 152-153, 158, 159, 162, 205, 208, 209, 231, 233, 234, 272, 273, 287
Lipitz, Louis, Russian-born cantor and teacher, 16
List, Emanuel (1891-1967), Austrian-born Jewish singer, 77
Liszt, Franz (1811-1886), 74, 146, 152, 284
Loeb (Lob), Otto (fl. mid 19th cent.), author of Jewish hymnal, 163, 261
Loew, Leopold (1811-1875), Hungarian-born rabbi and scholar, 288
Lovy, Israel (Lowy; Levy; Israel Glogow; Reb Yisroel Furth; Israel Strassburg), (1773-1832), Danzig-born cantor, composer, 74, 149, 150, 198, 283

Low, Leo (1878-1960), Russian-born composer, conductor, 167, 168, 212, 213, 214
Loewenstamm, Max (1814-1881), Trebitsch-born cantor and composer, 64
Lower East Side, Manhattan, New York, 15, 160, 161
Lubavitcher Rabbi, music of the court of the, 217
Lucas, Alice, 265
Luria, Isaac ben Solomon (1534-1572), Palestinian kabbalist and liturgical poet, 100, 188, 192, 252
Lustig, Moshe (1922-1958), Israeli composer, conductor, 202

Maccabees, The (Rubenstein), 70
Machtenberg, Meyer, Vilna-born American Jewish composer, choral conductor, 161
Madison Square Garden, New York, 39
Magrepha, 129
Maharil, see Jacob ben Moses Halevi Molin
Ma'oz Tsur (Heb. "Fortress Rock"), *Hanukkah* hymn, 66, 67
Ma'oz Tsur (Bruch), 70
Marek, Pesach (1862-1920), Russian-born historian and collector of Yiddish folk songs, 181, 210
Margovsky, Jacob Samuel (Zeidel Rovner) (1856-1940), Ukrainian-born composer, cantor, 161
Margulies, Jacob, choir leader, 161
Marks, E. B., music publishers, New York City, 215
Markson, Hadassah Binder (daughter), vii, 20
Marshaliks (Yid. from Ger. *marschal*—royal chamberlain), entertainers, jesters, 170
Mathias, Christian, 261
Magen Avot (Heb. "Shield of Our Father"), abridged from of *Amidah* prayer for Sabbath eve, 101